GLORIOUS FOOD

GLORIOUS

By CHRISTOPHER IDONE

Photographs by Richard Jeffery

FOOD

STEWART, TABORI
& CHANG, INC.
PUBLISHERS,
NEW YORK

Design: Nai Chang
        Jim Wageman
Editor: Marya Dalrymple

Photography Credits

Karen Radkai: 8, 11, 15, 42, 47, 49, 56, 57, 59, 60, 208,
236, 237, 238; Rico Puhlmann:4, 108-109, 118, 148, 149,
150-151, 152, 153; John Marmaras/Woodfin Camp:16,
17, 23, 32-33, 34-35; Horst: 71.

Recipe Credits

Jean-Claude Nedelec: 24, 26, 28, 31, 35, 38, 40 (except
fruits), 64, 68, 70, 71, 113; the Chartreuse Soufflé was
inspired by a recipe from Roy Andries de Groot: 61; Bridie
McSherry: 92; the Syllabub was adapted from a recipe by
Felicite Love Morgan: 93; Yorkshire Pudding, Anne Idone:
125; Marie-Christine Queval: 166; Paul Bocuse: 166; the
Chocolate Truffles were adapted from a recipe by Tom
Krön, Krön Chocolatiere: 239.

Library of Congress Cataloging in Publication Data

Idone, Christopher.
Glorious food.

Includes index.

1. Entertaining.   2. Cookery.   3. Caterers and catering—
New York (N.Y.)   I. Jeffery, Richard.   II. Title.
TX731.I3   642   82-5587
ISBN 0-941434-22-2   AACR2

Text © 1982 by Christopher Idone
Photographs © 1982 by Richard Jeffery

Published in 1982 by Stewart, Tabori & Chang, Inc.,
Publishers, New York.
Distributed by Workman Publishing Company, Inc.
1 West 39th Street, New York, New York 10018
Printed in Italy.

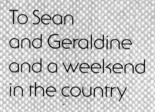

To Sean
and Geraldine
and a weekend
in the country

CONTENTS

FOREWORD 9

For ten years Glorious Food has created parties for an international list of clients and guests in the most international city in the world—New York. Founded in 1971 by Christopher Idone and Sean Driscoll (right and left, respectively), the company was later joined by Jean-Claude Nedelec (center). In 1981, Christopher Idone started Glorious Food 2, a food consulting company.

FOREWORD

FOR ME, the road to a career involving food was anything but direct. In my early twenties I was sent to school in Paris. That first year I lived with a family who employed a *femme de cuisine*. Before class, I would spend time in the kitchen, watching the old woman prepare the foods she had bought at the market that morning. After a while, she invited me to come to the market with her. I was fascinated. These markets had nothing to do with the supermarkets I was used to in America. They seemed an endless maze, miles of stalls filled with fresh produce. I was entranced by the sights, the presentation of the food. It was food as some sort of art form. I would watch this small, old woman wander in and out of the stalls, cajoling and berating the vendors as they would try to sell her a slightly bruised peach or a less-than-fresh piece of fish. She was adamant; she would accept nothing but their best. I had never seen such care. Eventually, I began to miss classes and spend more and more time with her in the kitchen, learning the techniques of good, straightforward French cooking.

The following summer I spent in Siena. As soon as I arrived in the city, I searched for the open markets. I found Italian markets to be as elaborately visual as their French counterparts. Unknown to me at the time, I had become hooked by the *look* of food, as well as its taste.

After I returned to New York from those two years in Europe, the idea of doing something with food continued to intrigue me. Years later, by a very circuitous route, Sean Driscoll and I founded Glorious Food.

This book has its genesis in the development of an attitude toward the preparation and serving of good food. Glorious Food's understated approach to food, and its emphasis on the visual, has been enthusiastically received by our public. We know our methods and techniques work, and therefore we feel we can offer valuable knowledge to hosts and hostesses.

Information about food can be presented in a variety of ways. There are cookbooks containing collections of recipes; there are books dealing with the history of food, its components and complements; there are books with recipes arranged in menus. This book is a distillation of my own varied experience with the preparation of food as appreciator, as practitioner and as consultant. Food doesn't have a solitary nature; it has never made sense to me without its surroundings. One of my first teachers was a chef who insisted, "You don't cook with books. You don't cook with your tongue. You cook with your eye." It was a wonderful clue to what makes a meal memorable. The eye, as well as the palate, has to be won. Therefore, this book is photographic, leading you by the eye through a variety of situations to show how everything—the food, setting, season and occasion—contributes to the rightness of things.

The menus in this book were inspired by the situations. The wines are merely suggestions of what might go with particular foods. You will discover that the philosophy that applies to a dinner for one thousand applies to a dinner for one. You will learn how all the elements of a meal can visually work together. I am offering advice, not a manifesto.

Years ago people followed hard and fast rules about entertaining. Now that one person often does the marketing, cooking, serving and hosting, these rules have disappeared. There are liberties. Once pretensions are put aside, you realize that entertaining is there to amuse, and that real success in entertaining comes from infusing your own personal style and whimsy into an occasion. Style isn't imitation; it's a revelation of yourself. Style is what you are comfortable with.

Because there has been a tidal wave of information about foods and their availability, hosts and hostesses—faced with countless choices —often feel paralyzed when they try to decide on a menu. One way to side-step all this is to get into the habit of considering the practicality of a menu. Will this particular food work or not work with respect to the number of guests, the setting or the service? In choosing a menu, be aware of color and texture. They can dazzle and they can dull. Use the plate as your palette. Finally, limit yourself to *one* bravura course. A competent cook can duplicate a range of tricky recipes, but accumulated knowledge and dexterity need not be shown off course after course at a single sitting.

I have seen people create a great deal out of nothing and similarly create nothing out of a great deal. My advice is: choose a menu, simplify things, then add some lift, an extravagance, to one of the courses, to the flowers or the setting. Combine a little sense and

The kitchen at Glorious Food in New York.

nonsense. Entertaining is a lifelong love, the felicitous part of your life. At its most successful, it stamps the memory. As Virginia Woolf said, "One cannot think well, love well, sleep well, if one has not dined well."

—Christopher Idone

BEING asked to tell the history of Glorious Food gave me a jolt. Was Glorious Food that old? Ten years flashed by. How does one recall and isolate events that were layered on one another so imperceptibly that the beginning seems only a few parties ago? I never watched any of it as *history*!

There are two parts to telling how this all came about. One part is simply blowing our own trumpets (mine and Christopher's), and we'll get to that almost immediately. But there is something else. The reason why Glorious Food succeeded was a combination of extraordinary ingredients present at the start. It was New York. It was our clients. And it was our love of food.

To begin with, Glorious Food was completely unintended. It was something to keep us going—a holding pattern. Christopher had bought a share in a Soho building in order to open a restaurant. He began to try out his food ideas at dinners for a few friends in his apartment. I was a television producer, between jobs, making up my mind about which ad agency to join.

I was strictly of the corned beef and cabbage, steak and potato school of food. You cooked something, put it on a plate and ate it. There was nothing mystical about it. But when Christopher produced those dinners for pals, I *noticed* something: the food *looked* different . . . and it certainly *tasted* different. He had brought an excessive, baroque style of cooking back to a natural, untampered form. Having done that, he simplified the food so that it appealed to all the senses at once with its colors, smells and tastes. In not too long a time we all knew that something exciting was happening at those meals on 48th Street.

We were smack in the middle of a recession. Christopher needed money for his new restaurant and he felt it was time he tried his ideas on someone other than friends. I think that the first dinner was for ten. The reaction was a shock. The phone calls came the next day, "Who are you? Where are you? What are you all about?" That is New York. There is an immediate enthusiasm for something new. Every time we got one of those calls, Christopher and I just looked at one another. Deep down I don't think either of us dared think it would take off. In fact, we held our breath . . . for about five years. I continued helping out, running the business end for about nine months, until one day I realized this could actually *be* a business. It *was* a business. So I stayed, and Christopher sold back his share in the Soho building.

Since none of this was planned, it's no surprise the business had no name. When a friend—who is a lyricist—came by one day, we asked her to think of a name. She answered emphatically, "Christopher's food is fresh and glorious. Call it Glorious Food." She refused to think of anything else, so that was the name.

Four clients who appeared that year were, in every sense, modern-day Medicis. These patrons supported, encouraged, championed, suggested and challenged us, and have remained with this odd little company all these years. One was Geraldine Stutz of Henri Bendel, who took us by the hand into the fashion world, where we learned the tempo of creating and realized the need to stay five minutes ahead of the last new idea. Another was Lily Auchincloss, who is deeply involved in just about every facet of New York's cultural life. Helen O'Hagan of Saks Fifth Avenue gave us the freedom to experiment with food for large occasions. Finally, the Metropolitan Museum of Art, whose evenings gave us the opportunity to blend entertainment and fantasy. Somehow all who came to us came through these four.

It seems as though in those first years we cooked on every free stove and used every friend's refrigerator. In 1975, we took two major gambles. We bought a coach house on 75th Street to build our own kitchen. And we took a six-week trip to France (which we could hardly afford) to compare firsthand our own direction with that of French cuisine. That summer we were the guests of the newly knighted geniuses—Bocuse, Chapelle, Vergé, Delaveyne, and the Troisgros brothers. The French have a wonderful attitude about food. Their best conversations are at meals, where business is conducted and romances are made. That summer we learned how the French seduce. For them, everything in life has to do with food. Every summer, after that tour, we traveled to see what was happening elsewhere. We were able to bring back ideas from every country we were in, edit them and contemporize them to the New York way of life.

Not too long after we moved to 75th Street, we got a call to do a party for 2,000. I remember putting the phone down, smoothing the hair that was standing straight up on my head, and thinking, "Are we ready for this?" But who's going to make that decision and say you're ready? You just go ahead and plunge in. By then Jean-Claude Nedelec had joined us as chef. His French and Swiss training, combined with his experience at the Plaza, made dinners for a thousand flow like a dinner for ten.

Today, the kitchen staff has increased to twelve full-time cooks, and the number expands to forty for a large party. On the average we serve two cocktail parties—ranging in size from thirty-five to a thousand guests—and two dinners for fifteen to forty people each night during the year. We have been part of thousands of dazzling nights: the opening of the East Wing of the National Gallery, the ninetieth birthday of Carnegie Hall, the Tony Awards, the Calder retrospective at the Whitney, the twentieth birthday of Lincoln Center, Yves St. Laurent's launching of "Opium" on the Peking at the South Street Seaport. There were nights honoring the Royal Ballet and Prince Charles, Chancellor Helmut Schmidt, Princess Margaret, the Rockefeller family, Prime Minister Thatcher, and thirty Saudi Arabian sheiks. There were the openings at the Metropolitan for Tutankhamen, the Temple of Dendur and the Michael Rockefeller Wing. There were days and nights creating celebrations for many of *Fortune*'s 500.

In the end, our history is really just a part of our clients' histories. We've spent these ten years in a wonderful adventure. All of us have learned from one another—Christopher, myself, later Jean-Claude, our clients and all the rest who came and joined us along the way. New York has its own peculiar bush telegraph—the drums beat for a new enterprise—and ours was food. We've been blessed. Imagine having a business *and* having the time of your life.

—Sean Driscoll

MY first acquaintance with Glorious Food was in 1975 when I was an executive *sous-chef* at the Plaza Hotel in New York. I was asked by Christopher and Sean to do an ice sculpture for a party at the Metropolitan Museum of Art. Two things impressed me that evening: the European elegance and manner of the cooks and waiters, and Christopher's creativity and ideas. After a few years of freelance work with Glorious Food, I became involved full time.

The trends, the logistics, the possibilities and limits of this business fascinate me. They change constantly. People seem to eat more now than they did ten years ago. At private parties, it's not unusual to pass the main course twice. We cook twenty percent more food than is actually needed for parties under one hundred people and about ten percent more for crowds over a hundred. This is our allowance for accidents, spilling and so on. When ordering meat we allow a half-pound per person. The most popular main courses among our clients are fish and chicken, probably for economic reasons, followed by veal and lamb. Pork is rarely served at large parties for health or religious reasons. Beef is not popular, except in the corporate world.

We can prepare nearly any dish—with the exception of soufflés—even if there is no kitchen at the location, but the logistics are trickier without. We once cooked a Pheasant Souvaroff, a braised pheasant with an elaborate puff pastry cover, in our kitchen on 75th Street and then had to drive it twenty blocks—v-e-r-y slowly—in New York traffic to the party. The crust remained intact! When we did the opening of the East Wing of the National Gallery, ten carved ice baskets were transported in a van from New York to Washington, D.C. without damage.

Whether it's a party for twenty-five or for two hundred and fifty, everything has to be planned, checked and rechecked. To give you an idea of the timing and preparation for large parties (about 500 guests), the food is ordered five to six days before and the preparation begins two to three days ahead. Four chefs and six pantry help come in two days before the party. For occasions with a thousand guests, there are five chefs and five pantry help working.

We have an obsession with detail. A few years ago, Mrs. Carter

Brown (the wife of the Director of the National Gallery) shared with us her recipe for a sauce we now use with our Three Berries dessert. We wanted to use that recipe at the opening of the East Wing. The sauce called for Grand Marnier and midway through the dinner course, I realized we had none of the liqueur on hand. Sean "kidnaped" a guest's limousine in front of the museum, found a liquor store that was just about to close and delivered the Grand Marnier to our "kitchen" ten minutes before the dessert was to be served. We forget—just like everyone else—just not too often.

—Jean-Claude Nedelec

BIG PARTIES

F IT IS true that everything has a reason, then the big party is the reason caterers exist. The sheer number of guests tends to daunt the host or hostess. To have another person responsible for the vast amount of coordination and planning needed for such a party is the beginning of relief, which is why the caterer is summoned.

Once the number of guests goes beyond twenty or twenty-five, it is unlikely that the host will have sufficient table and glassware, or sufficient kitchen and service staff. The caterer solves this also.

Three factors determine the form of the big party: the space, the menu and the service. With very large numbers, finding a space is the first problem to solve. Most of these parties are given as benefits or corporate events, and a committee chooses a suitable and preferably exciting location. In New York City the choice of public spaces is nearly endless—the New York Public Library, the Metropolitan Museum of Art, the Museum of Modern Art, the 79th Street Boat Basin, the armories, the zoos and even department stores. Depending on the charity or the clout of the corporation, parties are welcomed in these places. Once the location has been established, it is necessary to determine what mood should be created for the evening. If the location has architectural beauty, so much the better; everything is that much simpler. But even if the space is dull and vacant you can do a great deal with lighting, flowers and especially the food.

Creating a particular menu for a specific location is one of the most exciting aspects of catering. The process is like solving a puzzle. We have actually set up kitchens on stairwells, in basements and elevators, hallways and dressing rooms, and even in the back of trucks. No matter where the kitchen is set up, no matter how difficult it makes the serving of food, the tension and frustrations must be restricted to the "back room." The guests must see only ease and graciousness. It simply wouldn't be appropriate for the waiters and chefs to have stage fright in full view of the guests. (Maybe that is why so many of our waiters are actors!)

For every big party there is one thing we insist on: a plethora of waiters. We always employ one and a half to two waiters for every table of ten. (By one and a half we mean that one waiter is responsible for serving the meal to his ten people, while the other waiter pours the wine, clears the table, and aids in serving two tables of ten.)

Most large parties are seated dinners. Many of these are held to honor someone, or to celebrate an event. The traditional dais has all but disappeared. At the time for toasts and speeches, the host leaves the table and goes to the part of the room where a microphone has been set up and where he will be visible to everyone present. The arrangement is more egalitarian and makes for a more relaxed evening.

Cocktails almost always precede dinner. Depending on the number of guests, the dinner is announced fifteen minutes ahead for twenty to one hundred guests and twenty minutes ahead for two hundred guests or more.

As soon as the guests are seated at their tables, wine is poured. Only one-third of the glass is filled. The meal is served in either butler or French service. With butler service, the guests generally serve themselves the first course, the salad and the dessert. With French service, the waiter serves the guests the main course from the platter, the soup from a tureen and all other courses are presented on trays. After the dessert course, tables are cleared after the guests have left the room. This practice is good manners, and the guests don't feel as if they are being rushed out the door.

THE METROPOLITAN MUSEUM OF ART

With its extravagance, fantasy and elaborate display, there is no party quite like this ball at the Metropolitan Museum of Art in New York City. It is a reminder of the court balls of yore. After all, what more appropriate setting for such a gone-forever kind of party than a museum?

The Metropolitan Museum of Art is the supreme hostess in this great city. Each year in early December she welcomes guests to a grand ball in honor of her Costume Institute. Entrance to the dinner preceding the ball is the most sought-after ticket of the winter season. By July, the dinner for seven hundred is already sold out. With this party, the Metropolitan achieves what every hostess in the world aspires to: to lavishly entertain old guard society, artists, royalty, heads of state, Hollywood celebrities and scions of fortune. She also has something that no other hostess has—many noble benefactors who underwrite every morsel of food, every flower, every glass of wine.

Each year the party is organized around the theme of the Costume Institute's exhibit, which opens to the public a few days after the party. (For the event shown here, the theme was "The Eighteenth Century Woman.") The party "belongs" to the chairwoman and her committee. The dream chairwoman, and we've had many, is knowledgeable and aware of the problems inherent in feeding large numbers, which is why some years the planning for the following year's event has begun as early as the morning hours after the ball. To determine the menu, Glorious Food holds a tasting of possible selections months ahead of the party in our kitchen. By then the chairwoman has already given us her ideas for the menu, which we reinterpret. We take her suggestion for a soup, for example, which she may have served to ten or twelve people at home, and adapt her recipe to suit seven hundred guests. At the tasting, two main courses and two desserts are presented and final choices are made.

One month before the party a meeting is held with the staff of the Metropolitan, the various rental people and the Glorious Food staff (chefs, maitre d's and captains). At this meeting there is a basic walk-through and final decisions are made with budgets in mind. (Because this is a benefit, the purpose is to raise needed funds; a good chairwoman can charm the musicians, the caterers, the florists—everyone—to rally around her.)

The most important consideration in finally deciding the menu is its suitability to the museum. Because of the limited kitchen facilities at the Metropolitan, two hot courses at this dinner are out of the question, so we plan to start with a hot course and follow with cold courses. Since this party is given on

MENU

Coquilles Saint-Jacques*

Cold Fillet of Beef and Veal
with Mustard Sauce*
Potato and Cucumber Salad
with Julienne of Truffle*
Mélange of Fresh Vegetables
Vinaigrette*

Vacherin on Lettuce Leaves

Charlotte Russe*

Espresso

•

Mâcon-Lugny "Les Charmes"
1979 · Château Simard 1974

Serves Ten

The Metropolitan Museum of Art's cavernous restaurant (on pages 16 and 17) is transformed into one of the most beautiful dining rooms in the world by lighting, candles, flowers and *trompe-l'oeil* paintings. The menu, opposite, is a tribute to a nation whose "Eighteenth Century Women"—the theme of the 1981 party— were the most exciting in the world.

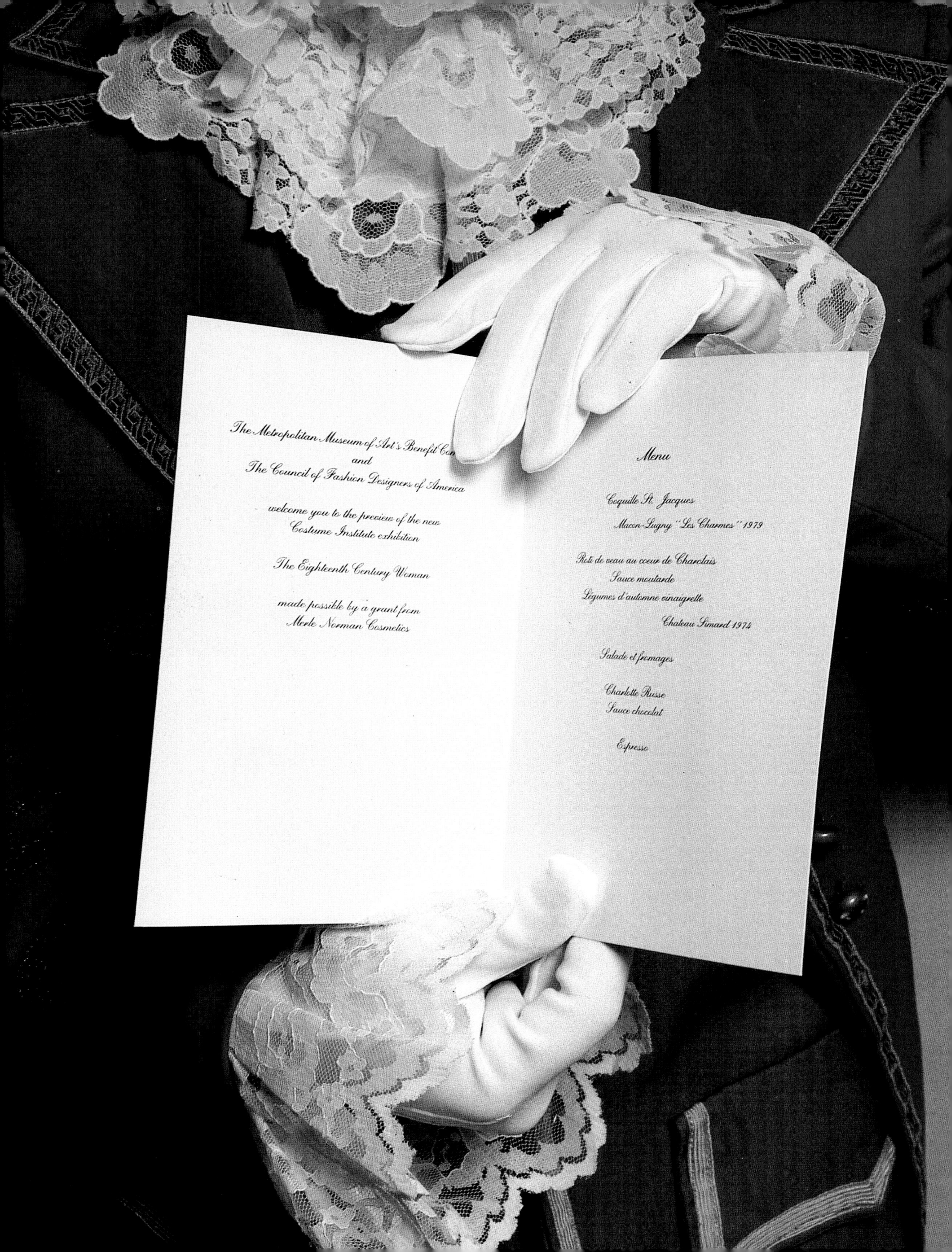

The Metropolitan Museum of Art's Benefit Com

and

The Council of Fashion Designers of America

welcome you to the preview of the new
Costume Institute exhibition

The Eighteenth Century Woman

made possible by a grant from
Merle Norman Cosmetics

Menu

Coquille St. Jacques

Macon-Lugny "Les Charmes" 1979

Roti de veau au coeur de Charolais
Sauce moutarde
Légumes d'automne vinaigrette

Château Simard 1974

Salade et fromages

Charlotte Russe
Sauce chocolat

Espresso

a cold winter night, we will begin the dinner with a piping hot Coquilles Saint-Jacques.

The day of the party round tables of ten are set up in the museum's public restaurant. Queen Victoria, when attending a dinner in her honor at Versailles, was quite struck by four hundred guests seated at such "intimate" tables of ten. As far as we know, this was the first time that official long banquet tables had been replaced by small round tables. We've always believed that seating more than ten at a table at large parties interferes with contact and destroys conviviality.

The one hundred and forty waiters hired for this party are not all scheduled to arrive at once: one third of the staff arrives to set up four hours before the party begins; the remainder of the staff comes two hours before. We spend one hour explaining the menu to the waiters and instructing them on serving the meal and wines. Once the food has left the kitchen the entire success of the party will depend on these men.

In producing this kind of party, there is always some stage fright and anxiety as the evening begins, but over the years we've come to realize that this tension adds life to the party. Serving the Coquilles Saint-Jacques hot to seven hundred guests

Flowers in glass vases tower over the heads of the guests but do not obstruct their view.

One hundred and forty waiters were hired to serve the seven hundred guests.

at once is the kind of challenge that demands extraordinary agility on the part of the kitchen staff and the waiters, triggering a momentum that lasts throughout the evening. The courses that follow are easier to serve, since they are prepared ahead, and the staff can then concentrate on pouring the wine and keeping the tables attractive by constantly clearing excess plates, unused glasses and used ashtrays.

A big party can be either a great success or a great flop. There is no such thing as a moderately good party. The hours, days and months of planning, the logistics, the numbers, the timing, are like staging a battle. Long ago we determined that catering big parties is the creation of the possible from an impossible situation.

The first course, Coquilles Saint-Jacques, is the only hot course served after the guests are seated.

COQUILLES SAINT-JACQUES

INGREDIENTS

6 ounces (12 tablespoons) unsalted butter
4 ounces (½ cup) unsifted all-purpose flour
4 cups (1 quart) court bouillon (see Appendix, page 246)
2 large shallots, chopped very fine
1 large leek, white part only, julienne sliced
¼ pound mushrooms, caps only, julienne sliced
1 cup dry white wine
3 pounds sea scallops, sliced in half if too large
2 cups heavy cream
Pinch of saffron (optional)
1 tablespoon finely chopped chives
2 egg yolks

TOOLS

Stockpot *or* heavy kettle
Oven-proof casserole *or* 10 individual serving shells

Salt and pepper placed in simple mussel shells eliminates the need for renting traditional cellars.

METHOD

In a stockpot, melt 8 tablespoons of the butter over low heat.

Gradually add the flour, stirring vigorously with a wire whisk. Stir the mixture constantly until it thickens, taking care not to let it brown.

Add the court bouillon, ½ cup at a time, incorporating it before adding more. Continue cooking over low heat, stirring constantly, until the white sauce has thickened and cooked through, about 30 minutes. Set aside.

In a large skillet, melt the remaining 4 tablespoons of the butter over moderate heat. Sauté the shallots in the butter, add the leek and, after about a minute, the mushrooms. Sauté briefly without browning.

Using a slotted spoon, transfer the vegetables to a bowl; set aside.

Pour the wine into the skillet and bring it to a simmer.

Add one third of the scallops and poach them in the wine for about 1 minute (the scallops should be undercooked).

Set them aside; poach the remaining scallops in two batches.

Increase the heat to high and reduce the poaching liquid by half. Over medium heat, slowly stir in the heavy cream. Add the saffron if you are using it and again reduce the liquid by half.

Pour the cream mixture into the white sauce and stir vigorously. Strain and reserve 1 cup for the glaze.

Gently fold the scallops, sautéed vegetables and chives into the remaining sauce.

In a small saucepan, combine the reserved cup of sauce with the egg yolks. Cook over low heat, stirring constantly with a whisk until the yolks are incorporated and the sauce warmed through. Do not boil.

Preheat the broiler. (If you do not have a broiler, set the oven for maximum temperature.) Spoon the scallop mixture into an oven-proof casserole or into 10 individual serving shells. Spoon with the glaze and broil until golden brown.

Serves 10

COLD FILLET OF BEEF AND VEAL WITH MUSTARD SAUCE

INGREDIENTS

A 3½-pound (net weight) fillet of beef, completely
 trimmed
A 3-pound (net weight) eye of loin of veal, completely
 trimmed
Olive oil
1 teaspoon salt
½ teaspoon white pepper
½ cup coarsely chopped celery
½ cup coarsely chopped onion
½ cup coarsely chopped carrot
2 cloves garlic, crushed

Mustard Sauce

1 cup dry white wine
1 bay leaf
½ teaspoon crushed black peppercorns
¼ teaspoon thyme
½ cup tarragon vinegar
2 shallots, finely chopped
½ cup Dijon-style mustard
½ cup *crème fraîche* (see Appendix, page 245)
½ cup chopped chives

TOOLS

Large roasting pan

METHOD

Preheat the oven to 450°.
Place the beef fillet next to the veal and cut off the
 ends of the beef so that the fillet is the same length
 as the loin of veal.
Quickly sear the beef on all sides and on both ends
 in a little oil. This should take no longer than
 1 minute. Set the beef aside to cool.
Split the loin of veal lengthwise without cutting it all
 the way through (butterfly cut).
Open the veal out flat and season the inside with the
 salt and pepper. Lay the beef down the center of
 the veal and wrap the veal around it to enclose it
 completely. (If the veal is not wide enough to wrap
 the beef entirely, open it up again and pound with
 the flat side of a cleaver to flatten it.) Tie the meat
 at intervals with kitchen string.

Place the meat in a lightly oiled roasting pan and
 roast it for 15 minutes. Remove the pan from the
 oven and reduce the temperature to 375°.
Remove the meat from the pan and scatter the
 celery, onion, carrot and garlic in the bottom of the
 pan. Place the meat on top of the vegetables and
 roast for an additional 25 minutes.

Two classic roasts and a colorful mélange of fresh vegetables are prepared ahead of time and served cold.

Set the meat and vegetables aside to cool.

To prepare the mustard sauce:

Deglaze the pan with the white wine and scrape the mixture into a small saucepan. Add the bay leaf, peppercorns, thyme, vinegar and shallots; reduce over high heat until about ¼ cup of liquid remains. Strain and set aside to cool.

In a mixing bowl, whisk the mustard with the *crème fraîche*. Stir in the cooled reduction.

Just before serving, stir in the chives.

When ready to serve, slice the meat into ½-inch slices and serve with the cooled vegetables. Serve the mustard sauce on the side.

Serves 10

POTATO AND CUCUMBER SALAD WITH JULIENNE OF TRUFFLE

INGREDIENTS

6 large Idaho potatoes
5 cucumbers
1 teaspoon salt

Sauce

1 teaspoon Dijon-style mustard
1 shallot, finely chopped
3 tablespoons mayonnaise (see Appendix, page 245)
¼ cup tarragon vinegar
¼ teaspoon white pepper
1 teaspoon salt
1 cup olive oil

Accompaniment

1 truffle, cut into matchstick julienne

TOOLS

Food processor *or* blender

METHOD

Wash the potatoes and cook them in their skins in salted boiling water to cover until a knife can be inserted easily. Drain, cool and peel.

When the potatoes have cooled thoroughly at room temperature, slice thin.

Peel the cucumbers, cut them in half lengthwise and remove the seeds. Place one half of a cucumber on top of another and cut into paper-thin slices. Repeat for each cucumber.

In a bowl, toss the cucumbers well with 1 teaspoon of salt. Let stand for several hours at room temperature or overnight in the refrigerator.

Drain, reserving the liquid for the sauce.

To prepare the sauce:

Combine the reserved liquid with the mustard, chopped shallot, mayonnaise, vinegar, pepper and salt in a food processor or blender. Purée thoroughly, slowly adding the oil. Continue to blend until mixed.

Pour the sauce over the potatoes and toss carefully. Fold in the cucumbers.

Just before serving, arrange the truffle julienne over the top of the salad.

Serves 10

Potato and cucumber salad is tossed in a creamy, pungent mustard sauce then dusted with truffles.

MÉLANGE OF FRESH VEGETABLES VINAIGRETTE

INGREDIENTS

2 medium carrots, peeled and trimmed
2 medium zucchini, trimmed
1 small cauliflower
1 bunch broccoli
5 ounces snow peas
5 ounces string beans
1 teaspoon salt
¼ cup lemon juice
Vinaigrette (see Appendix, page 245)

TOOLS

Large kettle

METHOD

Keep each vegetable separate until the final step.
Cut the carrots and the zucchini into 2-inch lengths and then into fine julienne.
Cut the cauliflower and broccoli into florets no larger than ½-inch in diameter. Remove any excess stem.
Wash the snow peas. Break off the stem end and remove together with any "string."
Wash the string beans. Using a sharp knife, cut off the stem end, then cut each bean lengthwise into 4 strips. (This is most easily accomplished by cutting it in half lengthwise using the "seam" as a guide, then holding the two halves together, turning the bean and making a second lengthwise cut.)
In a large kettle, bring a large quantity of water to a boil. Add the salt.
Pour some of the water into a 2-quart saucepan, in which you will blanch the vegetables.

Pour in the lemon juice. When the water returns to the boil, blanch the cauliflower florets. Cook briefly (the vegetables should retain their crispness); immediately drain and plunge the florets into cold water. Rinse until completely cooled and drain again.
Repeat the blanching process, omitting the lemon juice, with the broccoli, snow peas and beans, using fresh water from the large kettle each time. Cooking times will vary for each vegetable. Be especially careful not to overcook the broccoli.
Set the vegetables aside at room temperature until ready to serve.
Make the vinaigrette.
Just before serving combine all six vegetables. Pour the vinaigrette over them and toss gently. Taste for seasoning.

Serves 10

The bread is passed during the salad course—individual lettuce leaves with slices of vacherin eaten as finger food. *Overleaf:* Just before serving, miles of spun sugar, candied violets and fresh strawberries are added to the Charlotte Russe.

The dessert moves quickly from kitchen to table.

CHARLOTTE RUSSE

INGREDIENTS

½ cup candied fruit, diced
¼ cup *kirsch*
9 egg yolks
½ cup superfine sugar
4 teaspoons unflavored gelatin
1½ cups milk
3 cups heavy cream
½ vanilla bean
¼ cup confectioners' sugar
25 ladyfingers

Accompaniment

Unsweetened whipped cream
Candied violets
Large-stemmed strawberries

TOOLS

8-inch round springform pan

METHOD

Macerate the candied fruit in the *kirsch* for at least 4 hours or overnight.

In a bowl, beat the egg yolks with the superfine sugar until the mixture falls slowly in a ribbon from a raised whisk.

Sprinkle the gelatin over ½ cup of the milk, and set aside to let the gelatin soften.

In a heavy saucepan, combine the remaining 1 cup of milk with 1 cup of the heavy cream and the vanilla bean. Bring to a boil, remove from the heat and slowly whisk it into the egg mixture, beating vigorously. When the two are thoroughly combined, pour the mixture back into the saucepan and cook over low heat, stirring constantly. The cream will thicken as it cooks. Just before it starts to boil, remove from heat and stir in the softened gelatin.

Strain the cream mixture into a bowl set in a larger bowl of ice water. Stir until the mixture is almost cold.

Add the macerated fruit with all of the liquid.

In a mixing bowl, whip the remaining 2 cups heavy cream. When almost stiff, add the confectioners' sugar and keep beating until very stiff.

Fold the whipped cream into the cream mixture; do not overmix.

Line the bottom and sides of an 8-inch round spring-form cake pan with the ladyfingers. Spoon the cream into the pan and refrigerate for 6 to 8 hours.

To serve, remove the outside of the pan and with a large spatula, carefully transfer the charlotte to a serving platter. Decorate with the whipped cream, candied violets and large-stemmed strawberries.

Ambitious cooks may want to use spun sugar.

Serves 10

THE NEW YORK BOTANICAL GARDEN

MENU

Cold Mussel Soup*

Roast Loin of Veal with Sweetbread
Mousse*
Rosemary Potatoes and Garden
Vegetables*

Fresh Fruits and Three Sauces*

Chocolate Truffles* (see page 239)

Espresso

·

Meursault · A fine red Bordeaux

Serves Ten

For corporate entertaining, clients often ask for an unusual setting in which they might hold their parties. A unique setting offers the guests an adventure, a place they may never have been or at least a place where they have never been entertained. In many cities, you will find that museums, historic houses, botanical gardens and national trust houses may be rented in exchange for a donation to the institution.

For example, some of our most successful evenings have been dinners given at the New York Botanical Garden, located about twenty minutes from Manhattan in the Bronx. Because transportation to an out-of-the-way location can be inconvenient, we encourage the host to hire a bus for transporting the guests to and from the party.

The conservatory at this botanical garden is a crystal palace and an architectural gem. During cocktail hour, the guests may wander through the maze of greenhouses, where we have set up a series of bars, discovering and rediscovering the garden's exotic flowers and plants. The guests are encouraged to move around during cocktail hour, before they are assembled in one room for dinner. By bringing them all together for the meal, we eliminate the common, though often unwarranted, feeling among guests that there is an "A" and "B" room.

When deciding on the menu, thought must be given to kitchen facilities and equipment. Since the conservatory has no kitchen, foods must be prepared ahead and then transported in special insulated cabinets. For this particular occasion, the first course and the dessert are cold, the main course, hot. In serving large groups, fish should be served as a first course only, so we offered a mussel soup. The "roast" for this occasion is veal, served with a variety of vegetables to add color to the course. The fresh fruit for dessert, if mixed together, would be just another *macédoine*, or worse yet, a fruit cocktail. To avoid this, each fruit has been arranged separately on a silver tray, and is served with three complementary sauces, creating an attractive presentation.

For this kind of occasion, if china, linens and glassware must be rented and your choice is limited, choose simple white china, unembroidered cotton cloths and serviceable, pleasantly shaped glasses. Create the visual interest in the food instead.

The ordinary business dinner—so often given in a hotel—has been transformed into a generous treat by such an unusual setting. The host or hostess will be long remembered for inventiveness and ingenuity.

A mussel on a half-shell and julienne of leek and carrot decorate the cold mussel soup.

COLD MUSSEL SOUP

INGREDIENTS

100 mussels
1 leek, white part only
1 carrot
½ cup dry white wine

Stock

½ cup chopped leek, green part only
½ cup chopped celery
2 shallots, chopped
4 white peppercorns, crushed
Pinch of thyme
½ bay leaf, crushed

1 ounce (2 tablespoons) unsalted butter, at room
    temperature
1 tablespoon all-purpose flour
About 2 cups heavy cream

TOOLS

Large stockpot *or* heavy stainless-steel pot, each with
    cover
Food mill

METHOD

Wash and scrub the mussels and remove their beards.
Place the mussels in the freezer for 10 minutes before
    steaming so they will open faster.
Preheat a large covered pot for about 5 minutes over
    high heat. Add the mussels and cover. Shake the
    pot from time to time to allow the mussels to heat
    evenly. When the mussels open, allow them to
steam a minute or two, then remove them from
    the pot; do not overcook. Reserve all juices.
Remove the mussels from the shells, reserving ten
    uniformly sized, beautiful half-shells and ten of the
    plumpest mussels for the accompaniment. Discard
    the remaining shells.
Cut the leek and carrot into 2½-inch lengths, then
    julienne. You should have about 1 loosely-packed
    cup of each.
In a small pan, combine the white wine with ½ cup of
    water. Bring to a boil. Use this liquid to individually
    poach the leek julienne and then the carrot juli-
    enne. Poaching time should be about 30 seconds.
    Set the leeks and carrots aside, reserving the cook-
    ing liquid.
In a saucepan, combine the liquid reserved from the
    mussels with the stock ingredients, the remaining
    mussels and the vegetable poaching liquid. Bring to
    a boil then simmer to reduce the volume by half.
Knead together the butter and flour and add them to
    the soup, stirring constantly until blended. Cook for
    15 minutes over low heat, stirring constantly.
Pass the mixture through a food mill, cool. You should
    have 2 cups of soup base.
Stir the heavy cream into the soup base (if necessary,
    add more cream to make 1 quart). Strain; chill well.
To serve, pour the soup into bowls and accompany
    each serving with a mussel on a half-shell in the
    middle of the bowl and some julienne of leek and
    carrot placed decoratively at each end of the shell.

Serves 10

ROAST LOIN OF VEAL WITH SWEETBREAD MOUSSE

INGREDIENTS

Sweetbread Mousse

1 medium sweetbread
1 tenderloin of veal (about ½ pound or less)
1 shallot, finely chopped
3 dried morels, soaked, washed and dried
½ teaspoon salt
Pinch of ground white pepper
Pinch of cayenne
1 egg white
¼ cup heavy cream

Loin of Veal

A 3-pound eye of loin of veal, completely trimmed
1 teaspoon salt
½ teaspoon ground white pepper
8 large spinach leaves

½ cup coarsely chopped celery
½ cup coarsely chopped onion
½ cup coarsely chopped carrot
2 cloves garlic, crushed
½ cup dried morels, soaked overnight in 1 cup of water
1 cup dry white wine
1 quart veal or chicken stock (see Appendix, page 246)
1 teaspoon unsalted butter
2 shallots, finely chopped
1 cup heavy cream

TOOLS

Electric mixer with meat grinder attachment, fine
    blade, *or* manual meat grinder
Food processor
Large roasting pan

The veal roast with sweetbread mousse and rosemary potatoes transform a "meat and potato" course into a lofty presentation.

METHOD

To prepare the sweetbread mousse:

Follow the method for preparing sweetbreads on page 185 and increase the cooking time to 20 minutes. Do not refrigerate.

Pass the veal tenderloin, sweetbread, shallot and morels through the fine blade of the meat grinder until they are finely ground.

Place the mixture in the food processor with the salt, pepper and cayenne. Process by turning the machine on and off quickly two or three times to blend.

Add the egg white and the heavy cream and continue processing in the same way until the mixture is smooth.

Transfer the mixture to a bowl and refrigerate until ready to use.

To prepare the veal:

Preheat the oven to 450°.

Split the loin of veal lengthwise without cutting it all the way through (butterfly cut).

Open the veal flat and season the inside with the salt and pepper.

Wash the spinach and lay four of the leaves down the center of the loin.

Spread the sweetbread mousse over the spinach leaves so that the mousse covers only the middle section of the veal.

Cover the mousse with the remaining spinach leaves, encasing the mousse completely in the spinach.

Carefully roll the loin, keeping the mousse in place. Tie the roast at intervals with kitchen string and place in a roasting pan.

Roast the veal for 15 minutes and remove it from the oven. Lower the oven temperature to 375°.

Lift the veal out of the pan and scatter the celery, onion, carrot and garlic in the bottom of the pan. Place the meat on top of them and roast for 25 minutes.

While the meat is roasting, drain the morels, saving the water they have soaked in. Wash them well and set aside.

Remove the meat from the oven, take it out of the pan and keep it warm on a platter. Deglaze the roasting pan with the white wine.

Place the liquids and the vegetables from the roasting pan in a saucepan together with the veal stock and the reserved liquor from the morels. Cook over high heat until the liquid is reduced to about 2 cups. Strain the sauce through a fine sieve and set aside.

In a heavy saucepan, melt the butter and lightly sauté the shallots. Add the morels and the heavy cream, cooking until thickened.

Add the reserved sauce base slowly, stirring to keep the mixture smooth.

Serve immediately, to accompany slices of the veal.

Serves 10

ROSEMARY POTATOES AND GARDEN VEGETABLES

INGREDIENTS

Garden Vegetables
2 medium carrots
2 medium zucchini
1 small head cauliflower
1 bunch broccoli
5 ounces snow peas
5 ounces string beans
1 teaspoon salt
¼ cup lemon juice

2 ounces (4 tablespoons) unsalted butter
Salt and freshly milled white pepper, to taste

Potatoes
11 large Idaho potatoes, cut in half crosswise
½ cup clarified butter (see Appendix, page 245)
½ teaspoon crushed dried rosemary or ¼ teaspoon
   chopped fresh rosemary
Salt and freshly milled black pepper, to taste

METHOD
Prepare the garden vegetables following the method
   given on page 31, up to the point of adding the
   vinaigrette.
Instead of adding vinaigrette, melt the butter in a pan
   large enough to hold the vegetables and sauté
   them gently to heat through. Add salt and milled
   white pepper to taste.

To prepare the potatoes:
Preheat the oven to 400°.
Turning the potatoes as you pare them, cut them into
   22 2½-inch olive shapes.
Toss the potatoes and the clarified butter in a pan
   and roast for 15 minutes. Remove from the oven
   and sprinkle with the rosemary. Roast the potatoes
   for an additional 5 minutes or until cooked. Toss
   lightly with the salt and pepper.
Serve hot with the garden vegetables.

Serves 10

FRESH FRUITS AND THREE SAUCES

INGREDIENTS
Any combination of fresh fruits, such as:
   Orange and grapefruit sections
   Whole strawberries with stems
   Raspberries
   Sliced plums
   Fresh pineapple, peeled, cored and sliced extra thin
   Papaya, thinly sliced and sprinkled with some of its
      seeds
   Mango, thinly sliced
½ cup orange zest grenadine (see Appendix, page
   250)

Raspberry sauce (see Appendix, page 250)
Apricot sauce (see Appendix, page 250)
Caramel sauce (see Appendix, page 250)

METHOD
Attractively arrange the fruits on a serving platter.
   Sprinkle the fruits with the orange zest grenadine.
   Serve the sauces separately to accompany the
   fruits.

Serves 10

A mosaic of fresh fruit becomes a rich dessert
when served with caramel, apricot and raspberry sauces.

A TEA PARTY

MENU

Tea Sandwiches*
Scallops and English Cucumbers*
Brioche and Apricot Jam
Sandwiches*
Fruit Tartlets*
Scones*
Strawberry Basket
Lemon and Mint Sorbet*

Tea

Champagne · White Wine

Serves Twenty

A tea is a proper meal in bite-sized form. The sandwiches are typically English.

When a noted New York painter and sculptor invited us to do a party celebrating her New York opening in the spring, she decided to eschew the usual glass of wine in a smoke-filled gallery in favor of a far more festive party for her friends and collectors at her gingerbread house in Connecticut. The empty, turn-of-the-century greenhouse on her property would hold a hundred guests easily.

She wanted the best for the least, and we suggested a simple afternoon tea party. But she preferred more, a kind of stage set, so that people would dress up for the occasion. We suggested a *belle epoque* invitation to the tea party. Still she wanted more. We imagined creating a "conservatory," filled with palm trees and flowers, little clothed tables and white chairs, and a string quartet playing waltzes somewhere in a corner. But she wanted still more. As a result, this tea party would build to a crescendo.

As we decided it, from four to six o'clock we would serve tea and tea foods, a trio of Juilliard music students would play and a friend would sing *lieder* and art songs. As darkness approached hundreds of candles would be lit and champagne would be served. The music would shift to rock, people would dance and the guests would leave by 9 P.M. sharp.

The tea party became a carefully programmed event and the environment was transformed to suit the occasion. A few days before the party, the artist and a coterie of her friends whitewashed the floor and walls of the greenhouse. A planting shed behind the main greenhouse would function as a pantry for food and drink. One of our associates, a New York party and flower designer, decorated the greenhouse.

On the day of the tea, trees and ferns were borrowed from local nurseries and the flower designer supplied stencils of leaves and foliage, which were quickly sprayed on the floor and lower walls of the greenhouse. The roots and soil of the trees were bundled in white canvas duck and tied with gold rope. Pots of daisies were set in large baskets and tall, white vases held magnolia and forsythia branches. Pale beige cloths, covered with white eyelet, draped the small tables. We placed a small cage with a pair of finches on each table, while love birds in larger cages were suspended from the rafters. A two-tiered tea table was positioned at the side of the room.

The space became an enchanted garden.

TEA SANDWICHES

Cucumber Sandwiches

INGREDIENTS

2 medium cucumbers, about ½ pound each
Salt
1 ounce (2 tablespoons) unsalted butter
¼ cup mayonnaise (see Appendix, page 245)
12 slices thinly sliced white bread

METHOD

Peel the cucumbers and cut them in half lengthwise. Seed them with a small teaspoon.
Place one half of a cucumber on top of another and cut into paper-thin slices. Repeat with the other cucumber.
Lightly salt the cucumbers.
Place the cucumbers in a strainer over a bowl and refrigerate for an hour or more.
In a small bowl cream the butter with a wooden spoon and mix in the mayonnaise.
Lightly coat one side of each slice of bread with the mixture.
Squeeze the cucumbers in a tea towel to remove any excess liquid.
Spread the cucumbers on half of the bread slices.
Cover with the remaining bread slices.
Trim the crusts and cut each large sandwich into 4 triangles.

Yield: 24 small sandwiches

Watercress Sandwiches

INGREDIENTS

1 bunch watercress, bottom stems removed, finely chopped
Salt and freshly milled black pepper, to taste
16 slices thinly sliced white bread
¼ cup mayonnaise (see Appendix, page 245)

METHOD

Season the watercress with salt and pepper.
Lightly coat one side of each slice of bread with the mayonnaise.
Sprinkle the watercress on half of the bread slices.
Cover with the remaining bread slices.
Trim the crusts and cut each large sandwich into 4 triangles.

Yield: 32 small sandwiches

Chicken Sandwiches

INGREDIENTS

2 cups finely chopped poached, skinned and boned chicken
1 tablespoon finely chopped shallots
A few gratings of nutmeg
Salt and freshly milled black pepper, to taste
About ½ cup mayonnaise (see Appendix, page 245)
24 slices thinly sliced whole wheat bread
5 ounces (10 tablespoons) unsalted butter, creamed

METHOD

Combine all but the last two ingredients and mix well.
Lightly coat one side of each slice of bread with the butter.
Spread the chicken mixture on half of the bread slices.
Cover with the remaining bread slices.
Trim the crusts and cut each large sandwich into 4 triangles.

Yield: 48 small sandwiches

Egg and Tomato Sandwiches

INGREDIENTS

4 large eggs, hard boiled
Salt and freshly milled black pepper, to taste
1 teaspoon Dijon-style mustard
About ¼ cup mayonnaise (see Appendix, page 245)
5 ounces (10 tablespoons) unsalted butter, at room temperature
20 slices thinly sliced white bread
1 medium-ripe but firm tomato, cut into 10 thin slices and drained on paper towels

TOOLS

Food processor *or* blender

METHOD

Quarter the eggs and place them in a food processor or blender. Add the salt, pepper and mustard.

Process by turning the machine on and off a few times to blend the eggs into a crumbly mixture. Be careful not to purée.

Scrape the egg mixture into a bowl and add enough mayonnaise to bind.

Cream the butter in a bowl with a wooden spoon until very soft.

Lightly coat one side of each slice of bread with the butter.

Spread the egg mixture on half of the bread slices and cover each with a slice of tomato.

Cover with the remaining bread slices.

Trim the crusts and cut each large sandwich into 4 triangles.

Yield: 40 small sandwiches

Avocado and Bacon Sandwiches

INGREDIENTS

6 thin slices of bacon
½ cup mayonnaise (see Appendix, page 245)
1 tablespoon butter, softened
½ teaspoon Worcestershire sauce
A few drops of Tabasco
20 slices thinly sliced white bread
1 ripe avocado

METHOD

Render the bacon in a skillet over medium-low heat until golden brown. Drain and chop finely on a paper towel to keep it from forming into little lumps.

Mix the mayonnaise, butter, Worcestershire sauce and Tabasco in a bowl.

Lightly coat one side of each slice of bread with the mixture.

Peel and halve the avocado and slice thin directly over half of the bread slices. Sprinkle with the bacon bits.

Cover with the remaining bread slices.

Trim the crusts and cut each large sandwich into 4 triangles.

Yield: 40 small sandwiches

NOTES

Make the avocado and bacon sandwiches last. Place the sandwich triangles 4 to 6 deep in a container. Cover with damp paper towels. If you make them in the morning, seal the container with foil; they will stay fresh for hours and the bread will not dry out.

All tea sandwiches should be made with wafer-thin slices of bread. The combinations of fillings are endless but should always be light.

After arranging the sandwiches on a platter, sprinkle them with English cress or mustard cress. The seeds for these vegetables are available at good nurseries and through seed catalogues. They are easily grown on dampened felt and sprout in ten days.

BRIOCHE
AND APRICOT JAM SANDWICHES

INGREDIENTS

1 loaf brioche (see Appendix, page 248)
Apricot jam

METHOD

Slice the brioche into 14 (or more) thin slices.
Coat half the slices on one side with the jam. Cover
    with the remaining slices. Do not trim the crusts.
Cut each sandwich into 4 triangles.

NOTE

Serve the brioche on a separate platter from the tea
sandwiches.

Yield: 28 small sandwiches

SCALLOPS
AND ENGLISH CUCUMBERS

INGREDIENTS

½ pound tiny bay scallops
3 tablespoons lime juice
3 English cucumbers, at least 8 inches long
Dash of salt
Pinch of ground cloves
Pinch of cayenne
2 to 3 tablespoons *crème fraîche* (see Appendix,
    page 245)

TOOLS

1-inch round cookie cutter
Melon baller

METHOD

Cut the scallops in half. Toss them with 2 tablespoons
    of the lime juice and refrigerate for 2 hours.
Cut the cucumbers into 24 1-inch-thick slices, then cut
    these disks with a 1-inch cookie cutter to remove
    the skin and make perfectly round shapes.
Using a melon baller, make a shallow well in the
    center of each cucumber slice.
Drain the scallops, then mix them with the remaining
    1 tablespoon lime juice, the seasonings and enough
    crème fraîche to bind the mixture.
Place a little of the scallop mixture in the well of each
    cucumber round and serve.

NOTE

This recipe makes fine cocktail food as well.

Yield: 2 dozen

Palm trees, caged birds and a string quartet transform this once-empty greenhouse into a breathtaking garden.

SCONES

INGREDIENTS

2 cups unsifted all-purpose flour
1 tablespoon baking powder
½ teaspoon salt
1 tablespoon sugar
12 tablespoons (1½ sticks) unsalted butter, chilled
    and cut into small bits
About 1 cup heavy cream
2 eggs, lightly beaten
1/3 cup currants dusted with ½ teaspoon flour
1 egg yolk mixed with 1 tablespoon cold water for
    egg wash
Granulated sugar to dust the scones
Whipped cream or *crème fraîche* (see Appendix,
    page 245) and strawberry preserves (optional)

TOOLS

Electric mixer with paddle attachment
1-inch round cookie cutter
Large cookie sheet

METHOD

Preheat the oven to 450°.

Using the electric mixer, mix the flour, baking powder, salt, sugar and butter to a mealy consistency. Add the cream and eggs; do not overbeat. Fold in the currants.

Turn the dough out on a floured surface and pat it down by hand until it is 3/4-inch thick.

Cut out the scones with the cookie cutter, occasionally dipping the cutter in flour.

Place the scones on a large cookie sheet and brush them with the egg wash. Sprinkle with granulated sugar. Bake about 10 minutes or until golden brown.

Serve the scones with good farm butter or with whipped cream or *crème fraîche* and strawberry preserves.

Yield: 2 dozen

FRUIT TARTLETS

INGREDIENTS

Pâte brisée for tartlet shells (see Appendix, page 248)
Pastry cream (see Appendix, page 251)
Prepared fresh fruits (enough to fill 72 tartlet shells):
  Whole hulled strawberries
  Seedless grapes
  Raspberries
  Blackberries
  Poached apricots, halved
Apricot glaze (see Appendix, page 249)

METHOD

Make 72 tartlet shells from the *pâte brisée*.
Fill each shell with a full ½ teaspoon of the pastry
  cream.
The individual tartlet shell will hold one strawberry or
  one halved apricot, or use three grapes, raspberries
  or blackberries per shell.
Lightly spoon a little of the apricot glaze over each
  individual fruit.

NOTE

The tartlet shells and pastry cream may be prepared a
day ahead and stored in a covered container. The
finished tartlets are delicate and should be filled
shortly before serving. Do not refrigerate.

Yield: 72 tartlets

LEMON AND MINT SORBET

INGREDIENTS

12 lemons
2 packed cups stemmed fresh mint leaves
1 quart light sugar syrup, cooled (see Appendix,
  page 250)

TOOLS

Food processor *or* blender
Sorbet machine, if available (see page 131 for alternate
  instructions for food processor)

METHOD

Cut off the tops of the lemons about 1 inch from the
  stem end; reserve the tops.
Carefully remove the pulp from the lemons with a
  teaspoon, leaving the skin intact.
Drain the pulp through a sieve over a bowl and press
  the pulp gently to extract all the juice. Reserve 1
  cup of the juice (freeze the remainder for another use).
Put the lemon shells and the tops in a plastic bag and
  freeze.
In a food processor or blender, chop the mint until fine
  with ½ cup lemon juice.
Combine the mint mixture and the remaining ½ cup
  lemon juice with the light sugar syrup.
Pour the mixture into the container of the sorbet
  machine and freeze according to the manufacturer's directions.
Store the sorbet in the freezer until ready to fill the
  shells.
To serve, spoon the sorbet into the lemon shells
  and cap.

Serves 12

For guests who prefer something other than tea sandwiches, there
are cucumber rounds filled with scallops and miniature fruit tarts.

CHILDREN'S HALLOWEEN

Goblins and ghouls, gnomes and fairies, princes and princesses, supermen and tinmen arrive at Glorious Food every Halloween to bob for apples, pin tails on donkeys, to listen to ghost stories and, on occasion, to raise havoc with our array of pots and pans. This is a children's fancy dress carnival, celebrated with more aplomb and abandon than most adult masquerades.

Parties for children are important. At these occasions children learn to make new friends, to play games together, to take turns and to share; in short, to be considerate of others. They are introduced to the rudimentary social graces.

At Halloween children drink cider and hot chocolate, approaching every sweet put before them with unself-conscious curiosity. We watch them selecting and rejecting, already forming their own ideas about food. Children are tempted by visually attractive food in the same way adults are. They are eager to try what looks appealing and we vicariously experience their delight in discovering something new.

We also give them their old favorites. While the pumpkin is a familiar face, the marzipan pumpkin is the beginning of an acquired taste. The lollipop may be an old friend, but the ghost lollipop of white chocolate is a new acquaintance. Candy corn is candy corn. And brownies are always popular. The unabashed display of joy and excitement makes children of us all, for the pleasures of childhood are contagious.

MENU

Apples for Bobbing
Brownies*
Ghost Lollipops
Marzipan Pumpkins
Candy Corn

Warm Apple Cider

Hot Chocolate

BROWNIES

INGREDIENTS

Unsalted butter and flour for the pan
7 ounces unsweetened chocolate
½ pound unsalted butter, at room temperature
1¾ cups sugar, less 2 tablespoons
5 large eggs, at room temperature
1 cup sifted unbleached flour
2 tablespoons vanilla extract
¼ teaspoon salt
5 ounces imported (preferably Swiss) bittersweet
   chocolate, broken into bits
½ cup seedless raisins

TOOLS

Baking pan 13 x 9 x 2"
Waxed paper or baking parchment
Double boiler
Electric mixer with whisk or heavy balloon whisk
Sheet pan, lined with waxed paper

METHOD

Lightly butter the baking pan and line it with waxed paper or parchment. Butter the paper, dust with flour and shake off any excess flour. Set aside. Preheat the oven to 350°.

50

Slowly melt the unsweetened chocolate in the top of a double boiler over low heat. When melted, remove from the heat and let cool while you mix the remaining ingredients.

Cream the ½ pound of butter and the sugar in an electric mixer at a slow speed. When thoroughly blended, add the eggs, one at a time, and beat at a medium speed until the mixture is fluffy.

Add the flour and blend thoroughly.

Add the vanilla and salt.

Fold in the melted chocolate and blend thoroughly.

Remove the bowl from the mixer and fold in the chocolate bits and raisins.

Coat the baking pan evenly with the mixture and bake for 18 to 20 minutes or just until the center of the brownies has set.

Remove the brownies from the oven and, with care, turn them immediately onto a sheet pan lined with waxed paper.

Refrigerate until cold.

Cut the brownies into 1½- to 2-inch squares with a long, thin-bladed knife, cleaning the knife between cuts.

Store the brownies in an airtight container or wrapped in foil at room temperature. Eat within 24 hours. Serve at room temperature.

NOTES

The cooking time is important. The brownies should be slightly underbaked. This is a mousselike brownie.

Marzipan pumpkins and ghost lollipops offer intriguing new tastes for this young party-goer.

CELEBRATIONS

T IS customary for us to mark the occasions of birth, marriage and death with a demonstration of our joy or respect. Whether the gatherings for these occasions are large or small, the surroundings simple or ornate, the moment is intended to be memorable.

No matter what scale they may assume, these occasions take up a good part of a day and—in the case of the wedding festivities—a full two days. These events are exhausting for everyone. The people brought together—often strangers—bring different sets of emotions to these celebrations and must be made to feel comfortable. These details require an intimidating amount of advance planning.

More often than not, the group assembled is too large for the host or family to handle, and the event itself is distracting. For years Glorious Food has been asked to take over these celebrations. We concentrate on making the hours pass as smoothly as possible, alleviating any sense of strain. To accomplish this, extra help is paramount, a staff sufficient to ease and guide the flow of guests. Food is not the focal point here; the occasion is. A simple menu will suffice.

Wedding festivities are the most demanding. Prenuptial celebrations are usually signaled by a dinner reuniting close friends and bringing together the two families. The dinner may or may not be followed by music and dancing. Traditionally, the evening—which is full of toasts and ribaldry—comes to an end just before midnight, when the bride-to-be and groom separate until the following day's ceremony.

The wedding day brings another set of festivities, including a reception and meal after the marriage ceremony. How elaborate this is depends primarily on the size of the gathering and on the space available.

When we first became involved with weddings, we regretted that it was not more common to elope. During what seemed our every waking moment, the concerned mothers of the brides felt compelled to consult with us. Today, either the capacity of mothers to cope has improved or our reputation has put their worries to rest. We have attended to so many weddings that we have come to feel like the professional best man. We advise, suggest and cajole, and hope that, through our efforts, the day will happen just as the bride and groom had dreamed.

Planning and coordination are essential to the success of big celebrations. You must decide upon menus and cake decorations; select appropriate wines and liquors; choose the color scheme for tables and chair seats and determine the areas for tables and bars, musicians and dancing.

A couple of meetings with the musicians, flower arrangers and tent and lightning designers suffice. We mention the tent here because it can accommodate a large number of guests in the ''privacy'' of one's home, providing an atmosphere of festivity for everyone present seldom equaled by a hotel or other public accommodations. And finally, of course, the tent is an enormous umbrella in inclement weather. It can be erected almost anywhere—in gardens, around trees, at docks, on top of pools and over ponds. Most cities have a choice of tent companies capable of performing the seemingly impossible.

The christening celebration is usually a midafternoon gathering of the family, when fathers and mothers of all generations, siblings and godparents, closest friends and the church official join to celebrate the blessed event. The number of guests may be small or large, but the event need not be elaborate. A champagne reception, a festive lunch or a tea are appropriate. Between naps and feedings, the guest of honor is required to put in a token appearance only—a contented one, it is hoped.

A solemn event, the funeral is the third of our occasions. It is an expression of affection, respect and sorrow, and a demonstration of love and care for the family. It is customary to follow the funeral service with a reception for the family and close friends held at the decedent's house. We suggest relying on family members and friends who offer to assist on this occasion.

WEDDING EVE

MENU

Shucked Oysters
with
Caviar
Champagne Cocktail

Julienne Breast of Duck with Truffles,
Pears and Orange Cream*

Rack of Lamb* (see page 191)
String Beans
Potato and Truffle Tart*

Leaves of the Heart of Romaine
with Boursault*

Chartreuse Soufflé and
Crème Anglaise*

Espresso

·

Blanc de Noirs · Red Bordeaux
Vintage Champagne

Serves Ten

The thirty guests invited for this wedding eve dinner had to be accommodated in a long and narrow space. We lined up four standard twelve-foot banquet tables, covered each table with a cloth extending to the floor, and then ran one long bolt of shiny cotton fabric down the full length of the tables. For such an occasion, we felt lilac would be a suitable color.

We served shucked oysters with caviar and champagne cocktails before dinner. For the first course, a plate of duck julienne, poached pear and truffles was in place before each guest was seated. Although the combination of game and fruit is well known, this dish—a Glorious Food taste-teaser that is not a full course—is less known.

Spring lamb, fresh string beans and a truffled potato tart followed. Boursault cheese placed on a leaf of Romaine accompanied what remained of the red wine. The dessert was a chartreuse soufflé with warm *crème anglaise* and more champagne.

Determined to bring spring indoors, we "plant" wild violets and lilies of the valley on mosses and nestle quail eggs here and there. *At right:* The first course of julienne breast of duck with truffles, pears and orange cream makes a delicate introduction to the meal.

JULIENNE BREAST OF DUCK WITH TRUFFLES, PEARS AND ORANGE CREAM

INGREDIENTS

Duck
A 5- to 6-pound fresh Long Island duck
Salt and freshly milled black pepper

Pears
5 small ripe pears
⅓ cup lemon juice
1 cup white wine
½ cup sugar

Duck Marinade
4 oranges
1 tablespoon sugar
3 medium truffles, sliced into matchstick julienne
2 tablespoons walnut oil
1 tablespoon lemon juice
Salt and freshly milled black pepper, to taste

Orange Cream
½ cup mayonnaise (see Appendix, page 245)
Juice of ½ lemon
1 tablespoon Grand Marnier
Salt and freshly milled black pepper, to taste
½ cup heavy cream, whipped stiff

10 sprigs fresh mint, for accompaniment

TOOLS

Roasting pan and rack
Food processor *or* blender
1½-inch round cookie cutter
Melon baller

METHOD

To prepare the duck:
Preheat the oven to 450°.
Wash and dry the duck. Salt and pepper the cavity.
Place the duck, breast side up, on the rack in the roasting pan and roast for 30 minutes.
Reduce the heat to 375° and roast for 40 minutes more.
Remove the duck from the oven and set aside to cool.

To prepare the pears:
Peel, halve and core the pears. Brush them with some of the lemon juice.
In an enamel saucepan, bring 2 cups of water, the wine, the remaining lemon juice and sugar to a boil. Reduce the heat to a simmer and add the pears.

Place a round of waxed paper the size of the interior of the pan over the pears and poach for about 8 minutes, or until the pears can be pierced easily with a sharp paring knife. Cool the pears in the syrup.

To prepare the duck marinade:
Remove the zest from the oranges and julienne it.
In a small pan of boiling water, simmer the zest with the sugar for 5 minutes. Drain and reserve.
Remove the pith of the oranges with a sharp knife and separate the segments. Select 20 of the best sections and refrigerate. Purée the remaining sections in a food processor or blender and strain the juice. Reserve.
Remove the skin and any fat from the duck. Working carefully to keep the meat intact, remove the duck breasts from the bones. Discard the carcass or save for stock. Save the legs and skin for stock if desired.
Cut the breasts lengthwise into thin slices and then crosswise into thin strips. Place the strips in a large bowl and pour ⅔ cup of the strained orange juice over them.
Add the truffles, oil, lemon juice, salt and pepper and mix well. Set aside.

To prepare the orange cream:
In a separate bowl, mix the mayonnaise, lemon juice, Grand Marnier, salt and pepper.
Whisk ½ cup of the strained orange juice into the mayonnaise mixture. Fold in the whipped cream slowly and blend. Refrigerate.

Remove the pears from the syrup and reserve the syrup. Cut each pear half with a 1½-inch round cookie cutter, then pare the rounds so they are all ½-inch thick. Scoop out the center of each round with a melon baller.
Return the rounds to the syrup and set aside until ready to serve.

To assemble:
Remove the pear rounds from the syrup and drain. Place the pear rounds on individual plates. Arrange two orange sections opposite each other on the round. Toss the duck mixture again and remove from the marinade. Fill each round with a generous tablespoon of the duck mixture. Sprinkle some of the orange zest over the duck mixture. Decorate with a sprig of mint and serve with the chilled Orange Cream.

Serves 10

POTATO AND TRUFFLE TART

A truffled potato tart is served with the lamb.

INGREDIENTS

5 large Idaho potatoes, peeled
Salt and freshly milled black pepper, to taste
¾ cup clarified butter (see Appendix, page 245)
2 to 3 truffles, thinly sliced

TOOLS

10-inch pie pan

METHOD

Preheat the oven to 500°.

Slice the potatoes very thin (preferably on a mandoline). Place them in a bowl of lightly salted ice water. Drain and pat dry. Toss with salt and pepper.

Generously coat the pie pan with 2 tablespoons of the butter.

Arrange the potato slices in an overlapping spiral on the bottom of the pie pan. After one layer is complete, place some truffle slices on top and coat with butter.

Continue alternating layers of potatoes, then truffles and then butter (reserve some butter) until the pie pan is completely filled, ending with a layer of potatoes.

Place a towel over the pan and with a second pie pan press down firmly on the potatoes.

Remove the towel and pan and pour the remaining butter over the tart.

Bake for 45 minutes or until golden brown. After removing from the oven, let the tart rest for 3 minutes.

Place a heated serving platter over the tart and invert. If the potatoes do not immediately release, run a narrow metal spatula around the rim of the pan.

Slice the tart into wedges and serve.

Serves 10

CHARTREUSE SOUFFLÉ
AND CRÈME ANGLAISE

INGREDIENTS

Unsalted butter and granulated sugar for the
   soufflé pan
9 egg whites
Pinch of salt
6 tablespoons superfine sugar
Pinch of cream of tartar
4 egg yolks
½ cup green Chartreuse
Confectioners' sugar
1 quart of *crème anglaise,* (see Appendix, page 251),
   for accompaniment

TOOLS

Electric mixer
A 9 x 13½ x 1½" tin-lined oval copper pan

METHOD

Preheat the oven to 400°.
Butter the soufflé pan and dust with sugar.
Beat the egg whites with a pinch of salt until fluffy,
   then add 3 tablespoons of the sugar and the cream
   of tartar; continue to beat until the whites are stiff
   and glossy.
In another bowl, beat the egg yolks until smooth and
   lemon colored. Fold in the remaining 3 tablespoons
   of sugar. Fold in the Chartreuse.
Beat one heaping spoonful of egg whites into the yolk
   mixture, then lightly fold in the remaining whites.
Transfer the mixture to the soufflé pan, shaping the
   mixture into peaks.
Place the pan on the lowest shelf of the oven and
   bake 12 to 15 minutes or until the soufflé is puffed
   and browned on top.
Dust with confectioners' sugar and serve with warm
   crème anglaise.

NOTE

If serving 10 guests, prepare two soufflés. For
best results, prepare the ingredients for each soufflé
separately.

Serves 6

LEAVES OF THE HEART OF ROMAINE
WITH BOURSAULT

Using a thin, sharp-bladed knife (and dipping the knife
into hot water before each slice is made), cut the
refrigerated cheese into long thin slices (about ten to
each small Boursault). Arrange the slices on small,
pale green leaves of romaine (it is a crunchy contrast
to this soft and creamy cheese and will support the
cheese well). Place the romaine and cheese on a tray
and return it to the refrigerator covered with waxed
paper. Remove the tray about 15 minutes before
serving. Pass the tray to your guests while the dinner
plates are still on the table. The romaine can be picked
up with the fingers.

Other double and triple crème cheeses such as
Explorateur or St. André may be served, but they
are usually too soft and difficult to slice thin.

Chartreuse soufflé.

WEDDING RECEPTION

A champagne and tea-sandwich reception that ends with the cutting and sharing of the wedding cake often follows the traditional wedding ceremony. Sometimes strawberry baskets and white *petit fours*—small, square iced cakes—with the initials of the bride and groom are passed rather than the traditional wedding cake.

In this particular instance, the reception was a grand, seated lunch served under a white tent. We covered the tables with two shades of pink cloths, and placed a weeping birch, its roots and soil wrapped in purple cloths, in the center of each table. The tent was lit by paper lanterns that had been painted to match the other decorations. In the late afternoon, everything glowed soft pink.

Because the activities of the day were fatiguing, the lunch menu was chosen specifically to provide efficient service. The cold shrimp pâté, dill sauce and cucumber salad were presented together on silver trays brought to each table. Meanwhile, a second waiter poured the wine. The roast breasts of chicken with lemon-mustard sauce were offered on rustic clay platters, followed by the vegetables and spaetzle in copper pans. These ceramic and copper serving platters—appropriate in a country setting—reflected the pink theme. While the bride and groom cut the cake, lemon sorbet was served. The cake was then offered with champagne. Coffee ended the lunch.

After the bridal bouquet (a mixture of wild ferns) was tossed, the guests departed. The following day, each centerpiece was planted in the garden as a special reminder of the event.

MENU

Cold Shrimp Pâté with Dill Sauce*
Cucumber Salad

Roast Breasts of Chicken with
Lemon-Mustard Sauce*
Glazed Vegetables*
Spaetzle*

Wedding Cake* (see page 93)
Lemon and Mint Sorbet*
(see page 48)

Espresso

Vouvray · Champagne

Serves Ten

The tent, which covers a fourteen-foot drop of lawn, was erected the day before the event. The bar, set on the terrace, leads the guests from the house to the reception.

The shrimp pâté.

COLD SHRIMP PÂTÉ WITH DILL SAUCE

INGREDIENTS

Dill Sauce
⅔ cup mayonnaise (see Appendix, page 245)
⅔ cup *crème fraîche* (see Appendix, page 245)
⅔ cup sour cream
2 tablespoons lemon juice
Salt and freshly milled white pepper, to taste
Dash of cayenne
3 tablespoons chopped fresh dill

Shrimp Pâté
Court bouillon (see Appendix, page 246 and use
    entire quantity)
2 pounds medium shrimp
1 tablespoon unflavored gelatin
Sprigs of fresh dill
2 ounces (4 tablespoons) butter, at room temperature
½ cup *crème fraîche* (see Appendix, page 245)
2 teaspoons finely chopped chives
Dash of cayenne
½ cup heavy cream

TOOLS
Large stockpot *or* heavy kettle
Cotton cheesecloth
1-quart porcelain *or* metal mold *or* loaf pan, chilled
Food processor *or* blender

METHOD

To prepare the dill sauce:
Combine all the sauce ingredients and mix well. If the
    sauce is too thick, thin it with a little white wine or
    more lemon juice. Refrigerate until ready to use.
    Thin again if necessary just before serving.

To prepare the shrimp pâté:
In a large stockpot, bring the court bouillon to a full
    boil. Add the shrimp to the boiling stock and
    remove the pot from the heat. Let the shrimp cool
    in the stock (the shrimp will cook during this cooling
    period).

After the shrimp have cooled, remove, peel and devein them and reserve. Strain the stock through a double layer of damp cheesecloth. Chill 2 cups of the stock for the pâté. Save the remainder for other uses.

In a medium heavy saucepan, combine the 2 cups of chilled stock with the gelatin and heat, stirring constantly, until the gelatin has dissolved completely. Do not let it boil. Set aside to cool and thicken.

When the aspic has thickened enough to coat a spoon, pour it into the chilled mold or loaf pan. Rotate the mold so that the entire inside is coated with aspic; pour off any excess.

Refrigerate the mold to allow the aspic to set. Repeat the process until the desired aspic thickness is obtained. Set aside ½ cup of the aspic.

Decorate the bottom and sides of the mold with a few shrimp split lengthwise and with sprigs of dill. (They will adhere to the aspic.) Refrigerate until ready to serve.

Chop the remaining shrimp coarsely and combine in a food processor or blender with the reserved ½ cup of aspic and the butter. Purée, turning the machine on and off quickly, until the mixture becomes a fine paste.

Transfer the shrimp paste to a large bowl, add the *crème fraîche*, chives and cayenne and mix well.

Whip the heavy cream until stiff and fold it in. Taste for seasoning.

Carefully spoon the shrimp mixture into the prepared mold. Cover and refrigerate for at least 8 hours before serving.

NOTES

To unmold the pâté: Briefly dip the mold in hot water reaching almost to the rim. Invert a serving platter over the mold, hold firmly and turn the pâté and platter right side up. The pâté should slip out of the mold onto the platter without difficulty. If the pâté does not unmold, you can run a knife around the edge to help loosen it and dip into hot water again. Do not keep the mold in the hot water so long that the aspic melts. This can destroy the decoration.

Serve the shrimp pâté with the Dill Sauce and a Cucumber Salad.

Serves 10

Backstage: The service station and, overleaf, the kitchen.

ROAST BREASTS OF CHICKEN WITH LEMON-MUSTARD SAUCE

INGREDIENTS
6 double breasts of chicken

Marinade
1 medium onion, coarsely chopped
1 clove garlic, chopped
3 teaspoons dry mustard
1 cup lemon juice
¼ teaspoon ground white pepper
½ teaspoon salt
½ cup olive oil

Sauce
1 cup chopped onion
1 cup chopped celery
1 cup chopped carrot
1 cup dry white wine
1 quart veal or chicken stock (see Appendix, page 246)
3 tablespoons dry mustard
1 teaspoon arrowroot
¼ cup lemon juice
2 ounces (4 tablespoons) unsalted butter, chilled

Accompaniment
Grated zest of 2 lemons
1 teaspoon finely chopped chives
Fresh chanterelle mushrooms, if available

TOOLS
Food processor or blender
Large roasting pan
Large stockpot

METHOD
Cut the chicken breasts in half.
Combine all of the marinade ingredients in the food processor or blender and process until smooth.
Brush the breasts on both sides with the marinade and refrigerate for 24 hours.
Preheat the oven to 400°.
Remove the breasts, reserving all of the marinade.
Place the breasts in a large roasting pan, skin side down.
Brush with the marinade and roast for 15 minutes.
Turn the breasts, brush again with the marinade and roast 25 minutes more.
Transfer the breasts to a platter and set aside to cool.
Scatter the chopped onion, celery and carrot into the roasting pan.
Lower the oven temperature to 350° and bake the vegetables for about 15 minutes, or until they are lightly browned.
Remove the pan from the oven and deglaze with the white wine. Transfer the contents to a large saucepan or stockpot, taking care to scrape out all of the particles.
Remove the meat from the bones and add the bones to the saucepan. Add the stock and simmer over medium heat for 30 minutes.
Strain the stock, pressing out as much of the liquid as possible. Skim the fat off the top and return the stock to a saucepan. Simmer until the sauce base is reduced to 3 cups.
Mix the mustard and the arrowroot with the lemon juice until smooth and whisk into the sauce base.
Remove the pan from the heat and add the chilled butter, stirring vigorously until it is incorporated.
Reheat the chicken in a moderate oven until golden brown.
Arrange the meat on a platter and ladle the sauce over it. Sprinkle with the zest and chives immediately before serving with lightly sautéed chanterelles.

Serves 10

Roast breasts of chicken with lemon-mustard sauce are served on rustic clay platters, appropriate in a country setting.

Glazed vegetables and spaetzle.

GLAZED VEGETABLES

INGREDIENTS

22 small white onions
5 to 6 large carrots
4 to 5 large turnips
22 snow peas
22 small mushrooms
¼ cup salt
4 ounces (1 stick) unsalted butter
⅓ cup red wine vinegar
⅓ cup sugar
½ teaspoon salt
Pinch of white pepper

METHOD

Peel the onions and make an ''X'' in the root end of
     each.
Pare the carrots and turnips into 1½-inch olive shapes,
     making 22 of each.
Wash the snow peas, break off the stem end and
     remove, together with any ''string.''
Cut off the mushroom stems even with the caps.

Bring 2 quarts of water to a boil in a large saucepan;
     add the salt.
Using the same water, separately blanch the onions
     for 10 minutes, the carrots for 10 minutes, the
     turnips for 5 minutes and the snow peas for 30
     seconds. As you remove each vegetable from the
     boiling water, plunge it immediately into cold
     water. Drain and set aside to cool.
Melt 2 ounces of the butter in a small skillet and sauté
     the mushrooms in it. Set aside.
In a skillet or saucepan large enough to hold all of the
     vegetables, cook the vinegar, sugar and the remain-
     ing 2 ounces of butter over high heat until the
     mixture is somewhat reduced and takes on a
     caramel color.
Add all the vegetables except the snow peas and
     continue cooking, stirring occasionally until the
     liquid has evaporated and the vegetables are
     glazed, about 10 minutes. Add the snow peas and
     stir to glaze. Season with the salt and pepper.
Remove from the heat and transfer to a serving dish.

Serves 10

SPAETZLE

INGREDIENTS

1 pound (about 3 cups) unsifted all-purpose flour
8 eggs
2 teaspoons salt
Grating of nutmeg
½ cup cold water
Unsalted butter for sautéing.

TOOLS

Electric mixer with dough hook
Large pasta pot *or* kettle
Colander with large holes, which fits on top of the pot

METHOD

Combine all of the ingredients in the bowl of the
    mixer. Using the dough hook, mix on medium
    speed until the dough comes away from the sides
    of the bowl.
In a large pasta pot bring 8 quarts of water to a boil
    and add 2 tablespoons of salt. Place a colander
    with large holes in it on top of the pot.
Put the spaetzle dough into the colander and, using a
    rubber spatula, press it through the holes into the
    boiling water.
Remove the colander and stir the spaetzle to separate.
Cook for about 2 minutes.
Using a skimmer or slotted spoon, remove the spaetzle
    from the pot into a bowl of cold water. Rinse until
    cold and drain well.
Refrigerate the spaetzle in a flat container until ready
    to serve.
Before serving, sauté lightly in butter and taste for
    seasoning.

Serves 10

The wedding cake, a three-tiered bouquet of icing and violets is, underneath it all, a fruit cake.

71

CHRISTENING

The pastel hues of this afternoon meal suit the occasion.

What words come to mind at a christening? Gentle, pure and light. Pale pastels are fitting food colors for the occasion.

A puréed soup—light green—sparked with mint and served either hot or cold depending on the season is a simple beginning. Next, we offered a poached fish with green sauce and a cucumber salad. And, finally, a refreshing sorbet to accompany the christening cake. This simple meal in hues of greens and yellows is cooled by a glass of champagne or white wine. It is a meal that suits the occasion in its mildness.

MENU

Purée of Fresh Pea Soup with Mint*

Poached Bass with Green Sauce*
Cucumber Salad

Christening Cake
Fresh Fruit Sorbets*
(see page 130)

Espresso

·

Champagne · Veuve Clicquot

Serves Ten

PURÉE OF FRESH PEA SOUP WITH MINT

INGREDIENTS

5 cups hulled, fresh peas (about 5 pounds)
5 cups chicken stock (see Appendix, page 246)
Salt and freshly milled black pepper, to taste
1 to 1½ cups heavy cream
1½ tablespoons fresh mint leaves, cut into thin juilenne

TOOLS

Food processor *or* blender

METHOD

Cook the peas and chicken stock in a saucepan over a medium heat until the peas are tender. Strain the peas into a bowl; reserve the stock.

Purée the peas in a food processor or blender until smooth.

Stir the purée into the stock until blended. Push the mixture through a strainer and season with salt and pepper. Refrigerate until chilled.

Just before serving, whisk in a cup or more of the cream until the soup is the desired consistency.

Pour the soup into individual chilled bowls and sprinkle each with some of the mint juilenne.

Serves 10

POACHED BASS WITH GREEN SAUCE

INGREDIENTS

Green Sauce

1 bunch watercress leaves and the stems, chopped
½ cup chopped parsley
1 scallion (white and some of the green), chopped
1 tablespoon fresh tarragon leaves (or tarragon packed in vinegar)
1½ cups mayonnaise (see Appendix, page 245)
About 1 tablespoon lemon juice
About ½ cup sour cream
Salt and freshly milled black pepper, to taste

Bass

A 10-pound striped bass, cleaned with head and tail intact
6 quarts court bouillon (see Appendix, page 246, and double the recipe)
Dry white wine

Accompaniment

Watercress
2 lemons, thinly sliced

TOOLS

Food processor *or* blender
Fish poacher

METHOD

To prepare the green sauce:

Place the chopped greens and herbs in a food processor or blender and purée until smooth. Add half the mayonnaise and purée until only small flecks of green remain. Transfer the mixture to a bowl. Fold in the remaining mayonnaise, the lemon juice and sour cream.

Season with salt and pepper.

If the sauce is too thick, add more sour cream. Refrigerate until ready to serve with the fish. Thin again if necessary just before serving.

To prepare the bass:

Wash the fish and place it in a fish poacher.

Add the cold court bouillon. If the liquid does not cover the fish, add equal parts of white wine and water to cover.

Cover the poacher, place it over medium heat and bring the liquid to a light boil. Immediately reduce to a simmer. Skim the liquid once and poach for 10 minutes.

Remove the poacher from the heat and allow the fish to cool uncovered in the poaching liquid. Do not refrigerate.

Remove the fish from the poaching liquid and place it, bottom side up, on a platter. Peel off the skin with a sharp paring knife. Turn the fish over and peel the top side.

Remove all of the fin bones and as much of the belly lining as you can. Soak up any excess liquid with a paper towel and clean the platter.

Decorate simply with watercress and thinly sliced lemons.

Serve with the chilled green sauce.

NOTES

Once cooked, the fish will not spoil if left covered for a couple of hours before serving. Once refrigerated it begins to toughen.

Leftovers are good for a salad.

Serves 10

HOLIDAYS

GLORIOUS FOOD has never worked during holidays. When the company was first formed, we made a pact that holidays were meant to be private, family occasions, and we were determined to keep them that way. Our clientele tend to treat these occasions in just that spirit: after the intensity and merry-go-round of preholiday parties, they return to their private lives, their families and close friends.

These are a few of my own memories—in recipe form—which I enjoy recreating during these special moments of joy and celebration. The menus are, indeed, traditional, something remembered and repeated. They evoke the past. They recall former experiences—a smoked fish I once ate on New Year's in Berlin, a cake brought to me by Russian friends and the flaming plum pudding presented at the end of every Christmas dinner throughout my childhood. After all, memories make holidays. They are most easily elicited and enriched by the food we cook and serve and share.

Since we are speaking here of entertaining at home, a word about hors d'oeuvres and cocktail foods should be said. Hors d'oeuvre means literally "outside of the work"—outside of the main course. Therefore, it is the first course, not a cocktail food. When you have invited guests and have gone to the trouble of preparing a splendid meal, cocktail foods should be minimal. A dish of salted nuts is sufficient for the drink hour. And be sure to keep cocktails to that—one hour— so that your guests will arrive at the table with an appetite, not a hunger.

For a variation on the traditional champagne cocktail, perfect for any holiday gathering, add a drop of *framboise* and a drop of raspberry syrup to a glass of champagne.

THANKSGIVING

Thanksgiving celebrates the bounty of autumn, so let that bounty function as your holiday decoration. Colored leaves, autumnal fruits, squash and gourds, all sorts of berries and dried flowers can be strewn around the house or clustered on the dining room table. Pile apples high in bowls or stack pomegranates in pyramids; whatever strikes your fancy.

The pumpkin is one of the symbols of this rich time of year. We use a pumpkin shell as a "tureen" for serving the pumpkin soup. By oiling the pumpkin, you will give the "tureen" a rich bronze gloss when it is baked.

The cornsticks are actually cornbread baked in corncob-shaped iron molds, a tribute to the time when the Indians shared their "maize" with the Pilgrims.

For those who seek relief from the relentless appearance of turkey, substitute the more exotic roast pheasant, stuffed with sage leaves, orange zest and juniper berries. These leaves and berries will infuse the bird with a fruity taste. The rich brown sauce is laced with Madeira, and just before it is presented, the pheasant is flamed with the brandy of Armagnac.

All the vegetables for this feast are puréed and the combinations are determined by taste and color—the brown, white and orange of chestnuts, turnips with pear and sweet potatoes.

Always serve wine with cheese; they complement each other and bring a shading of tastes often missed when cheese is served alone. Port—the dark, sweet red wine of Portugal—is the ideal accompaniment for a rich cheddar cheese, a course designed to allow the guests to linger.

As a nice change from the usual overabundance of pies and cakes after all these courses, offer syllabub, the frothy old English dessert. There are scores of recipes for this creamy concoction, but many result in a cloying dessert. By adding lemon and sherry you will cut the syllabub's potential overbearing sweetness, creating a culmination to the meal that demonstrates your thought and inventiveness.

MENU

Pumpkin Soup*

Corn Sticks
Pheasant with Juniper Berries,
Orange Zest and Sage*
Puréed Vegetables*
Lingonberries

New York State Cheddar,
Grapes and Nuts

Syllabub* (see page 93)

Espresso

•

California Sauvignon Blanc or
California Champagne · Port

Serves Ten

A thoughtful tribute to our Pilgrim fathers.

PUMPKIN SOUP

INGREDIENTS

A 10- to 12-pound pumpkin (preferably round), for the "tureen"
Salt and pepper, for the "tureen"
2 quarts chicken stock (see Appendix, page 246)
Vegetable oil
A 5- to 6-pound pumpkin
2 quarts heavy cream
Nutmeg and mace, to taste
Salt and freshly milled white pepper, to taste
½ cup clarified butter (see Appendix, page 245)

TOOLS

Large baking pan that will comfortably hold the
    pumpkin "tureen"
Large soup kettle or stockpot
Food processor

METHOD

To make the tureen:
Preheat the oven to 375°.
Cut a "lid" in the top of the large pumpkin. The stem
    will serve as the "handle." Scoop out the seeds and
    loose fibers; reserve the seeds.
Lightly salt and pepper the inside of the pumpkin.
    Pour in ½ cup of the chicken stock and replace the
    lid to fit exactly. Rub the exterior of the pumpkin
    with vegetable oil and place it in a well-oiled pan.
    Bake for 1½ to 2 hours depending on size. The
    pumpkin is done when the flesh is tender and the
    exterior skin firm.

Meanwhile, make the soup:
Seed the smaller pumpkin, reserving the seeds,
    and cut it into cubes. Remove the outer skin. Place
    the cubes in a soup kettle and add the remaining
    stock to cover.

continued

79

Place the kettle over high heat and bring to a boil. Simmer for 1 hour or until the pumpkin cubes are very tender and soft (the smaller the cubes the quicker the cooking time). Stir from time to time to keep the mixture from sticking.

Strain the mixture and reserve the juice. Purée the pulp in a food processor.

Mix the purée with the reserved juice and return the mixture to the kettle. Add the cream, nutmeg, mace, salt and pepper, keep warm over low heat.

To toast the seeds:

Preheat the oven to 375°.

Coat the reserved seeds with the clarified butter and spread them out on a baking sheet. Place the baking sheet on the upper shelf of the oven. Toss the seeds from time to time until they are golden brown, about 18 to 20 minutes.

Place the seeds in a brown paper bag, add some salt and shake vigorously. Reserve.

To assemble:

Remove the "tureen" from the oven and carefully transfer it to a serving platter. Pry off the lid with a sharp paring knife (the steam inside the "tureen" will have almost sealed the lid).

Pour the soup into the cavity (it will not hold the entire amount) and mix the soup with the juices inside the "tureen." Replace the lid.

Serve the soup in heated soup plates, scraping some of the pumpkin meat from the "tureen" into each plate.

Sprinkle the soup with the pumpkin seeds or, if you do not like pumpkin seeds, substitute hot, butter-fried croutons.

NOTE

The seeds and soup can be prepared a day ahead. Add the cream when reheating.

Serves 10

PHEASANT WITH JUNIPER BERRIES, ORANGE ZEST AND SAGE

INGREDIENTS

4 pheasants (about 3 pounds each)
Salt and freshly milled black pepper
4 strips orange zest
4 sprigs fresh sage
2 tablespoons crushed juniper berries
Vegetable oil for coating
3 cups pheasant or chicken stock (see Appendix, page 246)
1 cup dry white wine

TOOLS

2 ovens
2 roasting pans and racks

METHOD

Preheat the ovens to 400°.

Wash and dry the birds. Salt and pepper the cavities.

Fill each cavity with one strip of orange zest, one sprig of sage and ½ tablespoon of crushed juniper berries. Truss the birds.

Coat the skin with oil and sprinkle with salt and pepper.

Place the birds on the racks in the roasting pans and place one pan in each oven. Immediately reduce the heat to 350° and roast the birds for 25 to 30 minutes per pound or until a meat thermometer placed between the leg and thigh reads 185°. Baste the birds every 15 minutes with their own juices.

Transfer the birds to a warm platter and keep them warm while you make the sauce.

Drain off most of the fat in the pans. Evenly divide the stock and wine between the pans and deglaze. Strain the sauce and serve with the birds.

NOTES

Pheasant stock can be made from the carcasses of previously cooked birds. Follow the same method as for duck stock (see Appendix, page 247) or reduce 1 quart of brown sauce (see Appendix, page 247) with the wing tips from the pheasants, 4 well-scrubbed feet and ¼ cup of Madeira. Reduce this stock by half and strain.

Flame the birds with Armagnac and serve with this sauce.

Serves 10

PURÉED VEGETABLES

Chestnut Purée

INGREDIENTS

1 pound fresh chestnuts
About 2 cups chicken stock (see Appendix, page 246)
1 teaspoon sugar
2 tablespoons unsalted butter
Salt and freshly milled white pepper, to taste

TOOLS

Food processor
Double boiler

METHOD

Using a sharp paring knife, score the chestnuts with an "X" on the round, soft side. Place the chestnuts in a pot and cover with cold water. Bring the water to a boil over high heat and boil for 2 minutes. Drain.

When the chestnuts are cool enough to handle, peel off the shells. Place the shelled chestnuts in a saucepan and cover with the stock. Add the sugar and bring the stock to a simmer. Continue to simmer for 45 minutes or until the chestnuts are tender. Strain, reserving the stock; remove all of the light brown fuzz from the nuts. (You may prepare this recipe up to this point a day in advance. If you do, refrigerate the chestnuts in the stock. When ready to cook, bring the chestnuts in the stock to a boil and simmer for 5 minutes. Drain, reserving the stock.)

Purée the chestnuts in a food processor until smooth. Thin the purée with a few tablespoons of the stock. Add the butter, salt and pepper.

Transfer to the top of a double boiler and keep hot over simmering water until ready to serve.

White Turnip and Pear Purée

INGREDIENTS

1 pound white turnips, peeled and quartered
1 ripe pear (about 7 ounces)
1 tablespoon lemon juice
1 tablespoon unsalted butter (optional)
Salt and freshly milled white pepper, to taste

TOOLS

Food processor

METHOD

Place the turnips in a saucepan with lightly salted cold water to cover. Bring to a boil over high heat, cook until tender, and drain.

Peel, halve and core the pear and place the pear in a small saucepan with the lemon juice and cold water to cover. Set over medium heat and bring the water to a simmer. Cook until tender and remove the pear from the liquid.

Purée the turnips and the pear in a food processor until smooth. Stir in the butter and season. Reserve in a double boiler and keep hot over simmering water until ready to serve.

Purée of Sweet Potatoes

Use about 1 pound of sweet potatoes. Bake the potatoes in their skins while the pheasants are cooking. When cooked, remove the potatoes from their skins and purée in a food processor with a bit of unsalted butter, salt, pepper and a touch of scalded heavy cream.

Serves 10

CHRISTMAS EVE

Christmas is the most delicious holiday, the one that appeals to all the senses at once. The scents of pine needles, spices, sizzling logs, baked pies and breads and roasting birds permeate every room. Christmas allows us to fill the entire house with flowers and garlands of evergreens. It's a time for splurging on luxury foods, as we pursue perfection for family and friends. Everyone has a special time for celebrating Christmas—some prefer Christmas Eve, others Christmas Day. I treasure a luxurious Christmas Eve dinner with a few friends.

Bring your guests to the table for smoked salmon and champagne. The salmon should be sliced thin and served with a creamy, whipped fresh horseradish sauce. By all means, avoid chopped onion for an accompaniment; it is a detail that overwhelms the delicate salmon and ruins the taste of all that follows. If you really want an additional variety of condiments to accompany the salmon, choose from last year's food gifts instead: pickled cherries, *cornichons à l'ancienne*, capers, Niçoise olives marinated in oil and herbs, Malaga raisins in vinegar, wild apricots preserved in Armagnac. Even a spoonful of caviar with nothing more than a squeeze of lemon would be splendid.

Wild game is synonymous with winter feasts and holidays, and quail is the most tender and sweet of all the birds in the game kingdom. Quail need only slight braising in butter and a brief roasting to seal in their delicious juices. Because there is so little meat on the bird, pick the fine bones clean. Quail should be eaten rare. It deserves a strong glaze sauce with cubes of *foie gras* tossed in. If *foie gras* is too much of an extravagance, sauté the quail's livers in butter, purée with a lesser grade of goose liver, and serve on thin slices of toast.

According to tradition, game birds should be served with the foods the birds themselves are most likely to eat, such as berries and wild rice. The cabbage dish—a mixture of thick *crème fraîche*, seedy mustard, crusty lardons and strips of cabbage—is a combination of wonderful textures. Myrtilles or bilberries, small blueberries that are quite common in jams and preserves in Europe, are prepared with very little sugar, and their extremely tart taste is an unusual relish for the quail. If they are unavailable lingonberries provide a very good substitute. (Cranberries are too large.) Crush rose geranium leaves, a pungent and almost exotic herb, and line the serving bowl with these leaves to perfume the berries.

MENU

Smoked Scotch Salmon
with
Fresh Horseradish Sauce*
(see page 125)
Red and White Pickled Cherries
Cornichons à l'ancienne
in Champagne vinegar
Capers
Niçoise Olives Marinated in Oil
and Herbs
Malaga Raisins in Vinegar
Wild Apricots Preserved
in Armagnac
Warm Toast and Sweet Butter

Baby Quail with Juniper
Berry Sauce*
Sautéed Red Cabbage
with Lardons*
Wild Rice*
Unsweetened Myrtille with Rose
Geranium Leaves

Vacherin Mont d'Or

Miniature Croquembouche*
Raspberry Sorbet* (see page 131)

Espresso

·

Vintage Champagne · White
Burgundy from Puligny-
Montrachet · Burgundy from
the Vosne-Romanée · A Great
Armagnac

Serves Four

This miniature croquembouche is
pure fancy. A simple alternative is
a plate of caramelized cream puffs.

The Vacherin Mont d'Or is a delicate, soft cheese from the Jura in southwestern Switzerland. Produced only during the latter months of the year, this cheese is at its peak during the holiday season. By serving it with such a grand meal, you encourage your guests to sip the wine and enjoy the company for a while longer. As for serving bread, avoid big blotter breads because they are too heavy for this meal. A slice of warm toast with the salmon and a cracker with the cheese will suffice.

Remember, Christmas is a festival of light. Use many shimmering candles to illuminate the appointments you have placed throughout the room and on the table. Never use scented candles in the dining room; save them for elsewhere in the house. Christmas is the time to bring out the best china and silver and all those favorite, precious things stored and unused the rest of the year for fear of breakage. It's the time to be lavish.

Juniper branches mixed with holly and pine boughs are strewn on the table and a lacquered Regency whirly-gig is filled with crystallized fruits from Cannes.

BABY QUAIL WITH JUNIPER BERRY SAUCE

INGREDIENTS

12 quails (5 to 5½ ounces each), cleaned, necks cut
off and reserved
2 cups brown sauce (see Appendix, page 247)
10 juniper berries, crushed
½ cup clarified butter (see Appendix, page 245)
8 ounces *foie gras*, cubed and chilled

TOOLS

Large wooden tongs
Oven-proof pan for sautéing

METHOD

Preheat the oven to 350°.
Truss the birds with strong thread.
Place the brown sauce, necks and juniper berries in a
saucepan and simmer over medium heat until the
sauce is reduced by half.

Using large wooden tongs so that the flesh will not be
pierced, sauté the birds in the clarified butter over
moderately high heat, in an oven-proof pan, until
they become lightly browned on all sides.
Place the sauté pan in the oven for 15 minutes and
baste the quails two to three times. Remove the
birds to a warm platter and cover lightly to keep
them warm.
Spoon off the excess butter and deglaze the sauté pan
with the reduced brown sauce. Strain the sauce
back into the pan and add the *foie gras*.
Pour the sauce over the birds and serve.

NOTES

Quail should be juicy and, for true lovers of game,
served rare. This is not to everyone's liking however. If
it is not to yours, extend the cooking time.

Serves 4

SAUTÉED RED CABBAGE WITH LARDONS

INGREDIENTS

½ pound fresh country or Black Forest lean bacon, cut
into ¼-inch slices and cubed for lardons
1 small head red cabbage, outer leaves removed
½ cup *crème fraîche* (see Appendix, page 245)
1 tablespoon whole grain French mustard
Salt and freshly milled black pepper, to taste

METHOD

In a skillet, render the lardons until they are golden
brown, removing some of the fat as they cook.
Drain on paper towels and reserve the fat. Do not
clean the skillet.

Cut the cabbage in half, remove the core and cut the
cabbage into thin strips.
Pour ½ cup of the rendered fat back into the skillet and
sauté the cabbage over low heat until it is tender.
Add more fat if the cabbage is not thoroughly
coated. Mix in the *crème fraîche*, mustard and salt
and pepper.
Warm the lardons briefly in a pan and fold them into
the cabbage.
Serve hot.

Serves 4 to 6

WILD RICE

INGREDIENTS

10 ounces (1¼ cups) wild rice
1 quart chicken stock (see Appendix, page 246)
Salt and freshly milled black pepper, to taste

METHOD

Rinse the rice thoroughly under cold running water.

Drain and place it in a saucepan with the stock and
a little salt. Cover the pot and bring to a boil.
Reduce the heat and simmer for about 45 minutes.
Drain off any excess liquid, season with pepper and
serve.

Serves 4

MINIATURE CROQUEMBOUCHE

INGREDIENTS

Pastry cream (see Appendix, page 251, and double
    the recipe)
Pâte à choux (see Appendix, page 249)
Unsalted butter, for the baking sheets
2 cups sugar
Vegetable oil, for the baking sheets

TOOLS

Pastry bag with ¼-inch plain tube and ⅛-inch or
    smaller plain tube
4 baking sheets
Double boiler

METHOD

Prepare the pastry cream and refrigerate.
Preheat the oven to 400°.
Make the *pâte à choux.*
Butter the baking sheets.
Using the ¼-inch tube, fill the pastry bag with the
    pâte. Pipe dime-size balls onto the buttered baking
    sheets. Use all the *pâte;* there should be about 112
    little puffs.
Bake for 30 minutes, or until golden brown; cool.
Fit the pastry bag with the ⅛-inch (or smaller) tube
    and fill the bag with the pastry cream.
Pierce the bottom of each puff and fill each dent with
    some of the cream.

To assemble the croquembouche:

Lightly oil 2 baking sheets.
Heat 1 cup of the sugar and ½ cup of water in a
    heavy saucepan over medium heat. Stir with a
    wooden spoon only until the sugar has dissolved.
    When the sugar begins to turn golden, rotate the
    pan to even the color. Caramel burns quickly;
    watch it carefully. When the color is amber, keep
    warm over simmering water in a double boiler and
    dip each puff, one at a time, into the caramel.
    (When none of the first batch of caramel remains,
    repeat the caramel recipe and continue.) As each
    puff is dipped, arrange it on a baking sheet as
    follows:
Starting with 7 puffs for the base, arrange them in a
    circle about 4 inches in diameter. Top with a second
    layer of 6 puffs, a third layer of 5 puffs, and so on,
    all the while forming a cone that resembles a little
    Christmas tree. Use 28 puffs for each tree.
The croquembouche will keep for about 8 hours in a
    cool place. Do not refrigerate.

NOTES

Caramelized pastry (and fruits) do not keep in humid
weather.

If you wish to "spin" the tree with additional caramel,
prepare one more batch of caramel and "drip" it over
the croquembouche with a four-pronged fork.

Serves 4

The main course of baby quail and sautéed red cabbage is placed on the sideboard.

NUTCRACKER TEA

The Sunday that usually falls between Christmas and New Year's can be set aside for a very simple gathering—an afternoon tea. This is a fine occasion for enjoying your holiday decorations at leisure, for exchanging presents and for entertaining those friends you may have overlooked during the holiday frenzy.

This Christmas tea recalls the dreamlike confection of the Nutcracker Ballet. It is a "fantasy" tea, a menu of sugarplum visions for children of all ages. It includes recipes for a variety of rich holiday sweets, although we don't suggest you prepare all of them.

Some of this tea fare may be prepared days, weeks and even months in advance. We came up with our fruit cake packed with fruits and nuts after years of adding and subtracting a variety of ingredients. Its rich, dark color comes from espresso coffee, melted bitter chocolate and a long period of aging. To make this a truly delicious cake, douse it every so often with Cognac, so that it is completely "inebriated" before being brought to the table. You might wish to steam it, as you would a Christmas pudding, and serve it flamed in a Cognac bath. (In the South, fruit cakes are often doused with corn whiskey instead of Cognac. It's a nice change.) Stored in tight containers and "basted" from time to time with Cognac or other liquor, fruit cakes keep for years.

Bridie McSherry's Christmas pudding is a dark, spicy cake, easy to prepare and the most delicious pudding we know. (The traditional suet-based puddings seem outdated today.) Although there happen to be grated carrots in the ingredients, it does not resemble any type of carrot cake and should not be associated with it. This is an old-fashioned blend of dried fruits and spices, whose full flavor emerges when steamed. Bridie's pudding should be presented like the fruit cake—flamed with warm Cognac or with dark rum, and accompanied by a rum- or Cognac- based hard sauce or *crème anglaise*. Frozen *crème anglaise*, a splendid, rich vanilla ice cream (see page 251), provides a worthy contrast when served with Bridie's hot, hot pudding.

Many Christmas cookies may be baked, then carefully wrapped and stored in airtight containers at least a month before the holiday, and those gaily wrapped tins of sweetmeats and bonbons that arrive at Christmas can be opened for this afternoon.

The Nikolashka is a Russian drink with an accompanying ritual. Bite down on a tissue-thin slice of lemon—which has been sprinkled with sugar and instant espresso—and swallow it with neat shots of icy cold vodka. To fully benefit from vodka's warming and restorative value, drink it icy and no other way. A

A sip of Christmas spirit: the Nikolashka.

89

Russian friend flavors his vodka with everything from orange and lemon peel to peppercorns and beach plums, ices it to an Arctic freeze, and drinks it ounce after ounce. He is able to consume formidable quantities and claims never to have had a hangover. In fact, we have found it to be a *cure* for hangovers.

On a low table for the children, set little saucers and cups for frothy hot chocolate (whisked with milk and fine, imported cocoa) and within their easy reach arrange bowls of candies and Christmas cookies.

Brew a strong tea. No pale, perfumed Oriental leaf will do for this party. Keep it hot on an alcohol burner and set aside another pot of hot water for those who prefer a milder tea. We suggest this Russian method of presenting tea: Place some whole black cherry preserves or red plum preserves in a glass, and then fill the glass with the tea. Sipped with an added slice of clove-studded lemon, this beverage evokes Christmas spirits. The final taste of warm cherries or plums becomes an additional dessert.

The syllabub and Mont Blanc are included for those with hearty appetites. Although it may be an acquired taste, the chestnut may be eaten in many guises—in soup, in soufflé, roasted or sautéed, served whole or puréed with stock and butter. The supreme concoction, however, is the chestnut Mont Blanc. Here the chestnuts are puréed and pressed through a ricer (or passed through the fine blade of a meat grinder), scented with vanilla and sweetened with a thick sugar syrup. In its paste form, the nut purée is heavy, but once it is passed through the ricer, the strands become light and airy. These fine strands piled high form the Mont Blanc, its peak capped with bitter chocolate shavings, its valley flavored with unsweetened whipped cream. The violets, sparkling candy crystals, brighten the chestnut mountain.

The Seckel pears are poached in red wine. Do not use too much wine, or the pears will resemble beets.

Ask your guests to arrive at different hours throughout the afternoon to eliminate overcrowding. During the course of the party you might decide to bring out different confections rather than presenting them all at once. No matter what you do, rest assured that all these foods can sit out untended as the guests come and go. Just be sure to keep a good supply on hand so that you can replenish the tables and spirits throughout the day.

A Lilliputian view of the children's table.

NUT AND BUTTER COOKIES

INGREDIENTS

1 pound (4 sticks) unsalted butter
2½ cups sugar
3 tablespoons vanilla
5 cups all-purpose flour, sifted
2½ cups finely ground pecans

TOOLS

Electric mixer with paddle attachment
Cookie sheets and baking parchment

METHOD

Preheat the oven to 325°.
Cut the butter into chunks and cream it thoroughly with the electric mixer. Add 1½ cups of the sugar and the vanilla; blend thoroughly. Fold in the flour. Fold in the nuts and blend thoroughly.

Line the cookie sheets with baking parchment. Place balls of cookie dough the size of a rounded teaspoon 1½ inches apart on the cookie sheets.

Bake for 20 minutes; the cookies will puff up and remain light in color.

Remove the cookies from the oven and sprinkle them with the remaining 1 cup of sugar.

Do not touch the cookies until they are thoroughly cooled or they will crumble.

When cool, pack them in an airtight container to retain their freshness.

Yield: 12 dozen cookies

The dessert table laden with a selection of Nutcracker sweets.

BRIDIE MCSHERRY'S CHRISTMAS PUDDING

INGREDIENTS

1½ cups grated carrots
1½ cups fresh bread crumbs
1½ cups dark brown sugar
4 large eggs
2 tablespoons vanilla
3 tablespoons ground cinnamon
1 teaspoon ground cloves
1 teaspoon nutmeg
¾ pound (3 sticks) unsalted butter, melted and the
   foam removed
1¾ cups all-purpose flour, sifted
1½ teaspoons baking soda
¼ teaspoon salt
¾ cup raisins
¾ cup pitted, chopped dates
1 tablespoon unsalted butter, to butter the molc and
   cover
Dark rum or Cognac, for flaming
Hard sauce, for accompaniment

TOOLS

2-quart fancy mold with a cover or use foil
Large pot and cover to hold the mold when steaming

METHOD

Combine the carrots, bread crumbs and sugar in a
   large bowl.
In another bowl, beat the eggs until they are smooth
   and lemon colored. Add to the carrot mixture.
Fold in the vanilla, spices and melted butter and blend
   thoroughly.
Fold in 1½ cups of the flour, the baking soda and salt.
Dust the raisins and dates with the remaining ¼ cup
   of flour and add to the batter. Mix well.
Turn the batter into the buttered mold. It should fill the
   mold to within 1 inch of the top (the pudding will
   rise during the cooking process).
Cover the mold tightly with the buttered cover. Place
   the mold in a large pot and add enough boiling
   water to come halfway up the sides of the mold.
Cover the pot and steam the pudding over low heat
   for 1 hour. Cool the pudding and refrigerate for up
   to a month. When serving, steam the pudding in
   the same manner for 1 hour.
Unmold and flame with dark rum or Cognac. Serve
   accompanied by hard sauce.

Serves 12

FRUIT CAKE

INGREDIENTS

1 pound (4 sticks) unsalted butter, at room temperature
1 pound dark brown sugar (soft, not granular)
12 large eggs
1 pound (about 4 cups) sifted all-purpose flour
1 teaspoon ground cinnamon
¾ teaspoon mace
⅛ teaspoon ground cloves
½ teaspoon baking soda
2 ounces bitter chocolate
½ cup strong espresso, chilled
2 pounds raisins
1 pound candied red cherries
1½ pounds currants
½ pound sultana raisins
½ pound citron, grated
½ pound candied orange peel, grated
½ pound candied lemon peel, grated
½ pound candied pineapple, cut into eighths
½ pound whole hazelnuts
½ pound walnut pieces
1 cup unsifted all-purpose flour to dust the fruit
Unsalted butter for the brown paper
Cognac, bourbon or corn whisky for aging
Apricot sauce (see Appendix, page 250)

TOOLS

Electric mixer with paddle attachment
Double boiler
An extra-large bowl *or* stockpot for the fruit and nut mixture
6 2½-cup fancy molds (fluted tube pans)
Brown paper, buttered
Cotton cheesecloth

METHOD

Using the electric mixer, cream the butter until it is light and fluffy. Add the sugar and blend thoroughly. Add the eggs, one at a time, and mix them in thoroughly. Fold in the flour, spices and baking soda and blend thoroughly.

Melt the chocolate over simmering water in the top of a double boiler; remove from the heat and cool.

Fold the chocolate and coffee into the batter (this will loosen the batter and give it a rich color as well). Set aside.

In an extra-large bowl, combine the fruit and nuts, dust with the flour and toss to mix. Pour in the batter and mix thoroughly.

Preheat the oven to 275°.

Line the molds with buttered brown paper. (Cut the buttered paper into blunted triangles to fit.)

Fill the molds to within ½-inch of the tops with the batter mixture.

Bake for 1 hour and 45 minutes to 2 hours, or until a kitchen needle comes out clean.

Sprinkle the cakes with the liquor and allow them to cool in the oven with the oven door slightly ajar.

When cool, unmold the cakes, leaving them wrapped in the paper.

Wrap the cakes in cheesecloth, then in foil. Place the cakes in plastic bags or airtight containers.

Unwrap and douse the cakes with liquor every 7 to 10 days for at least six weeks.

Brush the cakes with warm Apricot Sauce when you are ready to serve them.

NOTE

If using this recipe for the Wedding Cake (see page 93) use three round cheesecake pans lined with brown paper measuring: 12 x 3", 8 x 3", and 6 x 3". Preheat the oven to 250° and bake the cakes for 2½ to 3 hours, or until a kitchen needle comes out clean. Unmold the cakes and leave them in their paper. Douse them with Cognac and wrap them in cheesecloth, then wrap in foil and place them in plastic bags or in tightly covered containers. Douse with Cognac every 7 to 10 days for at least six weeks. As long as the cake is "drunk," it will last forever.

Have the cake decorated by a local confectioner.

Yield: 13¼ pounds.

SYLLABUB

INGREDIENTS

2 cups confectioners' sugar
2 cups heavy cream
⅔ cup good-quality medium-dry sherry
½ cup lemon juice
Grated zest of 1 lemon

TOOLS

Food processor

METHOD

Whirl the sugar in a food processor to fluff it up. Add the cream and beat for about 1 minute, scraping the sides of the bowl once or twice. Add the sherry and lemon juice and beat for another 15 seconds.

Pour the mixture into another bowl, then fold in the zest. Refrigerate for two days.

The longer the syllabub sits, the more it will "ripen" and thicken.

NOTE

For ten to twelve persons, double the recipe and make in two separate batches.

Serves 5 to 6

MONT BLANC

INGREDIENTS

2 pounds fresh chestnuts
4½ cups milk
1 vanilla bean, split lengthwise
1 cup sugar
Bitter chocolate, shaved into curls
1½ cups heavy cream, whipped
Candied violets

TOOLS

Food processor
Electric mixer with paddle attachment and fine meat
    grinder attachment *or* a ricer
Pastry bag and star tube

METHOD

Using a sharp paring knife, score the chestnuts with an
    "X" on the round, soft side. Place them in a pot and
    cover with cold water. Bring the water to a boil and
    boil for 2 minutes. Drain. When the chestnuts are
    cool enough to handle, peel off the shells.
Place the chestnuts in a saucepan and cover with the
    milk. Add the split vanilla bean and heat the
    mixture to a simmer. Cook for 45 minutes. Strain
    the chestnuts and reserve the milk. Remove all the
    light brown fuzz from the nuts.
Purée the chestnuts in a food processor in three
    batches.
Transfer the purée to a mixing bowl and reserve.

Place the sugar and ⅓ cup cold water in a saucepan
    over medium heat and stir with a wooden spoon
    until the sugar has dissolved. Bring the syrup to a
    low boil and cook for 3 minutes; do not let it
    caramelize.
Allow the syrup to cool and then mix it with the
    chestnut purée using the paddle attachment on
    an electric mixer.
Thin the mixture, 1 tablespoon at a time, with not
    more than ⅓ cup of chestnut milk until it is creamy
    and holds its shape. Refrigerate. (The purée can be
    made a day ahead.)

To assemble:

Using the grinder or ricer, push the chestnut purée
    into a mound on a serving platter. (Hold the platter
    directly under the grinder and swirl the purée into
    a high, cone-shaped mound, slowly turning the
    platter as you do so.)
Decorate with the chocolate curls and pipe the un-
    sweetened whipped cream around the base of the
    purée, using the pastry bag and star tube.
Place a few candied violets on top of the whipped
    cream.
Serve the extra whipped cream in a sauceboat.

NOTES

The chestnut purée can also be presented in large or
individual meringue shells and decorated as above.

The remaining chestnut milk works as a delicious base
for hot chocolate.

Serves 12 to 16

SECKEL PEARS IN RED WINE

INGREDIENTS

1 quart light sugar syrup (see Appendix, page 250)
Juice and zest of ½ lemon
2 cups good-quality dry red wine
1 cinnamon stick
4 cloves
12 Seckel pears

METHOD

Place the sugar syrup in a stainless steel or enamel
    saucepan that will comfortably hold the pears.
Add the lemon juice, zest, wine and spices.
Peel the pears, leaving the stems intact. Place the
    pears in the pan as you peel them. Cover the pears

with a round of waxed paper cut to fit the inside of
    the pan. Bring the pears to a light boil and reduce
    the heat to a simmer. Poach for 12 minutes or until
    the pears can be pierced easily with a sharp paring
    knife.
Cool the pears in the juice.
When cool, remove the pears to a serving dish and
    strain the juice over them before serving.

NOTE

If serving as a dinner dessert, serve two pears per
person.

Serves 6 to 12

NEW YEAR'S EVE

MENU

Pasta with Caviar*

Green Grapes and Macaroons

Espresso

•

Vintage Champagne

Serves Two

We salute those who enjoy a night on the town with paper hats and horns and the strains of Guy Lombardo's "Auld Lang Syne" on December 31st. We salute the late, late movie-goers who picnic at the theater and the concert-goers who sup at midnight. But for those who spend the evening at home, welcoming a respite from the holiday crowds and chaos, we suggest this dinner to greet the New Year.

For our celebration we chose the library, a small cozy room. We selected the plates and tray from a shelf of souvenirs, a reminder of days past, to suggest confetti, those cheerful and colorful paper bits scattered on festive occasions.

Our menu is light but lavish, simple but splendid. Pasta, that plainest of culinary pleasures, with caviar, that undeniably grand joy, is a sublime combination. Fresh pasta should be made or bought especially for this dish. Unless the pasta is fresh, the grave insult done to the caviar is beyond repair. Sevruga caviar is preferable for this recipe. It is slightly less expensive than Beluga, with finer and blacker eggs. (Reserve Beluga for the thinnest slices of black bread or buttered toast and a sprinkle of lemon juice—never anything more.) The amount of caviar you use depends on your generosity. A satisfactory portion is one heaping teaspoon (and certainly not more than a full tablespoon) for every three ounces of pasta.

Complete the meal with green grapes, chewy macaroons and a cup of strong espresso. For those who shy away from after-dinner coffee, there is a decaffeinated espresso bean on the market which makes an excellent substitute. (Few people can tell the difference.)

Of course, the champagne may accompany the dinner or be opened for the midnight toast. We prefer to sip it at leisure, welcoming in the New Year with the last glass.

PASTA WITH CAVIAR

INGREDIENTS

6 to 8 ounces fresh fettuccine
4 ounces clarified butter (see Appendix, page 245)
Grated zest of 1 lemon
7 ounces fresh Sevruga caviar

TOOLS

5-quart pot
Colander *or* strainer

METHOD

Cook the pasta in unsalted boiling water until it reaches the desired doneness (fresh pasta is done when all the noodles float to the top of the pot).

Drain in a colander and return to the pot. Toss with the butter and zest.

Turn the pasta out onto heated plates and nest as much caviar as you like in the center.

NOTES

A pound of pasta will adequately serve five as a first course. Some cooks recommend six persons to the pound; it is a bit shy.

As a main course figure on ¼ pound of pasta per person (this dish is rich; three ounces of fettuccine is quite an adequate serving).

Never rinse or shake pasta.

Serves 2

A simple but splendid dinner to welcome the New Year.

NEW YEAR'S DAY

MENU

Smoked Mussels, Eels and Scallops

Cassoulet*
Baked Sugar-Cured Virginia Ham
A Variety of Mustards
Endive, Julienne of Beets and Bibb
Lettuce Salad Vinaigrette
Brie
Braided Bread

One Floating Island*
Fruit Cake* (see page 93)
Bridie McSherry's
Christmas Pudding*
(see page 92)
Poached Oranges*

Espresso

•

Iced Beaujolais   Iced red and
white Côtes-du-Rhône
Vin de Cahors
(if available)

Serves Fifty

Start the New Year with a bang (not a whimper)! Invite friends for three in the afternoon. For some, this will be breakfast; for others, lunch; for still others, dinner. You will need a good deal of food, for people will probably come and go all afternoon and eat what and when they like. Your friends will be eternally grateful that they did not have to cope with the dreaded Morning After.

Only with careful planning will a relaxed and congenial atmosphere be guaranteed. By now, we assume your fruit cake has been aging for months. The next step is the *cassoulet*, which may be made days or even weeks in advance. (It freezes well, but you must defrost it thoroughly before reheating it. We suggest that you defrost it for two and a half days under refrigeration and for four to six hours out of the refrigerator to bring it up to room temperature.) *Cassoulet* is a warming and hearty dish. Although the uninitiated might regard *cassoulet* as a pot of beans, it is far from that; nor is it Hopping John, the traditional New Year's Day dish from the South made almost exclusively of black-eyed peas. *Cassoulet* is a delicious concoction of dried beans, tomatoes, wine and stock, pork, lamb and duck, and wonderful spicy sausages. Fables about this Languedoc dish abound (possibly because it is the only great recipe of Toulouse, a region that produces *foie gras* and truffles). There is a tale about a *cassoulet* in Toulouse that has been bubbling in an iron pot over a wood-burning stove for some hundred odd years. *Cassoulet* is a three-star dish and well worth the efforts it takes to make it.

You can prepare other parts of this meal, such as the *crème anglaise*, a day in advance as well. And you may want to cook the beets, mix the vinaigrette and poach the oranges then too. Set out a brie to soften at room temperature overnight. You might even decide to set your tables the evening before.

The day of the party, put the *cassoulet* into its serving casserole, dust it with the bread crumb mixture and put it in the oven; bake the ham; prepare the salad greens; steam the pudding; and poach the One Floating Island.

Serve the smoked fish with cocktails. Serve the main course from the dining room buffet and the desserts from a living room table. The coffee pot may be put on a heating stand on another table. Surround it with plenty of cups and saucers, cream and sugar.

A buffet need not be synonymous with eating on laps. Dining tables are set up throughout the house.

The *cassoulet*—a festive holiday filler.

CASSOULET

INGREDIENTS

Cassoulet

About 8 quarts chicken stock (see Appendix, page 246, and double the recipe)

8 pounds Roman (cranberry) beans or Great Northern beans

3 ducks (4½ pounds each)

Salt and freshly milled black pepper

½ cup vegetable oil

An 8-pound leg of lamb, boned and cut into 3-inch cubes, with bones reserved, or 6 pounds of lamb shoulder, boned and cut into 3-inch cubes, with bones reserved

6 pounds of pork loin, boned and cut into 3-inch cubes, with bones reserved, or 6 pounds of pork shoulder, boned and cut into 3-inch cubes, with bones reserved

1½ cups rendered goose or duck fat

6 cloves garlic, finely minced

4 pounds onions, finely chopped

6 pounds tomatoes, peeled, seeded and chopped with the juice reserved, or substitute canned whole peeled plum tomatoes

½ gallon dry white wine

8 sprigs parsley

2 sprigs fresh thyme *or* 2 teaspoons dried thyme

5 to 6 carrot tops

4 bay leaves

3 medium leeks (the white and some of the pale green), washed

3 large carrots, peeled, halved and sliced lengthwise

1 medium yellow onion, peeled and studded with 24 cloves

3 pounds pancetta or lean bacon, cut into ½-inch cubes

4 pounds Toulouse sausage or sweet Italian pork sausage

Gratin and Accompaniment

2½ cups dried bread crumbs

1 cup finely chopped parsley

4 cloves garlic, finely minced

4 pounds garlic sausage

TOOLS

20-quart stockpot

Roasting pans and racks

1 large sauté pan

Cotton cheesecloth

15-quart casserole *or* two 8-quart casseroles

METHOD

Bring the stock to a rolling boil in a large stockpot.

Wash the beans in cold water and drain.

Add the beans to the stock and boil for 10 minutes, stirring with a spoon from time to time; skim.

Remove the pot from the heat and allow the stock and beans to cool.

Preheat the oven to 450°.

Wash and remove the excess fat from the ducks. Pat them dry. Salt and pepper the cavities and rub the skin with the oil.

Place the ducks on racks in the roasting pans and roast for 20 minutes. Remove the partially cooked ducks from the oven and let cool. Do not turn the oven off.

Place the lamb bones and pork bones in a roasting pan and bake for 20 minutes or until golden brown.

Meanwhile, melt ½ cup of the goose fat in a large sauté pan. Brown the lamb in the fat and reserve. Add more of the fat and brown the pork; reserve.

Add the remaining fat and sauté the garlic and onions until they wilt, scraping up any browned particles that stick to the pan. Add the tomatoes to the onion mixture and cook about 10 minutes or until thoroughly heated. Add one quart of the wine and cook 5 more minutes.

Remove any stock that has settled above the beans and reserve.

Pour the tomato mixture into the pot of beans and set aside.

Bone the cooled ducks following the boning process given on page 222. Refrigerate the meat until the final assembly.

Cut the backbones of the ducks in half and place them, with the tails and wing tips, in a packet made from a double thickness of damp cheesecloth. Tie closed with kitchen string.

Prepare the lamb and pork bones in the same way.

Divide the parsley, thyme, carrot tops, bay leaves, leeks and carrots into two packets and tie in the same way.

Place all of the packets and the clove-studded onion into the bean mixture. Bring to a simmer over medium heat.

In a skillet, briefly sauté the pancetta lardons until lightly browned, then remove with a slotted spoon and mix into the bean mixture. Fold in the reserved lamb and pork.

Stir the mixture from time to time, making sure it does not stick to the bottom of the pot.

Cook until the beans are almost tender, about 1½ to 2 hours.

Add some of the reserved bean stock if the beans have absorbed most of the liquid during the cooking.

Remove the beans from the heat and cool for 1 hour, then refrigerate overnight (to prevent a refrigerator

continued

The buffet allows guests to nibble or feast.

full of beans, store the pot out-of-doors if the weather is cold enough).

Final assembly:

Preheat the oven to 350°.

Place the bean mixture over medium heat and add the remaining 1 quart of white wine. Cook to heat the beans through.

Cut the duck meat into small pieces, leaving the legs whole, and reserve.

Pierce the Toulouse sausages with a fork or small paring knife and brown in a pan with a little water. Set aside.

Press down on the packets in the bean mixture to release all their liquid and remove the packets.

Alternately layer the bean mixture, the duck legs and meat and the Toulouse sausages in the casserole(s), finishing with a layer of beans.

Toss together the bread crumbs, parsley and garlic; sprinkle over the top of the *cassoulet*.

Bake the casserole for 2 hours, or until a crust has formed on top.

While the *cassoulet* is in the oven, prepare the garlic sausages.

Prick the sausages with a kitchen fork or paring knife, place them in a pan with cold water to cover. Bring the water to a boil, reduce the heat to a simmer and cook the sausages for 45 minutes.

To serve the *cassoulet*, peel the sausages, slice them and arrange the slices around the perimeter of the *cassoulet*.

Serves 50

NOTES

Shop for the *cassoulet* ingredients at least two days in advance of your party. The bean mixture can be prepared three to four days ahead and the ducks two days ahead. The final assembly should be done on the day of the party.

Cassoulet should always be moist but not soupy, and, above all, not dry when served. Different varieties of beans absorb different amounts of stock; have extra stock on hand. Since the beans should rest at least a full day before the final assembly, they will absorb most of the liquid. Therefore you will want additional liquid on hand. You may add more stock with the white wine on the day of assembly.

Cassoulet freezes very well. It can go from stove to freezer for weeks on end and become more tasty each time. Always remember to add more liquid when reheating.

Cassoulet may be considered a peasant dish, but it is an expensive one. For bean lovers, however, it is heaven.

ONE FLOATING ISLAND

INGREDIENTS

24 egg whites (1 quart)
1/4 teaspoon salt
4 cups sugar
2 quarts *crème anglaise* (see Appendix, page 251)

TOOLS

Large roasting pan
Electric mixer with a 5-quart bowl and balloon whisk attachment
Wire rack covered with paper towels
2 large wire-mesh skimmers

METHOD

Fill the roasting pan 3/4 full of water and bring the water to a simmer.

Using the electric mixer, whisk the egg whites with the salt until they turn completely white. Gradually add 3 cups of the sugar until the whites are stiff and glistening.

Smooth the top of the egg whites so you have a flat surface and then turn the egg whites out of the bowl into the simmering water. The weight of the meringue will cause them to slide easily out of the bowl.

Gently poach the meringue on the flat side for 10 minutes.

Carefully turn the meringue over and poach for 10 minutes more, turning it occasionally to cook all the sides.

Return the meringue to the flat side and remove it to the rack using the skimmers. Let it rest for about 15 minutes, then carefully transfer it to a serving platter.

Pour enough *crème anglaise* around the meringue to coat the platter.

To prepare the caramel:

Heat the remaining 1 cup of sugar with 1/2 cup of cold water in a heavy saucepan set over medium heat. Stir with a wooden spoon only until the sugar has dissolved. When the sugar begins to turn golden, rotate the pan to even the color. Caramel burns quickly; watch it carefully. When the color is amber, drizzle the caramel over the meringue directly from the saucepan.

Serve the One Floating Island with additional *crème anglaise*.

Serves 25

The One Floating Island, Christmas pudding and poached oranges with orange zest grenadine are dessert.

POACHED ORANGES

INGREDIENTS

25 medium navel oranges
1 quart orange zest grenadine (see Appendix, page 250)
2 quarts light sugar syrup (see Appendix, page 250)
3 cups Grand Marnier

TOOLS

A large pot

METHOD

Using a sharp vegetable peeler, peel the zest from 18 of the oranges in long strips.

Reserve the oranges and use the zest to make the orange zest grenadine, following the recipe.

Slice the ends off of each orange and remove all the peel and pith.

Place half of the oranges in a pot. Pour in all of the light sugar syrup and Grand Marnier. Place the pot over high heat and bring the liquid to a simmer. Reduce the heat and continue simmering for 15 minutes. Remove the oranges with a slotted spoon and reserve them in a bowl.

Place the remaining oranges into the pot and bring the liquid back to a simmer and cook for 15 minutes. Remove the oranges to the bowl with the others.

Cool the syrup, then pour it over the oranges. Chill the oranges until ready to serve. Serve with the orange zest grenadine as an accompaniment.

NOTE

Because there are a variety of desserts on hand, it is unnecessary to have 50 servings of each one.

Serves 25

EASTER

Long before the Christian Easter holiday came into being, the rites of Spring celebrated rebirth. Before written history, eggs—the perfect symbol of new life—were painted in Eastern Europe. As Christianity flourished, the Russian Orthodox Church embraced Easter as its most cherished celebration. We have only to look at the bejeweled Fabergé eggs created for the czars to appreciate the importance of this holiday. Foods served at Easter were meant to be celebratory dishes, selected to enrich and satiate the body after a long fast. This Easter menu was created around the Paskha, the traditional Russian Easter cake, the most delicious of cheesecakes. We don't think any other national cuisine has developed a more unique festival cake for this holiday.

This late afternoon lunch is an amalgam of early spring foods and religious tradition. Shad and shad roe—that early spring delicacy found along the east coast—is a rich starter for this lunch. (The shad makes a wonderful main course on occasion, but remember that a little goes a long way.) By incorporating the puréed roe into the sauce, everyone can have a taste. For every person who likes shad, there is always one who doesn't, perhaps because the roe is so often grilled to the point of toughening and is so overwhelmed with bacon. Those who do not like shad are probably unfamiliar with its truly subtle flavor, and will be pleasantly surprised by the delicate sauce. If the shad and roe are unavailable, begin the lunch with raw oysters or oysters served hot on a bed of julienned leeks, steamed in cream, butter and champagne.

In Russia, Easter ham is served wrapped in a rye crust. We have chosen a savory pastry to envelope a sugar-cured Virginia ham. The pastry is light and flaky and complements the glazed ham. Preslicing the ham before covering it with the pastry and baking is a surprise trick that makes serving the meal easier.

Asparagus is one of the true spring vegetables and needs only to be served with clarified butter and lemon.

Make the Paskha with only the freshest farmer's cheese and eggs, the richest butter and heaviest cream. A friend of mine gave me a hand-carved mold for the Paskha and I particularly like its shape: a pentagonal obelisk carved with cross, chalice, wheat sheaves, flowers and the letters "XB"—"Christ is Risen." The mold is made of porous wood and the decoration appears in relief on the Paskha. Blunted pyramid shapes are the customary Paskha form and a clay flower pot, as described in this recipe, will do very nicely as a mold.

MENU

Baked Shad and Shad Roe Sauce*

Baked Ham in Savory Pastry*
Asparagus with Lemon Butter

Paskha*

Espresso

·

White Wine from the Loire
or Alsace   ·   Champagne

Serves Eight

BAKED SHAD AND SHAD ROE SAUCE

INGREDIENTS

Fillet
A 4- to 5-pound fillet of shad, with the skin
4 tablespoons unsalted butter
Salt and freshly milled black pepper

Sauce
1 pair of small shad roe
4 to 5 tablespoons unsalted butter
¼ cup finely chopped shallots
1½ to 2 pounds tomatoes, peeled, seeded and
    pureéd, with their juice (enough for 2 cups)
1½ cups *crème fraîche* (see Appendix, page 245)
1 tablespoon lemon juice
Salt and freshly milled black pepper, to taste
1 teaspoon red peppercorns

TOOLS

Oven-proof baking dish
Food processor *or* blender

METHOD

Preheat the oven to 400°.
Remove as many of the fin bones from the shad fillet
    as you can with tweezers.
Butter the baking dish, place the fish in it and dot the
    top with the remaining butter. Season lightly with
    salt and pepper.
Cover the dish with foil and place it on the upper shelf
    of the oven.
Bake for 18 to 20 minutes.

Meanwhile, make the sauce:
Poach the roe in lightly salted simmering water for 2
    to 3 minutes. Remove the roe with a slotted spoon
    and cool under cold running water.
Carefully remove the outer membrane and reserve
    the roe.
Melt 4 tablespoons of the butter in a saucepan over
    medium heat. Sauté the shallots until the mixture is
    almost a paste; do not allow the shallots to brown.
    Add the tomato purée and simmer the mixture for
    15 minutes.
In a food processor, purée the roe, gradually pouring
    in the tomato mixture until it is very smooth. Return
    to a saucepan and place over moderate heat for 5
    minutes.
Remove the sauce from the heat, whisk in the *crème
    fraîche*, add the lemon juice and season with salt
    and pepper. Warm thoroughly.
Place the shad fillet on a heated serving platter
    and cover it with sauce. Sprinkle with the red
    peppercorns.

NOTES

This exquisite spring delicacy from the East Coast is a
very bony fish. It is well worth the effort to remove as
many of the needle-like bones as possible.

Use only whole flaky red peppercorns (*not* pink).

Serves 8

BAKED HAM IN SAVORY PASTRY

INGREDIENTS

Savory pastry dough (see Appendix, page 247)
1 cup apricot jam
¼ cup dark brown sugar
1 tablespoon soy sauce mixed with 2 tablespoons dry English mustard
A 12- to 15-pound sugar-cured Virginia ham, fully cooked
2 eggs

TOOLS

Roasting pan and rack
Boning knife

METHOD

Prepare the savory pastry dough and refrigerate.
Preheat the oven to 325°.
Warm the jam in a saucepan over low heat.
Add the brown sugar and soy sauce mixture and stir constantly until the mixture is thoroughly blended and melted. Reserve.
Trim the ham of its dark outer skin, leaving about 4 inches around the bone area. Partially trim away the fat, leaving a ½-inch layer; score the fat.
Place the ham on the rack in the roasting pan, brush with the apricot glaze and bake for 2 hours.
Remove and allow to cool for 1 hour.
Preheat the oven to 400°.
Using a sharp boning knife, cut off the top of the ham, in an oval or "well" shape, from the shank to the butt and back. The knife should be inserted into the ham at a 45° angle, 4 to 5 inches below the shank

until you reach the bone. Use the bone as a guide and cut the ham to the bone, leaving a 2½-to 3-inch perimeter around the side of the ham. The hip bone is in the butt end and you will want to cut above this section when completing the oval. The whole process should be accomplished in one cut. Bring the knife down snugly against the bone to release the oval.
Remove the oval of ham and slice it thin.
Replace the slices one by one, filling the well.
Place the ham on a baking sheet.
In a small bowl, lightly beat the eggs with 2 tablespoons of water. Reserve.
On a floured surface, roll out the pastry to a ⅛-inch thickness. Drape the dough over the ham and tuck it in around the base. Leaving a 1-inch flap around the base, cut away any excess dough and reserve for decoration. Tuck the flaps underneath the ham.
Brush the entire ham with the egg wash.
Using the excess dough, make a few "grape leaves" and roll small balls of dough to about the size of peas to look like grapes. Place a cluster of "grapes and leaves" in the center of the ham and brush the ham again with the egg wash.
Bake for 50 minutes to an hour or until the pastry is golden brown.
Carefully run a spatula around the base and transfer the ham to a heated platter.
Cut away the crust from the oval area only and serve the slices of ham with some of the crust.

Serves 8 to 12

PASKHA

INGREDIENTS

2 pounds large curd (pot style) farmer's cheese
6 large eggs
¾ pound (3 sticks) unsalted butter
1 cup sugar
1 cup heavy cream
1 vanilla bean, split lengthwise
⅓ cup candied fruits, chopped and mixed with 3 tablespoons vodka
Grated zest of 1 lemon
⅓ cup sultana raisins
¼ cup slivered, blanched almonds

TOOLS

Electric mixer with paddle attachment
Double boiler
1 wooden paskha mold or a new 2-quart clay flower pot that is conically shaped
Cotton cheesecloth

METHOD

If you are using the clay pot, wash it thoroughly with light soap and water and rinse it well.
Bake it in a 300° oven for 45 minutes or until dry. Allow to cool.

Let the cheese, eggs and butter stand at room temperature for 2 hours. (If the cheese is particularly moist, drain, unpackaged, in a sieve.)

Place the cheese in a bowl and beat it with an electric mixer set at the lowest speed for 15 minutes or until smooth.

In a separate bowl, beat 6 egg yolks until they are smooth and lemon colored. (Reserve whites for another use.) Gradually add the sugar and blend thoroughly.

Meanwhile, scald the cream.

Continuing on the lowest mixer speed, add the egg mixture to the cheese, beat, then slowly add the scalded cream. Whip until fluffy.

Scrape the mixture into the top of a double boiler and place over medium heat. Add the vanilla bean.

Cook, stirring constantly with a wooden spoon, for about 20 minutes or until the mixture thickens.

Remove from the heat and strain through a fine sieve, pressing out all the small curds.

Drain the vodka off the candied fruits and fold in the lemon zest, candied fruits, raisins and almonds. Scrape the mixture into another bowl and chill thoroughly.

Using the electric mixer, cream the butter. Fold the chilled cheese mixture into it and blend thoroughly at a slow speed, scraping the sides of the bowl. Refrigerate for 1 hour.

Line the prepared mold with a double layer of dampened cheesecloth, leaving enough extra cloth at the top to cover the mold. Fill the mold with the cheese mixture and fold the overhang over the top.

Place a weight on top of the cheesecloth; this will force out the whey. Set a small pan beneath the mold and refrigerate for 2 days.

To unmold the paskha: Unwrap the cheesecloth, place a serving dish over the top of the mold and invert. Hold the cheesecloth down tightly and gently pull it away from the mold. Remove the cheesecloth and allow the paskha to rest in a cool place for 1 hour before serving.

The paskha will keep for 2 weeks refrigerated.

NOTE

This ''cheesecake'' is rich and demands the smallest of servings.

Serves 8 to 10

Apricot tulips in a brass bucket highlight the golden ham crust and the ivory Paskha.

BREAKFAST

THE WAY in which you break your nighttime fast need not be complicated. While everyone has a preference in wake-up foods, you are unlikely to find a wide range of breakfast menus. At Glorious Food, efforts are turned toward the visual presentation, making this simple meal as attractive as possible.

I like to recall my weekend visits to friends in Bléneau, a charming village on a tributary of the Loire, where breakfast became the highlight of the day. Its arrival was signaled by a light tap on the bedroom door. Served on a tray, this breakfast consisted simply of a crusty slice of warm bread, a pot of jam, some freshly churned butter from the local dairy across the field, and a piece of fruit. While the fare was simple, it represented an elegant greeting to the day. These mornings probably established my attitude toward breakfast for life.

Ideal fare for a late morning fashion show: miniature crêpes filled with banana and papaya. Or a variation: a filling of sautéed apples or fresh berries and a sprinkling of fresh ginger.

CORPORATE

The corporate breakfast is not meant to be a meal, but a light filler served by a considerate host before "getting down to business." Some corporate breakfasts are held early; others, at mid-morning. Neither should be elaborate. The menus are, essentially, reinterpreted cocktail foods adapted to the morning hours.

The early breakfast need be no more than an offering of orange juice, a basket of fresh strawberries, miniature croissants and brioches, and hot coffee and tea.

The midmorning breakfast might be more substantial, but again, uncomplicated. The food should be both gentle and pretty. Figs and apricots served in baskets add a pleasant touch.

The corporate breakfast is a business affair, and breakfast is secondary. Whether served before a fashion show or a general meeting, the food is a compliment and a complement.

MENU

Sparkling Mineral Water
with Lemon Slices
White Wine
Aquavit Danish Mary with Dill
Orange Juice and Vodka

Tartlets with Scrambled Eggs
and Caviar*
Fresh Figs with Ham Mousse
Crêpes Filled with Papaya
and Banana*
French Toast with Cinnamon Sugar
Baskets of Strawberries

Scrambled-egg-filled tartlets are topped with caviar.

TARTLETS WITH SCRAMBLED EGGS AND CAVIAR

INGREDIENTS

Savory pastry (see Appendix, page 247 and halve
    the recipe)
12 large eggs
Salt and freshly milled white pepper, to taste
6 tablespoons unsalted butter
Sevruga caviar

TOOLS

Nonstick crêpe pan

METHOD

Make 72 tartlets from the savory pastry recipe.

Beat 2 of the eggs with a little salt and pepper.
Melt 1 tablespoon of the butter in the crêpe pan and
    scramble the eggs over low heat until they are soft
    and creamy. Divide the eggs among 12 of the
    tartlets and top each with a demitasse spoonful
    of caviar.
Serve immediately and repeat.

NOTES

The scrambled eggs should be served hot and the
caviar cold. Two eggs yield enough mixture to fill 12
tartlets. Therefore serve a dozen tartlets at a time.

Yield: 72 tartlets

CRÊPES FILLED WITH PAPAYA AND BANANA

INGREDIENTS

Batter
6 eggs
½ pound (about 1½ cups) sifted all-purpose flour
1¾ cups milk
1 tablespoon sugar
⅛ teaspoon salt
Clarified butter for frying crêpes (see Appendix, page
    245)

Filling
1 ripe papaya
2 ripe bananas
1 tablespoon unsalted butter
2 tablespoons sugar
3 teaspoons lemon juice

Topping
Superfine sugar
Confectioners' sugar

TOOLS

Nonstick crêpe pan, 6 to 7 inches in diameter
Ladle or measuring cup that will hold ¼ cup of batter

METHOD

Beat the eggs, add the flour and gradually stir in the
    milk, sugar and salt. Mix well; refrigerate for 1 hour.

Using this batter, make 25 crêpes, as follows:

Brush the crêpe pan with clarified butter and place it
    over moderately high heat. When the butter is hot,
    remove the pan from the heat and pour in about
    ¼ cup of batter. Coat the bottom of the pan with a
    thin film of batter (pour off any excess). Return the
    pan to the heat and cook the crêpe for about 1
    minute or until it can be loosened from the bottom
    of the pan and is light brown underneath. Turn the
    crêpe and cook for another 30 seconds on the
    other side. Remove the crêpe to a plate and
    continue frying the rest of the crêpes in the same
    manner, buttering the pan lightly each time if
    necessary. Set aside to cool.

Peel, halve and seed the papaya. Peel the bananas.
    Cut the fruit into small cubes.

Melt the butter in a small pan and lightly sauté the
    fruit.

Remove the fruit to a bowl and sprinkle with the
    sugar and lemon juice. Stir gently, being careful not
    to break up the fruit.

One by one, place each cooled crêpe on a flat work
    surface. Fill with a teaspoonful of fruit filling placed
    near the bottom edge of the crêpe. Fold in the sides
    and roll into a shape resembling a small egg roll.
    Transfer the filled crêpes to a buttered baking sheet.

To serve, sprinkle the crêpes with superfine sugar and
    heat at 400° until warmed through. Remove from
    the oven, sprinkle with confectioners' sugar and
    arrange on a serving platter.

Yield: 25 crêpes

LUXE

In many respects, breakfast can be the most pleasant meal of the day if it is enjoyed at a quiet hour when there is time to gather energies. Breakfast is a luxury, if there is time to spare. Taking that extra time to create something special is an extravagance, an example of a self-indulgence that happens to be *good* for you as well.

This is a three-course breakfast, so elegant you may choose to go without lunch. Or you may decide to sleep late and try this as a mid-morning lunch instead.

As you are already going to open a bottle of pink champagne for the pink *beurre blanc* you can also prepare a dazzling morning cocktail by mixing chilled orange juice with champagne.

Most of us are familiar with Eggs Benedict sitting on soggy English muffins; some of us are acquainted with Eggs Benedict resting on the stylish, but nonetheless soggy brioche. To avoid either, we prefer to serve the brioche with our orange juice and coffee, and the eggs resting on an artichoke heart instead.

Dessert is composed of poached Italian plums with a Grand Marnier sauce and another cup of coffee. Indulge yourselves and refuse intrusions.

Iced orange juice with champagne and a warm brioche, followed by . . .

...Artichokes Benedict at a table for two.

ARTICHOKES BENEDICT

INGREDIENTS

2 large artichokes
1 lemon, halved
2 small carrots, peeled and sliced
Salt and freshly milled white pepper, to taste

Pink Beurre Blanc

½ cup blood orange juice, or substitute juice from a
    navel orange
½ cup pink champagne
¼ pound (1 stick) unsalted butter, chilled and cut into
    bits
1 tablespoon tarragon-flavored white wine vinegar
2 eggs
1 teaspoon chopped chives

TOOLS

Food processor *or* blender
Double boiler
Steamer *or* improvised steamer

METHOD

Bring a large pot of water to a boil.
Cut the stems off the artichokes and rub with the
    halved lemon. Cut off the top leaves just above the
    choke and discard them. Rub the tops of the
    artichokes with lemon. Squeeze any remaining
    juice from the lemon halves into the boiling water.
Cook the artichokes in the boiling water for about 25
    minutes or until the bottoms can be pierced easily
    with a sharp paring knife.
Cook the carrots in lightly salted boiling water until
    tender. Drain and purée in a food processor or
    blender. You may season with salt, pepper and a
    little butter if you like. Reserve the carrot purée in a
    double boiler over simmering water.
When the artichokes have cooked, cool them briefly
    under cold running water. Remove all the remain-
    ing leaves and chokes and trim the hearts to a nice
    round shape. Shave the bottoms flat so the hearts
    will sit level on a plate.
Place the artichoke hearts in a steamer over simmer-
    ing water to keep them warm, or place them on a
    plate over a pot of simmering water and cover
    (don't use foil to cover).
Bring a pan of water to a simmer in preparation for
    poaching the eggs.

To prepare the pink beurre blanc:

Place the orange juice and champagne in a heavy
    saucepan and reduce the liquid over low heat until
    it becomes a glaze (reduce by ¾ or more). Remove
    the pan from the heat and whisk in about 2
    teaspoons of the cold butter. Return to the heat
    and whisk in the remaining butter bit by bit, beating
    vigorously. When all of the butter is incorporated,
    the sauce will have the consistency of a Hollan-
    daise. Remove the pan to the warm side of the
    stove and reserve.
Add a bit of salt and the vinegar to the simmering
    water and poach the eggs. Drain them on paper
    towels and trim the whites so the eggs will sit neatly
    on top of the artichoke hearts.

To assemble:

Place each artichoke heart on a warm plate. Fill each
    well with a spoonful of the carrot purée; place an
    egg on top of it. Pour the pink *beurre blanc* evenly
    over each egg and sprinkle with the chives.

NOTES

This recipe is easily doubled, tripled, etc. You can
prepare the poached eggs before making the pink
beurre blanc. Reserve the eggs in a pan of ice water
with some ice cubes. Keep a pan of simmering water
on the stove. When the pink *beurre blanc* is complet-
ed, return the eggs to the simmering water to heat
through. Make a couple of extra eggs in case any
should break.

The artichokes may be prepared the night before and
refrigerated with the leaves on. Remove the leaves
and choke before heating the heart.

Serves 2

SAUTÉED ITALIAN PLUMS

Use half the amounts indicated for the ingredients on
    page 215 and follow the recipe.

GRAND MARNIER SAUCE

Use half the amounts indicated for the ingredients on
    page 192 and follow the recipe.

Artichoke Benedict.

FOR ONE

MENU

Fresh Fruit
Tea
Croissant
Preserves

Breakfast is a personal affair, the one occasion when we can revel in being labeled creatures of habit. Any variation of the breakfast menu is often regarded as an invasion of privacy. We have established a pattern that suits us and—whether breakfasting in bed or at the table, at home or out—our notion of what fare is appropriate for breakfast tends to be rather inflexible. With all due respect to those who eat eggs and bacon, pancakes and sausages, hot cereals or cold, muffins or toasts, I submit my own breakfast menu. It seldom varies and it always suits me.

To begin, I like fruit or fruit juice. Fresh. Following this, I prefer a cup of tea made with Earl Grey tea leaves. (I eschew all tea bags. Although I don't deny their practicality, I do think the fine flavor of the brew is sacrificed to convenience.) Sometimes I like a lemon slice in my tea, or sometimes I sweeten the tea with sugar or honey.

If there is a bakery nearby, and if I'm in an extravagant mood—with hunger to match—I venture out for a croissant or brioche. Either of these, spread with homemade preserves, is an unequalled breakfast treat.

Elements of the breakfast ritual.

LUNCH

LUNCH, that once gratifying midday repast, has become a victim of the demands of our lives. Unless it is a corporate event, this simple meal is now considered a luxury and has been forced into exile between two slices of bread or banished to a diet.

Not being the first or last meal of the day, lunch is a stop-gap, a bridge between breakfast and dinner. Although lunch is a modest meal, not a feast, it should not be ignored. Its possibilities are vast, particularly in the summer months, with time available and afternoons free for lingering. By tradition, the formal luncheon has a more defined pattern of courses: a clear soup, lightly grilled meat, fish or poultry, and a bit of salad and cheese; any of these—alone or in combination, followed by fresh fruit, sorbet or mousse—provide a perfect menu.

So let us welcome that stranger called lunch back into our lives, and let us reacquaint ourselves with its many variations.

Pistou, a Mediterranean vegetable soup, is served from a glass beaker and presented with shaved truffle.

SUNDAY

Very few find escape from the inevitable family gathering, the Sunday lunch, an event that may include parents, grandparents, children and in-laws. Surviving this chaotic meal is the chief goal of the host or hostess, and keeping the menu simple is the single means to this end. However simple, the fare should be ample. The afternoon lunch is often the main meal of the day.

You may buy the belons late in the afternoon on Saturday. (They can be opened at the fish market and kept overnight on ice.) You can substitute a crock of shrimp or a clear consommé if belons are not available. Or you can eliminate the first course altogether, because the menu has been planned with plenty of hearty food.

As cooking has become more sophisticated, light, reduced sauces have become popular, but the roast beef accompaniment is the exception. Roast beef deserves gravy—the rich, traditional kind made from pan drippings and flour.

Some details are worth noting. The Yorkshire pudding takes the place of bread. The Stilton cheese should be served with port, some grapes and nuts—ideal savories for the elders. The bittersweet endive goes well with the Stilton, too.

The Tarte Tatin is a stylized apple pie, a felicitous twist on the American version; its crust is thin, and the apples are sliced thin and sprinkled with lemon zest.

MENU

Maine Belons on Ice

Roast Beef*
with
Fresh Horseradish Sauce*
Yorkshire Pudding*
Brussels Sprouts and Dill

Ribbons of Endive Vinaigrette
Stilton, Green Grapes and Nuts

Tarte Tatin*

Espresso

·

Saint-Émilion · Vintage Port

Serves Eight

A "still life" cornucopia on the sideboard.

124

ROAST BEEF

INGREDIENTS

4- to 5-pound beef rib roast
Kosher salt
Freshly milled black pepper

TOOLS

Roasting pan

METHOD

Bring the rib of beef to room temperature.
Preheat the oven to 500°.
Place the meat in a roasting pan lightly greased with
vegetable oil. Season the roast with salt and pepper
and put it into the oven. Immediately reduce the
heat to 350°.
For rare meat, roast 18 minutes per pound (or until a
meat thermometer registers 140°).
After removing the roast from the oven, allow it to rest
for half an hour before slicing. This further tender-
izes the meat and makes slicing easier.
Reserve 1 cup or more beef fat for the Yorkshire
Pudding.
Serve the roast with its natural juices or a good
pan gravy.

NOTES

Prepare the Yorkshire Pudding while the roast rests.

Serve cold leftover roast beef with Mostarda fruits and
a good potato salad.

Serves 8

YORKSHIRE PUDDING

INGREDIENTS

2 large eggs
Pinch of salt
1 cup milk
1 cup all-purpose flour, sifted
About 1 cup hot beef fat

TOOLS

A 12-inch-square oven-proof pan or a 12-inch oval,
tin-lined copper pan

METHOD

Preheat the oven to 400°.
Combine the eggs, salt and milk and beat thoroughly.
Add the flour and mix it into the egg and milk
mixture. Set aside for 30 minutes.
Pour 1/3 inch of hot beef fat into the pan. Pour in the
batter without stirring. Bake for 30 minutes or until
the pudding is puffed and golden brown.

Serves 8

FRESH HORSERADISH SAUCE

INGREDIENTS

2 tablespoons freshly grated horseradish
Juice of 1/2 lemon
1 pint (2 cups) heavy cream

METHOD

Squeeze the grated horseradish dry in a paper towel.
Combine the horseradish with the lemon juice.
Whip the heavy cream and fold the horseradish
mixture into it. Serve cold.

Yield: 2 cups

TARTE TATIN

INGREDIENTS

1/2 cup sugar
8 apples (Granny Smith, Cortland, Rome Beauty or
Idared)
Grated zest of 1 lemon
Pâte brisée (see Appendix, page 248), or puff pastry
(see Appendix, page 249)

TOOLS

A 9-inch round metal *or* glass pie pan

METHOD

Preheat the oven to 325°.
In a heavy saucepan set over medium heat, melt the
sugar in 1/4 cup cold water, stirring with a wooden
spoon only until the sugar has dissolved. When the
sugar turns a golden color, rotate the saucepan to
ensure that the color is uniform. Caramel burns very
quickly; watch it carefully. When the caramel becomes an amber color, carefully pour it into the pie
pan, rotating the pan to coat its surfaces evenly with
the caramel. Reserve.
Peel, halve and core the apples; slice thin. Toss the
apple slices with the lemon zest.
Arrange one layer of apples in pinwheel fashion on
top of the carmel. Layer the remaining apples
evenly on top.
Roll out the pastry dough on a floured surface and
place the dough over the pie pan. Trim off any
excess dough with a sharp knife.
Bake the tart on the middle rack of the oven for 35 to
40 minutes or until the crust is golden brown.
Place a serving plate over the tart and invert. Allow
the tart to set for 5 minutes before removing it from
the pan.

Serves 8

CORPORATE

Ten years ago, the corporate lunch was deeply entrenched in a pattern of forty-five minutes of hard drinking followed by a meal that was invariably excessive. It included shrimp cocktail, Beef Wellington, a variety of vegetables, potatoes, bread and a rich dessert, sending executives off for a sluggish afternoon or a nap. When *nouvelle cuisine* beached itself on these shores, some —particularly in the fashion world—insisted on the restrained *salade composée*. It looked pretty and appealed to the visually oriented. Unfortunately, although the eye was satisfied, the palate was only teased. We offer a compromise between the two extremes.

Corporate lunches are working sessions and business is not usually put aside. Lunch must function around work. In fact, in this situation function *determines* the menu. Efficient service will assure success, just as the intrusion of placing, passing and clearing an endless line of courses will guarantee a disaster. It's a lunch that should not be a distraction.

MENU

Carpaccio*

Pistou and White Truffles*

Hothouse Lettuce Salad
Grilled Bleu de Bresse

Fresh Fruit Sorbets*

Espresso

·

Mineral Water · Iced Beaujolais

Serves Six

Grilled Bleu de Bresse on a slice of crusty bread is served with a simple salad.

In this office setting the menu was affected by
the need to transform the red-lacquered desk
into a dining table. (The colors of the foods
might clash or pale on such a vibrant background.) Carpaccio, paper-thin slices of raw
beef, served with a Pollock-like dribbling of
sauce, blends easily.

CARPACCIO

INGREDIENTS

2 pounds top round, trimmed of all fat (see Notes)
⅓ cup strong beef bouillon
1 cup mayonnaise (see Appendix, page 245)
1 teaspoon Worcestershire sauce

METHOD

Set the top round in the freezer for 20 minutes to facilitate slicing. Slice the meat tissue-thin and place 1 to 2 slices on each of 6 plates.

Heat the bouillon and gradually whisk it into the mayonnaise. Add the Worcestershire sauce and mix thoroughly (you want a creamy sauce that will dribble easily). Dip a three-pronged dinner fork into the sauce and drizzle the sauce in a zigzag pattern over the meat.

NOTES

Top round is the most flavorful cut of meat to use for this dish. You will need a fairly thick piece for easy balancing when slicing. The meat may be cut with a razor-sharp knife if you do not have a meat slicer, or ask a friendly butcher to do it for you.

Be aware that like beef tartare, top round discolors quickly. If you do not plan to serve immediately, keep the slices tightly wrapped.

Serves 6 to 8

PISTOU AND WHITE TRUFFLES

INGREDIENTS

4 to 5 cloves garlic, finely minced
5 ounces puréed fresh basil
¼ cup chopped walnuts
½ cup freshly grated Parmesan cheese
2 tablespoons tomato paste
¼ cup fruity virgin olive oil plus 5 to 6 tablespoons
¾ cup dry white beans
1 pound very ripe tomatoes, peeled, seeded, chopped, with the juice reserved
3 quarts chicken stock (see Appendix, page 246)
2 to 3 medium carrots, sliced thin on the bias
2 medium leeks, cut into 2-inch julienne
¼ pound string beans, trimmed and cut into 1½-inch lengths
2 medium zucchini, cut into small cubes
½ cup broken vermicelli
1 cup chopped inner celery leaves
⅛ teaspoon saffron
Freshly milled black pepper, to taste
1 fresh white truffle, shaved into paper-thin slices

continued

129

TOOLS

Food processor
Heavy stockpot

METHOD

Purée the first 5 ingredients in a food processor until smooth. Gradually add 5 to 6 tablespoons of the olive oil and blend until the mixture becomes a smooth paste. Reserve in a tightly covered container.

Wash the white beans in cold water; drain. Bring a quart of water to a boil, add the beans and cook for 5 minutes.

Cool the beans in their liquid, then return them to the heat and simmer about 1 hour or until tender.

When the beans are cooked, heat the ¼ cup olive oil in a stockpot and set over moderate heat. Add the tomatoes and their juice and cook for 1 minute. Add the stock and bring it to a boil. Add the carrots and leeks; simmer for 15 minutes. Add the string

beans and the white beans with their liquid; simmer for 3 to 4 minutes more.

Add the zucchini, vermicelli, celery leaves and saffron; simmer for 5 minutes. Add 1 or 2 tablespoons of the reserved purée and taste for seasoning.

Pour the soup immediately into a heated beaker or tureen and ladle into heated soup plates.

Serve the *pistou* with a shaved white truffle as accompaniment, if available.

NOTES

Adding salt to the soup is not necessary.

This soup will serve eight as a first course. When served as a main course, it will serve six with second servings.

The basil purée will keep for weeks under refrigeration and is an excellent addition to pasta sauces and tomato-based meat or fish stews.

Serves 8

FRESH FRUIT SORBETS

Pear Sorbet

INGREDIENTS

6 large ripe pears
Juice of 1 lemon
½ cup sugar (more or less depending on the sweetness of the pears)

TOOLS

Food processor
Sorbet machine, if available.

METHOD

Peel, core and quarter the pears. Place them in a saucepan with 2 cups cold water and the lemon juice.

If necessary, add more water to cover; add the sugar.

Cover the pears with a round of waxed paper to fit the interior of the pan and poach the pears for about 8 minutes until they can be pierced easily with a sharp paring knife. Cool the pears in the liquid. Strain, reserving the liquid.

Purée the pears in a food processor until smooth, adding the reserved syrup, as necessary, to make a quart of the mixture.

Pour the purée into the container of a sorbet machine and freeze according to the manufacturer's directions, or if a sorbet machine is unavailable, follow

the directions for using a food processor in Notes, below.

Peach Sorbet

Using 8 large ripe peaches, follow the directions given in the recipe for Pear Sorbet.
Note: Peel and pit the peaches *after* poaching.

Cantaloupe Sorbet

Melons need neither sweetening nor poaching.
Using 2 small or 1 large ripe cantaloupe, halve the melon, scoop out the seeds, remove the skin and purée the flesh.

Pour the purée into the sorbet machine and follow the manufacturer's directions, or follow the directions for using a food processor in Notes, below.

Honeydew Sorbet

Using 1 large honeydew melon, follow the directions given in the recipe for Cantaloupe Sorbet.

Pomegranate Sorbet

INGREDIENTS

3 cups freshly squeezed pomegranate juice (6 to 8 large pomegranates)
Light sugar syrup, to taste (see Appendix, page 250)

Fruit sorbets refresh and cool the palate.

TOOLS

Electric *or* hand juicer

METHOD

Squeeze the pomegranates with an electric or hand juicer. Add the sugar syrup to taste and pour it into the sorbet machine. Freeze according to the manufacturer's directions, or follow directions for using a food processor in Notes, below.

NOTES

It is important to make sorbet close to the time of serving. It should be soft when served. Sorbet can be stored in the freezer; if you do so, you must completely defrost it and put the purée through the sorbet machine process again before serving. This may be done once and *only* once.

Alternatively, you may place the frozen sorbet in the refrigerator to soften for an hour before serving. This method tends to make the sorbet somewhat grainy and its velvet texture is sacrificed for convenience.

Sorbets may be made with a food processor if a sorbet machine is unavailable. It is a time-consuming task, but it works. After puréeing the fruits, freeze the mixture in a shallow pan. When frozen, cut it into small cubes, return it to the food processor and purée again—2 cups at a time. Return the icy purée to the freezer for about 1½ hours. Just before serving, purée the mixture once again in the food processor

Apple Sorbet may be made by following the directions given in the Pear Sorbet recipe. Simply substitute apples for the pears.

Pineapple Sorbet may be made by following the directions given in the Cantaloupe Sorbet recipe. You will, however, need to add light sugar syrup (see Appendix, page 250) to taste before pouring the purée into the sorbet machine. In the same manner, berries, such as strawberries and raspberries, may be made into sorbet. However, they must be seeded through a fine sieve before adding the sugar syrup.

All of these sorbets may be served alone or in combination. Use a quenelle scoop or oval soup spoon to form egg-shaped mounds of each variety. Place the sorbets on chilled plates and accompany them with a selection of complementary fruits, such as berries, grapes, or orange and lime sections. You may also serve the sorbets with raspberry, apricot and caramel sauces (see Appendix, page 249-250).

Don't be intimidated by the process. Once you've made homemade sorbet, no other sorbet will seem quite so good.

GLORIOUS MELON

MENU

Glorious Melon*

California Chardonnay, Ventana
Vineyards or Minted Ice Tea

Serves Two

The Glorious Food ideal—simply stated and simply splendid—is the Glorious Melon. It is the *everything* of a meal in a single course.

Just as the pumpkin at the Thanksgiving dinner became the "tureen" for the soup, the melon at this lunch is the "bowl" for this salad. The Glorious Melon is an ideal refresher on a humid summer day when appetites are on the wane. Both quick and easy to prepare, it proves that a dish or a meal need not be difficult to make in order to delight the guests.

Because this is intended to be a light meal, it does not need to be preceded or followed by anything. Set this salad apart from typical salads by tossing the crabmeat with homemade mayonnaise. (The mayonnaise should be prepared that morning and will keep, refrigerated, for about ten days.)

Once the ingredients are chilled, serve the lunch immediately. These foods won't hold up well in the sun.

GLORIOUS MELON

INGREDIENTS

1 large, very ripe honeydew melon
½ cup mayonnaise, made with 1 extra tablespoon of
   lemon juice (see Appendix, page 245)
2 tablespoons gin, heated
1 pound fresh crabmeat, picked clean

TOOLS

Small melon baller

METHOD

Cut off the top of the melon, about ¼ of the way down, where the hollow seed section begins. Cut a small slice off the bottom of the melon so it will balance nicely when placed on a serving platter. Scoop out the seeds and discard them.

Scoop out as many melon balls as you can with a small melon baller; take care not to pierce the rind.
Set the melon balls in a strainer to drain off any excess juice, then refrigerate.
Invert the melon shell on a plate to drain. Refrigerate.
Prepare the mayonnaise with the additional lemon juice; thin it with the heated gin.
Reserve some of the choice crabmeat pieces to place on top of the melon.
Mix the melon balls with the remaining crabmeat and fill the honeydew cavity, spooning in some of the mayonnaise sauce as you fill it.
When filled, arrange crabmeat pieces around the opening.

Serves 2

Majolica

This lunch menu was inspired by a little whimsy. Pieces of the hostess's treasured Majolica collection were removed from their showplace on shelves in the living room and became the center of attention for this particular afternoon on the terrace. The *faïence*'s mixed and matched pieces, its exquisitely bizarre colors and Renaissance designs, inspired a menu. The garden was in full bloom and filled with foods whose colors complemented the shadings of greens, mauves and pinks in the pottery.

The buffet was set out on the terrace—a shaded area—to keep the food away from the noonday sun. (You can eat in the sun, if you like, but always serve food in the shade.) The beets, fresh out of the garden with their red-veined green leaves, were intended to be made into a cold soup, but the leaf pattern on the Majolica plate was nearly identical to the beet leaves, so we decided to serve the beets whole with their leaves to match the pattern. The smallest beet leaves, blanched, tasted delicious.

The vegetable sorbets—cucumber, beet, and tomato— were the same colors as the Majolica, their colors best shown off in clear glasses. These sorbets should be served as the first course as soon as the lunch begins, since they melt in the heat.

This entire afternoon lunch was composed with a sense of humor, fancy and imagination. It's the way menus should always be created.

MENU

Vegetable Sorbets and Sauces*

Salmon Mousse*
Toasted Brioche* (see page 248)
Brown Bread
Fresh Cream Cheese and Chives
Red and White Cabbage Salad*
Beets Glazed in Honey Mustard
Vinaigrette*
Cucumber Spears and Scallions

Vanilla Ice Cream and
Warm Melted Blueberries*

Iced Espresso

·

Sancerre

Serves Eight

Water lilies from a nearby pond decorate the table.

The buffet is set on the terrace for a leisurely afternoon meal.

VEGETABLE SORBETS AND SAUCES

Tomato Sorbet

INGREDIENTS

3 pounds very ripe tomatoes
Tabasco sauce, to taste
Salt and freshly milled black pepper, to taste

TOOLS

Food processor *or* blender
Sorbet machine, if available

METHOD

Blanch the tomatoes in boiling salted water; plunge
 into cold water and peel. Halve and seed the
 tomatoes, reserving the juice.
Purée the tomatoes in a food processor or blender.
 Combine the purée with the remaining ingredients.
Pour the purée and juice into the sorbet machine and
 follow the manufacturer's directions, or follow
 method for making fruit sorbets in a food processor
 (see page 131).

Serves 6 to 8 per quart

Curry Sauce for Tomato Sorbet

INGREDIENTS

1 cup mayonnaise (see Appendix, page 245)
1 teaspoon lemon juice
½ banana
1 teaspoon curry powder
2 tablespoons whipped heavy cream

TOOLS

Food processor *or* blender

METHOD

Purée all the ingredients except the cream in a food
 processor. Fold in the whipped cream and refrigerate.

Serves 6 to 8

Tart vegetable sorbets of cucumber, beet and tomato are a variation on cold soup.

Beet Sorbet

INGREDIENTS

2 pounds beets (enough beets to yield approximately
   3 cups of beet purée)
1 cup plain yogurt
1 tablespoon lemon juice
1 tablespoon white tarragon vinegar
Salt and cayenne, to taste

TOOLS

Food processor
Sorbet machine, if available

METHOD

Wash the beets thoroughly. Trim, leaving two or more
   inches of stem attached to prevent excessive bleeding while cooking.
Place the beets in a pot of lightly salted cold water.
   Bring the water to a boil and cook the beets until
   tender.
Remove the beets with a slotted spoon, reserving ½
   cup of the liquid. Allow the beets to cool.

Cut off the stems, pinch off the skins and chop
   coarsely. Purée the beets in a food processor.
Combine the puréed beets with all of the remaining
   ingredients.
Pour the mixture into a sorbet machine and freeze
   according to the manufacturer's directions, or use a
   food processor, following the directions on page 131.

Serves 6 to 8 per quart

Sour Cream Yogurt Sauce for Beet Sorbet

INGREDIENTS

½ cup sour cream
¼ cup plain yogurt
Grated zest of 1 lemon

METHOD

Combine the sour cream and yogurt.
To serve, sprinkle the lemon zest over the sauce.

Serves 6 to 8

Cucumber Sorbet

INGREDIENTS

4 to 5 medium cucumbers, peeled and seeded
Salt and freshly milled white pepper, to taste

TOOLS

Food processor *or* blender
Sorbet machine, if available

METHOD

Thinly slice the cucumbers and toss with salt and
pepper. Purée the cucumbers in a food processor.
Pour the purée into the sorbet machine and freeze
according to the manufacturer's directions, or use a
food processor, following the directions on page 131.

Serves 6 to 8 per quart

Dill Sauce for Cucumber Sorbet

INGREDIENTS

¾ cup plain yogurt
1 tablespoon lemon juice
1 tablespoon chopped fresh dill
Cayenne, to taste

METHOD

Combine all of the ingredients and refrigerate.

Serves 6 to 8

NOTES

If serving the three sorbets together, use a quenelle
scoop or a large oval soup spoon and arrange scoops
of each sorbet on a chilled plate in pinwheel fashion.
Place a spoonful of each sauce between the sorbets.

If serving the sorbets separately, pour a spoonful of
sauce over each portion.

SALMON MOUSSE

INGREDIENTS

1 pound Irish or Scotch smoked salmon
Dash of ground cloves
Cayenne, to taste
1½ cups heavy cream, whipped
Brioche (see Appendix, page 248)

TOOLS

Food processor
Fine drum- *or* bowl-shaped sieve

METHOD

Cut the salmon into small cubes.
Purée it with the cloves and cayenne in a food
processor, switching it on and off four or five times.
Do not overblend. Add 1 cup of the whipped cream
and purée.
Scrape the purée into a mixing bowl and fold in the
remaining whipped cream.
Press the purée, a little at a time, through a fine sieve,
scraping the bottom of the sieve from time to time.
(This process requires time, patience and some
muscle.)
Spoon the salmon into a serving bowl and refrigerate
for at least 1 hour.
Serve with toasted brioche.

NOTE

This mousse serves 16 with cocktails or champagne.

Serves 8

RED AND WHITE CABBAGE SALAD

INGREDIENTS

½ large, sweet red bell pepper, cleaned and seeded
½ head white cabbage, cored and thinly sliced
½ head red cabbage, cored and thinly sliced
Vinaigrette (see Appendix, page 245)
1½ teaspoons red peppercorns, slightly crushed, preferably deep red and flaky (not pink)

METHOD

Slice the pepper into long, thin julienne. Combine with
the two types of cabbage, toss with the vinaigrette
and dust the top of the salad with the peppercorns.

Serves 8

Baby beets and their leaves match the pattern of the plate.

Warmed blueberries accompany the ice cream.

BEETS GLAZED IN HONEY MUSTARD VINAIGRETTE

INGREDIENTS

16 small new beets with stems and leaves
Salt

Vinaigrette

2 tablespoons honey mustard
3 tablespoons good-quality apple cider vinegar
Salt and ground white pepper, to taste
4 to 5 tablespoons virgin olive oil

METHOD

Cut the choicest leaves from the beets, wash and reserve.

Wash the beets thoroughly, leaving 2 or more inches of stem attached to prevent excessive bleeding while cooking.

Place the beets in a pot of lightly salted cold water. Bring the water to a boil and cook until tender.

Meanwhile, prepare the vinaigrette:

Blend the mustard and vinegar with a whisk; season with salt and pepper. Gradually blend in the oil and set aside.

When the beets are cooked, remove them with a slotted spoon and set aside to cool. Plunge the reserved beet leaves into the hot beet water and remove immediately. Drain the leaves on a paper towel.

Pinch off the outer skins of the beets (they will slide off easily).

To serve, arrange the leaves on a plate. Toss the beets with the vinaigrette and mound the beets on top of the leaves.

Serves 8

VANILLA ICE CREAM AND WARM MELTED BLUEBERRIES

INGREDIENTS

1 pint blueberries, washed and drained
1 to 2 tablespoons sugar
1 quart vanilla ice cream (see *crème anglaise*, Appendix, page 251)

METHOD

Place the blueberries in a small saucepan and sprinkle them with not more than 2 tablespoons of sugar. Warm the berries over medium heat, gently tossing them with a wooden spoon. When the sugar has melted and the berries begin to give off their juices, remove them from the heat and serve immediately with the ice cream.

Serves 8

GARDEN

Because this garden lunch was surrounded by wall-to-wall flow-ers, our main concern was toning down a riot of color. Any table decoration added to the setting would have ensured visual chaos. We decided to leave the white wicker unadorned, feeling that wicker is, after all, the "summer Chippendale."

When entertaining in the country, even at a more formal luncheon, be sure to put most of the food out at once. This occasion should be a chance for the host to visit, not spend hours running back and forth from the garden to the kitchen. The plates are piled on the table; the knives and forks wrapped in napkins; iced wine and glasses at hand. In this menu all the foods are served cold, so that the guests can serve themselves at their convenience. For the first course, we served red and yellow peppers, which had been marinated in a crock, and followed it with the *vitello tonnato*, a rice salad, string bean salad and bread sticks and crusty bread.

The peaches are poached in their juices with sugar. Although zabaglione is usually served warm and alone or over fruits, for this summer meal it is cooled and mixed with unsweetened cream to produce a lighter sauce.

A poached peach with zabaglione cream and pistachios makes a refreshing summer dessert.

MARINATED RED AND YELLOW PEPPERS

INGREDIENTS

10 to 12 large, sweet red or yellow bell peppers
Fruity olive oil
4 cloves garlic, thinly sliced
Salt and cracked black pepper
Balsamic vinegar

METHOD

Char the peppers in the open flame of a gas range or
    under the broiler of an electric range. When thor-
    oughly black, place them in a brown paper bag to
    steam (so that they can be peeled easily).
When the peppers are cool enough to handle, remove
    the skin with a small paring knife.
Cut the peppers in half; core and seed them.
Pour a light film of oil into a small ceramic crock or
    bowl.
Layer the peppers in the crock, separating them with
    a little of the sliced garlic and oil. Cover tightly and
    refrigerate.
Serve with salt, cracked pepper and a splash or two of
    balsamic vinegar.

NOTES

These peppers are best prepared over a charcoal grill.
However they can be charred with equal success over
a gas flame or on a griddle. They will keep up to two
weeks under refrigeration.

Serves 8 to 10

STRING BEAN SALAD

INGREDIENTS

3 pounds green beans, trimmed
1 small red onion, very thinly sliced
Vinaigrette (see Appendix, page 245)

·METHOD

Blanch the beans in a large kettle of salted boiling
water. Rinse under cold running water and drain
thoroughly. Toss the beans, the red onion and the
vinaigrette together and serve.

Serves 8 to 10

RICE SALAD WITH ZUCCHINI FLOWERS

INGREDIENTS

3 cups whole grain white rice
3 ears fresh corn kernels, cooked
½ cup finely chopped fennel
2 tablespoons fennel leaves, chopped
1 pimiento or half a crocked marinated pepper
    (see page 140), drained, thinly sliced and diced
About ½ cup olive oil
About ⅓ cup lemon juice
Salt and freshly milled black pepper, to taste
Zucchini flowers or nasturtium flowers, if available

METHOD

Cook the rice in salted boiling water according to
    package directions. Do not overcook.
Drain the rice in a colander, then wash the rice under
    cold running water until it is cold; drain again.
Just before serving, mix the rice and the remaining
    ingredients and taste for seasoning. Toss a few
    zucchini or nasturtium flowers over the salad and
    serve.

Serves 8 to 10

The menu is a pastel version of the garden colors.

140

The whitest of meats, veal, is presented as *vitello tonnato* with white rice perked up by the yellow of zucchini flowers.

VITELLO TONNATO

INGREDIENTS

Veal

Vegetable oil for the roasting pan
1 5-pound (net weight) loin of milk-fed veal, boned
    and tied, at room temperature
Salt and freshly milled black pepper
2 ribs celery, chopped
2 carrots, chopped
1 medium onion, chopped

Tonnato Sauce

1 can (7 ounces) Genoa-style tuna fish in oil, drained

4 anchovy fillets, drained and patted dry
1 tablespoon capers, drained
4 cornichons, lightly chopped
1 tablespoon chopped Italian parsley
1 cup mayonnaise (see Appendix, page 245)
1 cup heavy cream

Accompaniment

1 tablespoon capers, drained
12 to 18 Niçoise olives

TOOLS

Roasting pan
Food processor

METHOD

Preheat the oven to 400°.

Brush the roasting pan with a light film of oil. Season the meat with salt and pepper.

Place the veal in the pan and surround the meat with the celery, carrots and onion.

Lower the oven temperature to 375° and roast the veal for 35 to 40 minutes or until the juices run slightly pink.

Let cool to room temperature; do not refrigerate.

Meanwhile, make the tonnato sauce:

Using the metal blade in a food processor, purée the tuna, anchovies, capers, cornichons and parsley until smooth. Add the mayonnaise and gradually pour in the cream. (Adjust the amount of cream depending on how light you want the sauce to be.) Set aside.

To serve, cut the veal into very thin slices, place it on a serving platter and pour a little of the sauce over it. Sprinkle with the capers and olives and pass the remaining tonnato sauce in a bowl.

Serves 8 to 10

POACHED PEACHES WITH ZABAGLIONE CREAM AND PISTACHIOS

INGREDIENTS

Zabaglione Cream

6 egg yolks
⅔ cup sugar
⅔ cup Marsala
2 cups heavy cream, whipped to twice its volume

Peaches

10 firm, ripe unblemished peaches
2 cups sugar, more or less depending on sweetness of fruit
Juice of 1 lemon

Accompaniment

Apricot glaze (see Appendix, page 249)
¼ cup pistachios, chopped

TOOLS

An improvised double boiler: a large copper or stainless-steel mixing bowl set over simmering water. This type of double boiler will prevent the egg from sticking and provides enough room for the egg mixture to increase in volume.
Food processor
Large stainless-steel pot

METHOD

To prepare the zabaglione cream:

Simmer water in the bottom of the double boiler. Off the heat, beat the egg yolks in the bowl with a wire whisk until they are smooth and lemon colored. Set the bowl over the simmering water and slowly add the sugar, whisking constantly.

As the eggs thicken and puff, gradually add the Marsala and continue to whisk for about 20 minutes. (If the mixture starts to curdle, remove the bowl from the heat and whisk in a bit of cold heavy cream and beat vigorously or restore it by blending for a minute in a food processor.) Cool the mixture over iced water and refrigerate.

To poach the peaches:

Place the peaches, in their skins, in the large stainless-steel pot with the sugar and lemon juice. Add cold water to cover. Cover with a round of waxed paper cut to fit the interior of the pot.

Set the pan over moderately high heat and bring the liquid to a simmer.

Simmer the peaches until they can be pierced easily with a paring knife. The cooking time will depend on the ripeness of the fruit. Remove the peaches from the heat and let them cool in the liquid.

When cooled, remove the skins with a sharp paring knife. Strain the cooking liquid over the peaches, cover and set aside.

To assemble the dessert:

Drain the peaches on paper towels.

Mix the whipped heavy cream into the chilled zabaglione mixture and pour it into a deep platter large enough to hold all of the peaches. Arrange the peaches in the cream.

Spoon some of the apricot glaze over the peaches and sprinkle each peach with pistachios.

NOTE

It is best to prepare the fruit just a couple of hours before you plan to serve it, since poached peaches do not retain their pretty blush once refrigerated.

Serves 8 to 10

SEASHORE

This attractive seashore cottage does just that: it attracts friends, neighbors and house guests all summer long, usually around mealtime. This lunch is geared toward these unexpected arrivals, and its ingredients should always be kept on hand. Sausages and salamis, cornichons, tuna fish, anchovies, capers, olives, eggs and pickled onions, oil, vinegar and cases of wine are staples for the summer larder. The Niçoise salad is the simplest lunch to make, and most of its ingredients derive from these easily stored items.

Arrange each ingredient on a table in separate bowls and on plates. The function of this is twofold. A salad tossed with all its ingredients soon becomes soggy; but when chosen one by one, all the foods remain crisp and fresh. Secondly, the ingredients here are not necessarily everyone's favorites. By setting out each item individually, you make it easy for the guests to pick and choose the foods in any combination.

The best of the lettuces for this salad are Boston, Bibb, Ruby Red, Oak Leaf and Butter Crunch. They can be served alone or in combination. After the lettuce has been washed and dried, cluster it and place it in a bowl with the base of the leaves in iced water. The bowl serves as wonderful table decoration and the water keeps the lettuce crisp. The same may be done with the leaves of red and green basil. Avoid serving butter in high summer heat, unless it is thoroughly iced. For those who do not like hard butter, just serve the bread warmed.

Preface the meal with a basketful of hard and soft sausages and salamis, bowls of red radishes and scallions, crusty French bread and bottles of iced rosé wine. End the meal with some creamy chèvre and then iced yellow watermelon.

The entire lunch is set on a table underneath a canopy of parachute fabric to keep the sun from "melting" the food.

Luncheon under the canopy.

Easy summer fare: hard and soft salamis and sausages...

...cornichons...

...pickled onions...

...and chilled yellow watermelon for dessert.

SALAD NIÇOISE

INGREDIENTS

4 heads lettuce (any combination of Boston, Oak
    Leaf, Ruby Red or Butter Crunch)
½ pound green beans, stem-end trimmed
½ pound yellow beans, stem-end trimmed
½ pound purple beans, stem-end trimmed

Pickled red onions

3 large red onions, very thinly sliced
1 cup tarragon red wine vinegar
1 teaspoon sugar
3 whole cloves
4 black peppercorns, crushed

Fresh red and green leaf basil with stems, washed and
    placed in a container of water
4 cans (7 ounces each) Genoa-style tuna fish in oil,
    drained
2 cans flat anchovy fillets, drained and patted dry
Capers, drained
12 hard-boiled eggs, peeled and halved
12 to 18 small new potatoes, boiled in their skins and
    left whole
Black Niçoise olives
Freshly milled black pepper and sea salt
Cruets of olive oil and red wine vinegar

METHOD

Wash and dry the lettuce.
Blanch the green and yellow beans separately in
    salted boiling water until tender, then cool under
    running water and drain. Do not cook the purple
    beans (if you do, they will turn green in the process).

To prepare the pickled onions:

Place the onions in a saucepan with the tarragon
    vinegar and enough cold water (about 1 cup) to
    cover. Add the sugar, cloves and peppercorns.
Simmer over medium heat for 10 minutes or until the
    onions are tender. Refrigerate until ready to serve.

Place all of the ingredients in individual bowls and on
    plates and let the guests make their own salads.

Serves 8 to 10

The Salad Niçoise.

BEACH HOUSE

In a rented summer house—where the living is supposed to be "easy"—improvisation is the only way to get anything done. Start the season by planting an assortment of herbs in a big clay pot set outside the kitchen door. Basil and rosemary thrive by the sea and your supply of fresh herbs should last all summer. Early in the season, make quarts of fish stock and freeze them. With these simple preparations you will be able to spend the rest of your sun-filled days at leisure. Assemble your utensils and tableware from ocean and beach, and from whatever exists in closets and on shelves, and let your imagination take wing. With a couple of pots, a casserole, a hodgepodge of plates and glasses and a few cotton dish towels for napkins, you can give a banquet-by-the-sea.

To begin the meal, serve little necks, always in season, steamed and sauced with cream and thyme.

Next a fish soup, which is neither a soup nor a stew. Its base consists of two quarts of the fish stock you have prepared and frozen ahead of time. The remaining ingredients include vegetables and herbs, white wine and Pernod. For extra dimension, make the *rouille*, a rosy pink version of *aïoli*, rendered fiery with the addition of hot red pepper and pimiento. The large croutons absorb both soup and *rouille*.

Because fresh corn on the cob may be served as a course, prepare grilled corn instead of a salad. Served with nasturtium butter, the corn becomes a salad. (The nasturtium, originally grown in an herb garden, is a plant that serves several functions: its seeds can be pickled and eaten in place of capers, its leaves and flowers eaten in salads.)

The dessert is the centerpiece decoration for the lunch: whole peaches and plums, eaten at the table or carried to the deck where hot coffee and gingersnaps await.

Fish soup, opposite, is followed by coffee and ginger snaps on the deck. *Overleaf:* A fire bucket holds iced wine, cotton dish towels become napkins, salt and pepper rests in clam shells and the fresh fruit makes a centerpiece for the table.

Fresh corn, ready for the coals.

STEAMED LITTLE NECKS IN CREAM AND FRESH THYME

INGREDIENTS

4 dozen little neck clams
1 pint (2 cups) heavy cream
1 teaspoon fresh thyme leaves

TOOLS

1 stainless-steel or heavy enameled-steel pot with lid

METHOD

Wash the clams thoroughly and place them in the
  freezer for 15 minutes. (The clams will open more
  quickly when they hit the hot pot.)
Simmer the cream in a saucepan and add the thyme.
  Continue to simmer until the cream is reduced by a
  third. Set aside.
Place the clam pot over a high flame for 5 minutes.
  Place the clams in the pot and cover, shaking the
  pot from time to time to allow the clams to heat
  evenly. As the clams open, remove them from the
  pot with a pair of tongs and reserve in a preheated
  bowl.
Strain the clam juice from the pot into the cream
  mixture and pour over the clams.
Serve the clams in heated bowls with a little of the
  sauce.

NOTE

Be sure to remove the clams from the pot as soon as
they open; they will become tough and chewy if
overcooked.

Serves 4

SOUTHAMPTON FISH SOUP WITH ROUILLE AND CROUTONS

INGREDIENTS

Rouille

½ sweet red pepper, roasted and seeded or 1 roasted
  pepper, packed in oil
1 thick slice fresh French bread, soaked in red wine
  vinegar and squeezed dry
4 cloves garlic, finely minced
2 egg yolks
¼ teaspoon hot red pepper flakes
Salt and freshly milled black pepper, to taste
1 cup fruity virgin olive oil

French bread croutons

½ loaf French bread

152

Fish Soup

1 cup finely minced onion

⅓ cup virgin olive oil

4 pounds fresh tomatoes, peeled, seeded and chopped, with the juice reserved

2 quarts fish stock (see Appendix, page 246)

1 cup dry white wine

2 small carrots, cut into 2-inch julienne

White inner celery ribs from 1 bunch, leaves reserved, ribs cut into julienne

2 small leeks, cut into 2-inch julienne and washed thoroughly

1 teaspoon packed fresh thyme leaves

1 teaspoon packed and lightly chopped fresh rosemary

1 teaspoon packed fresh tarragon leaves

½ cup packed and ribbon-cut fresh basil leaves

½ cup packed and lightly chopped Italian parsley leaves

½ teaspoon saffron

2 ounces Pernod

Freshly milled black pepper, to taste

TOOLS

Heavy enameled soup kettle *or* stockpot

Food processor

METHOD

To prepare the rouille:

In a food processor, purée all the ingredients except the olive oil until the mixture is smooth, scraping the sides of the processor with a rubber spatula from time to time. Gradually add the oil until the *rouille* has the consistency of thick mayonnaise. Scrape into a bowl and cover tightly. (*Rouille* keeps for weeks under refrigeration. It is an excellent, pungent sauce served with poached or steamed fish.)

Nasturtium butter.

To prepare the croutons:

Preheat the oven to 325°.

Cut the bread into ½-inch slices.

Place the slices on a baking sheet and bake 15 to 20 minutes or until golden brown. Set aside.

To prepare the fish soup:

Sauté the onion in the olive oil until wilted and translucent. Add the tomatoes and their juice and simmer for 5 minutes. Add the stock and wine and simmer for 5 minutes more.

Add the carrots, celery ribs and leeks and simmer for 10 minutes.

Stir in the herbs, saffron, Pernod and reserved celery leaves and simmer for 10 minutes more. Season with the pepper.

To serve, pour the soup into a heated tureen. Spread the *rouille* on top of the croutons and float them on top of the soup.

NOTES

This soup can become a heartier meal by poaching chunks of bass in the soup. It can also be turned into a delicious scallop stew.

To make the stew, strain the soup and purée the vegetable mixture. Fold the puréed vegetables back into the soup and whisk in 2 tablespoons of *rouille*. When the soup is simmering, add a pound or two of fresh bay scallops. Pour the soup immediately into a heated tureen and serve with additonal *rouille*.

Fresh herbs must be used when making these soups.

Serves 6 to 8

NASTURTIUM BUTTER

INGREDIENTS

1 pound (4 sticks) unsalted, good quality butter

6 nasturtium flowers

METHOD

Cream the butter with a wooden spoon or in an electric mixer.

Select a glass container that will comfortably hold the butter and place a nasturtium flower, face up, on the bottom of the container.

Arrange a few of the blossoms, facing out, on the sides of the container, using a bit of butter to hold them in place. Fill the container with the butter, pressing the butter carefully against the flowers.

When filled, place one blossom on top. Cover and refrigerate for 24 hours.

The butter will take on the perfume of the flowers and taste even richer.

Yield: 1 pound

BARBECUE

The barbecue is summer itself. From Memorial Day until the first cool days of September, cooking over a grill is the American way of life. Almost anyone with a watchful eye can master this method of cookery. And an outdoor kitchen is a fine space for entertaining. The word *barbecue* originally meant a grid of sticks. Although the American love of gadgetry has resulted in the development of charcoal broilers that are almost as complicated as professional stoves, here the simplest of grills will do.

Charcoal and charcoal briquets are easily managed by the beginner. Start cooking as soon as the lighted coals reach a dusty glow. For the more adventuresome, try grilling over sweet woods, such as mesquite and fruitwood.

The barbecue fare need not be encumbered by sauces, bottled or otherwise. If you prefer more flavor than that of the meat and char, you might make a marinade in which the meat may be placed before grilling. Any of your favorite combinations of fresh or dried herbs, good olive oil, wine and garlic will do. Do not marinate fish destined for the grill in lemon or wine, because their acid will "cook" the fish. Stalks of dried herbs—such as fennel, thyme or rosemary—may be thrown onto the hot coals just before the meats or fish are ready for serving.

Here we stuff the fish with lovage—a sharp, hot herb handed down from the Romans and used before peppercorns to "pepper" meats. We balance the skewered fish on the ears of corn and surround both with peppers.

The barbecue grill can serve a dual function, as stove and serving platter. Everything is prepared in one place so that there is no need to commute between "kitchens."

For dessert we serve cantaloupe, the sweetest of summer fruits, refreshed with ribbons of mint.

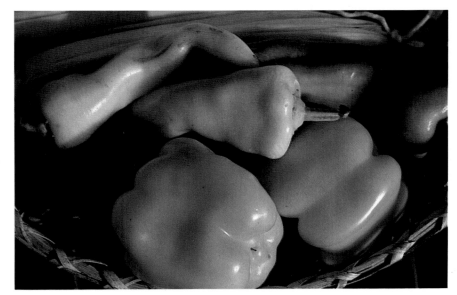

The red snapper is skewered and stuffed with lovage.

Balanced on the corn, the fish will not stick to the grill.

GRILLED RED SNAPPER WITH LOVAGE LEAVES

INGREDIENTS

A 4-pound red snapper, cleaned (scales and gills
   removed), with head, fins and spine intact
Salt and freshly milled black pepper
4 to 5 lovage stems and leaves (see Notes)
Fruity olive oil for basting the fish
2 tablespoons Pernod

TOOLS

A charcoal grill
2 12-inch (approximately) metal skewers

METHOD

Wash the fish and pat dry with paper towels. Push one
   skewer through the fish from mouth to tail along
   the backbone, and the other skewer through from
   tail to mouth in the same fashion. Salt and pepper
   the cavity and fill it with lovage stems and leaves.

Brush the fish all over with the olive oil.
When the corn (see next recipe) is almost cooked,
   balance the ends of the skewers on the ears and
   grill the fish 8 to 10 minutes on each side. Just
   before removing the fish from the grill, splash it with
   Pernod and serve after the flames have subsided.

NOTES

Lovage is a peppery herb tasting of anise and celery.
Fresh fennel leaves or sprigs of fresh tarragon may be
used in its place.

When you balance the fish on the corn it should be
about 2 inches above the grill and should cook
without sticking or losing its flesh.

Serves 3 to 4

GRILLED CORN AND PEPPERS

INGREDIENTS

4 ears sweet corn
¼ pound (1 stick) butter, melted
Kosher salt and freshly milled black pepper
2 whole yellow bell peppers
2 whole green bell peppers
4 to 6 whole frying peppers
Balsamic vinegar

TOOLS

A charcoal grill

METHOD

Husk the corn, leaving a double layer of husk attached at the stem of each ear. Brush the kernels with the melted butter and sprinkle with salt and pepper. Pull the husks up and tie them at the top with kitchen string.
Wash all of the peppers.
When the charcoal glows dusty red, place the peppers and corn on the grill.
The peppers should be turned with tongs to avoid piercing the skin; the corn can be turned easily by hand. Both vegetables should be turned often and will be slightly charred.

Serve with additional salt and balsamic vinegar to splash on the peppers.

Serves 3 to 4

CANTALOUPE AND MINT

INGREDIENTS

2 small ripe cantaloupes
About 8 to 10 mint leaves

TOOLS

Melon baller

METHOD

Cut a small piece off both ends of each melon and reserve.
Halve the melons and seed them.
Using the melon baller, scoop out melon balls; reserve in a bowl and refrigerate.
To serve, stack the mint leaves in a neat pile and cut them into thin julienne. Mix with the melon balls and serve on chilled plates with the melon ends for decoration.

Serves 4

Mint sparks the flavor of fresh cantaloupe.

BOAT PICNIC

Except for yachts and ocean liners, boats are not built for dining comfort. With tables and chairs notably absent, this movable feast must be served with as little stress and as few trappings as possible. Make a maximum effort to exert the minimum effort. Individual plates and tableware are unnecessary; a couple of knives, a corkscrew, wine glasses and big napkins, essential. Two large ice chests or Styrofoam containers—one for ice and drinks, the other for food—will suffice.

"Well-balanced" boat fare should consist entirely of finger foods, which may be prepared the night before departure. Keep the crudités crisp by storing them in plastic bags in the refrigerator. Marinate the cheese in oil and herbs. Steam, cool and refrigerate the mussels. Chill the cherries.

Have bottled water on hand the morning of the picnic and fill a thermos with iced tea or coffee. Before leaving for the dock, mix the mussels with the vinaigrette. Slice the bread on board.

MUSSELS VINAIGRETTE

INGREDIENTS

4 quarts small to medium mussels
½ cup finely sliced red onion
½ cup chopped Italian parsley
¼ cup olive oil
About 2 tablespoons tarragon red wine vinegar
Freshly milled black pepper

TOOLS

Heavy stainless-steel pot *or* other heavy, enameled pot, with cover

METHOD

Wash and scrub the mussels and pull away the beards. Place the mussels in the freezer for 10 minutes before steaming (they will open faster).

Heat a large, covered pot for 5 minutes over high heat. Add the mussels and cover. Shake the pot from time to time to allow the mussels to heat evenly. When the mussels open, allow them to steam a minute or two, then remove. Do not overcook.

Strain the mussel juice over the mussels; cover tightly when cool and refrigerate.

To serve, drain the liquid and toss the mussels in their shells with the remaining ingredients.

NOTES

You can freeze the juice for a mussel soup.

Transport the mussels to the boat in an ice chest.

Serves 4 to 5

MARINATED CHÈVRE

Choose a ½- to ¾-pound semi-soft chèvre log (such as a Montrachet without ash) and coat with olive oil.

Dust with any combination of chopped fresh herbs, such as thyme, rosemary, tarragon and chervil.

Splash with a little raspberry vinegar, but only after coating with the oil; the oil will keep the cheese from absorbing the vinegar. Cover tightly and refrigerate an hour or more.

Serve at room temperature.

Serves 4

AUTUMN PICNIC

There are no colors quite like those of the changing autumn leaves, and no other spectacle so irresistibly lures you into the woods. This picnic pays homage to the drama of autumn's display, enabling you to witness the magnificence of the season in style and comfort. Finding a quiet spot away-from-it-all is worth the trouble of lugging food. This portable feast is designed to sustain even the most vigorous hikers.

Although cold chicken and potato salad are admirable picnic fare, we prefer this more extravagant menu. If the weather happens to dampen the spirits, you can serve this indoors as well, by simply warming up the beans and pigs' feet. Low in alcoholic content, the hard cider gives an added lift to the picnic. The bread pudding is never refused!

MENU

Breaded Mustard Pigs' Feet*
Red Lentil and White Bean Salad*
Crusty Bread

Persimmons and Chèvre

Bread Pudding*

Thermoses of Hard Cider and Hot Coffee
Flask of Calvados

Serves Six

BREADED MUSTARD PIGS' FEET

INGREDIENTS

6 small pigs' feet or pigs' knuckles
2 bay leaves
8 black peppercorns
3 cloves garlic
1 tablespoon dried thyme
1 tablespoon dried rosemary
1 tablespoon fennel seeds
3 sprigs parsley
4 wide strips orange zest
1 carrot, chopped
2 carrot tops
1 medium onion, chopped
3 quarts apple cider
1 cup Dijon-style mustard

Bread crumb mixture
½ pound (2 cups) fine dried bread crumbs
3 cloves garlic, finely minced
1 cup chopped parsley
About ½ cup olive oil
Salt and pepper, to taste

TOOLS

8- to 10-quart heavy stockpot *or* soup kettle

METHOD

Wash the pigs' feet thoroughly in cold water and place in the kettle. Add all of the remaining ingredients except the mustard and add water to cover. Bring to a boil and continue cooking the pigs' feet at an easy boil for 1½ hours or until they can be pierced easily with a sharp knife. Cool the pigs' feet in the stock.

Mix together the bread crumbs, garlic and parsley. Moisten gradually with up to ½ cup of olive oil. Season with salt and pepper.

Preheat the oven to 375°.

Remove the pigs' feet from the gelatin-stock, coat them thickly with the mustard and dust them with the bread crumb mixture. Place the pigs' feet on a baking sheet and bake for one hour or until golden brown.

To serve, place in a covered dish and serve warm.

Serves 6

Persimmons served with chèvre.

RED LENTIL AND WHITE BEAN SALAD

INGREDIENTS

Red Lentils

½ pound red lentils
2 cups chicken stock (see Appendix, page 246)
Salt and pepper, to taste

White Beans

½ pound Great Northern, marrow or Navy beans
1 clove garlic, peeled
2 bay leaves
1 tablespoon dried sweet basil
1 tablespoon oregano
1 tablespoon fennel seeds
1 tablespoon thyme
Salt and freshly milled black pepper, to taste
1 quart chicken stock (see Appendix, page 246)

Salad

½ cup lightly chopped fresh fennel leaves
½ cup finely chopped sweet red peppers
2 shallots, finely chopped
1 cup vinaigrette (see Appendix, page 245)
Salt and freshly milled black pepper, to taste

METHOD

Simmer the red lentils in the chicken stock and 2 cups
of cold water for about 20 minutes. Add salt and
pepper. Reserve in the liquid.
Thoroughly wash the white beans.
Bring the beans and herbs to a boil in the stock and
1 quart of water. Boil for 5 minutes and cool.
Return the beans to the heat, bring to a simmer and
cook 1 hour or until tender.
Drain the lentils and white beans.
Mix them with all of the salad ingredients and serve at
room temperature.

Serves 6

Bread pudding.

BREAD PUDDING

INGREDIENTS

6 to 8 slices (1-inch thick) French or Italian bread
Unsalted butter
2 whole eggs
5 egg yolks
¼ cup sugar
½ teaspoon vanilla
A few gratings of nutmeg
2 cups milk
2 cups heavy cream
¼ cup sugar cubes, crushed
Confectioners' sugar

TOOLS

2-quart oven-proof casserole
Roasting pan

METHOD

Preheat the oven to 350°.
Lightly butter one side of each of the slices of bread.
Beat the whole eggs, egg yolks, sugar, vanilla and nutmeg together thoroughly.
Scald the milk and heavy cream. Pour the milk and cream into the egg mixture and whisk thoroughly, then pour through a sieve into the casserole.
Float the pieces of bread on top, buttered side up, and sprinkle with the crushed sugar cubes.
Place the casserole in a roasting pan on the middle shelf of the oven and pour boiling water into the pan until it reaches halfway up the sides of the casserole. Bake for 45 to 50 minutes or until a sharp knife inserted into the center of the pudding comes out clean.
Dust the pudding with confectioners' sugar.

NOTES

This pudding is best served at room temperature or warmed.

Apricot sauce (see Appendix, page 250) is an excellent accompaniment.

Serves 6

163

EVENT

There are times when you get the urge to put on a bravura performance for friends. When such a mood hits, you can create this dramatic surprise—an up-to-date version of a Four-and-Twenty-Blackbird Pie. Paul Bocuse made this "chicken pot pie" for us in his French restaurant, Collognes au Mont d'Or.

This show-off lunch is best displayed on a plain table because it needs no other embellishments. The highly polished table surface made the table settings glow. The shallow soup plates were white, decorated with small vegetable paintings. As soon as the guests were seated, we brought in the entrée itself, a large white tureen lidded with a domed *mille feuille* crust. Beneath the pastry mantle, a small whole chicken was nested on a bed of spring vegetables, diced *foie gras* and truffles.

To end the performance, we served another favorite: a chocolate mousse. Admittedly, there are as many recipes for this dessert as there are cooks, but this is the best one we have encountered, another gift from France. The mousse can be prepared, an hour before serving. You must, however, buy the very best chocolate, because the quality of the mousse depends on the quality of the chocolate.

The key to preparing this chicken pot pie is mastering the *mille feuille* pastry. For the timid, this same pastry may be store bought.

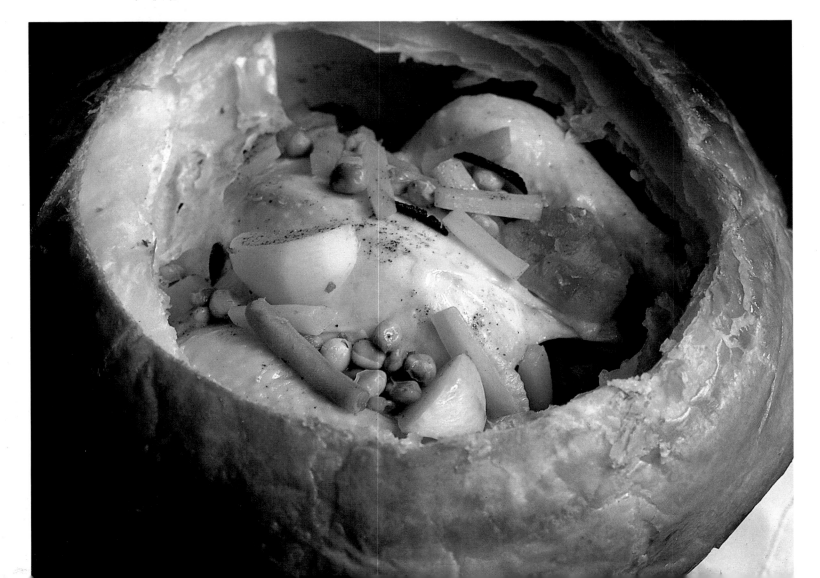

CHICKEN POT PIE

INGREDIENTS

A 3½- to 4-pound chicken
1 tomato
⅓ cup shelled peas
¼ pound (about 20) small string beans
3 carrots, cut into 2-inch julienne
4 small white onions, blanched and peeled
1 small turnip, peeled and quartered
2 cups chicken stock (see Appendix, page 246)
2 hearts of Boston or Bibb lettuce, quartered
3½ ounces (7 tablespoons) unsalted butter, cut into
    small chunks
4 ounces *foie gras*, diced
1 black truffle, sliced thin and cut into julienne
Milled rock salt and black pepper, to taste
Puff pastry (see Appendix, page 249), rolled to fit over
    the tureen with 1-inch extending all around the rim
1 egg, lightly beaten, for egg wash

TOOLS

A 3-quart oven-proof tureen

METHOD

Preheat the oven to 450°.

Wash the chicken and pat it dry. Place it in the tureen.

Blanch the tomato in salted boiling water, cool under
    running water, then peel it and cut it into eighths,
    removing the seeds.

One at a time, blanch the peas, beans, carrots, onions
    and turnips in the chicken stock. Cool each vegeta-
    ble under running water and drain.

Add the blanched vegetables, the lettuce, butter, *foie
    gras*, truffle and 1 cup of the stock to the tureen.
    Season with the salt and pepper.

Brush the rolled puff pastry with some of the egg
    wash, then fit it over the tureen, brushed side
    down. Brush the top side with egg wash and bake
    for 10 minutes. Cover the crust loosely with alumi-
    num foil and continue baking for 35 minutes more.
    Turn the oven off. Leave the tureen in the closed
    oven for 15 minutes, then remove.

To serve, bring the tureen to the table and, with a
    small knife, carefully cut off the crust, just inside the
    rim. Set aside. Remove the bird and carve it on a
    separate platter. Serve the chicken in heated soup
    plates with the vegetables and juices and a bit of
    crust.

Serves 4

MARIE-CHRISTINE'S MOUSSE LÉGÈRE

INGREDIENTS

10 ounces semisweet chocolate
10 ounces (2½ sticks) unsalted butter
8 eggs, separated
Pinch of salt

TOOLS

Electric mixer with balloon whisk attachment

METHOD

Cut the chocolate and butter into bits and melt in a
    pan over low heat, stirring until thoroughly blended.
Remove from the heat and refrigerate until cool.
One at a time, beat in the egg yolks until thoroughly
    blended.
In a mixing bowl, beat the egg whites with a pinch
of salt using the electric mixer until they form stiff
    peaks.

Vigorously beat a heaping spoonful of the whites into
    the chocolate mixture and fold this mixture into
    the remaining whites.

Place the soufflé mixture in a 2-quart bowl or glass
    beaker.

Refrigerate for 1½ hours before serving.

NOTES

For an even "looser" mousse, fold in two additional
tablespoons of unbeaten egg white after all the
ingredients have been blended.

The quality of the mousse depends on the quality of
the chocolate. Buy chocolate made with a high
percentage of cocoa butter, not shortening.

Serves 4 or more

SIMPLE

Even if you feel that "two's company and three's a crowd," this simple lunch will entertain *all three* of you admirably. In so small a group, your absence would be noticeable, so we suggest a menu that permits you to enjoy your guests and demands your presence in the kitchen only once, after completing the preparations.

Although the soufflé is one dish that must *not* be watched, it waits for no one when it is ready to be served. Lunch must be announced immediately. Contrary to the conviction of most cooks, the soufflé is not difficult, but it does require some practice.

At its most basic, the soufflé is a cream sauce into which beaten egg whites are folded. (Here the addition of mussels suggests the sea.) You may make the sauce in advance. Beat the egg whites just before the folding process (they will stay fluffy for fifteen minutes once beaten). *Always* butter and flour the soufflé bowl; if you forget, the soufflé will not rise. We prefer using a glass bowl, in order to see when the soufflé is done. Be sure to serve the soufflé from the center of the bowl; taking spoonfuls of it from the edge will cause the soufflé to sink.

California camembert and watercress salad, warm French bread and sweet butter follow, adding a taste, texture and color counterpoint.

After a fish entrée, any lemon dessert is appropriate. The tastes complement each other. Although a light dessert, the frozen lemon mousse is not at all like the soufflé, and it can be sliced. The mousse is sharp and very cold, and raspberry sauce sweetens it slightly.

The courses are small and simple, so set your table as lavishly as you wish.

MENU

Mussel Soufflé*

Watercress Salad
California Camembert
Crusty Warm Bread and Sweet Butter

Frozen Lemon Mousse*
with
Raspberry Sauce* (see page 250)

Espresso

·

California Chenin Blanc
Chappellet Vineyards

Serves Two

After the fish entrée, the lemon mousse is a light, sharp, complementary dessert.

MUSSEL SOUFFLÉ

INGREDIENTS

Butter and flour for the soufflé dish
1½ dozen small mussels
2 tablespoons unsalted butter
2 tablespoons flour
2 tablespoons dry white wine
5 egg yolks
7 egg whites
Pinch of salt
Pinch of cream of tartar
¼ cup finely chopped parsley

TOOLS

2-quart glass or porcelain soufflé dish
Foil collar for the soufflé dish. Butter and flour the foil
    and wrap it around the outside of the soufflé dish.
    The foil should extend at least two inches above
    the top of the dish.
Large heavy stainless-steel pot or other heavy,
    enamel pot, with cover.
Electric mixer with balloon whisk attachment

METHOD

Butter and flour the soufflé dish.
Wash and scrub the mussels and pull away their
    beards. Place the mussels in the freezer for
    10 minutes before steaming (they will open faster).
Heat a large covered pot for 5 minutes over high heat.
    Add the mussels and cover. Shake the pot from
    time to time to allow the mussels to heat evenly.
    When the mussels open, allow them to steam a
    minute or two, then remove them from the pot; do
    not overcook.
Strain the mussel juice and reserve. Remove the
    mussels from their shells and reserve.
Preheat the oven to 375°.
Melt the butter in a small saucepan until foamy. When
    the foam subsides, remove from the heat and
    whisk in the flour. Whisk in ⅓ cup of the reserved
    mussel juice and the wine and return to the heat.
    Stir the mixture with a whisk until it has thickened;
    reserve.
Beat the egg yolks until they are smooth and lemon
    colored. Add to the flour mixture and set aside.
Beat the egg whites with a pinch of salt using the
    electric mixer until they form stiff peaks. Add
    a pinch of cream of tartar just before finishing
    the whites.
Blend a large spoonful of the whites into the yolk and
    flour mixture, then fold this lightly into the remain-
    ing whites.
Half fill the soufflé dish with some of the mixture. Add
    the mussels and cover them with more, but not all,

of the soufflé mixture. Make a slight well in the
    center and add the parsley. Cover with the remain-
    ing soufflé mixture.
Bake about 30 minutes. When checking for doneness,
    the interior of the soufflé should look soft and
    creamy.
Serve immediately on heated plates.

Serves 2

FROZEN LEMON MOUSSE WITH RASPBERRY SAUCE

INGREDIENTS

1½ teaspoons unflavored gelatin
½ cup lemon juice
3 large eggs, separated
⅔ cup sugar
Grated zest of one lemon
Pinch of salt
½ pint (1 cup) heavy cream
3 stale macaroons, crumbled
Raspberry sauce (see Appendix, page 250)

TOOLS

Double boiler
Electric mixer with balloon whisk attachment
1- to 1½-quart glass beaker or soufflé dish
Foil collar, two inches high, attached to soufflé dish

METHOD

Dissolve the gelatin in the lemon juice in the top of a
    double boiler set over simmering water.
Beat the egg yolks with ⅓ cup of the sugar until the
    mixture is smooth and lemon colored. Fold the
    lemon mixture and the zest into the beaten yolks.
Gradually adding the remaining ⅓ cup sugar, beat
    the egg whites with a pinch of salt using the electric
    mixer until they form stiff peaks. Thoroughly blend
    a large spoonful of the beaten whites into the
    lemon-egg yolk mixture.
Whip the cream and fold the remaining whites and
    the cream into the lemon-egg mixture; do not
    overblend. Allow some of the white to show.
Fill the soufflé dish nearly to the brim with almost all of
    the mixture. Sprinkle with the macaroon crumbs
    and fill the dish with the remaining mixture.
Freeze for 2 to 3 hours.
Serve with raspberry sauce.

NOTES

If made in a sorbet machine, eliminate the macaroons
and gelatin, don't heat the lemon juice, and follow
the method above.

Serves 3 to 4

FOR ONE

MENU

Poached Asparagus and Fried Eggs*
A Glass of White Wine

This marvelous lunch came from a small office refrigerator and a two-burner stove. Just imagine the challenges presented by a lunch that must be prepared in such a small area. Try the menu out on a larger scale at home.

It takes minimum effort to peel the asparagus and cook them, to render the cracklings and to fry the egg. In just fifteen minutes—or less—you have a splendid, nourishing lunch.

The first step in developing a habit of entertaining is pleasing yourself, all by yourself. It is the beginning of what you will do for others. Play with tastes and experiment with combinations.

Fried eggs, asparagus, and a glass of wine.

POACHED ASPARAGUS AND FRIED EGGS

INGREDIENTS

1 thick slice pancetta (see Notes)
6 large asparagus spears
2 eggs
3 ounces (6 tablespoons) unsalted butter
Freshly grated Grana or Parmesan cheese
Freshly milled black pepper, to taste

METHOD

Dice the pancetta and render slowly in a small, heavy skillet. When golden brown, drain on a paper towel and reserve.
Peel the asparagus stalks and tie the spears into a bundle. Trim the bottoms evenly.
Cook the asparagus in salted, boiling water to the desired doneness, about 4 to 5 minutes. Drain them thoroughly and untie.
While the asparagus are cooking, fry the eggs in the butter.
To serve, place the asparagus spears on a heated plate and cover with the egg and butter drippings. Sprinkle with the pancetta cracklings, cheese and pepper.

NOTES

Pancetta is peppery rich bacon available at some Italian meat markets. Canadian bacon, Irish bacon or any good smoked bacon works as well.

Serves 1

169

COCKTAILS

MY APPROACH toward cocktail foods was inalterably influenced by the first party of size I ever served. That was in the early '70s, on a sweltering, humid New York evening when few guests wanted to eat. They were interested only in "tastes" to blot the drinks, before going on to dinner. They reached for the baskets of strawberries, pitted fresh apricots, halved black figs, iced red and white radishes and tiny red and yellow tomatoes. These baskets were the forerunners of the Glorious Food crudités basket, which eventually became our signature. We created the basket of crudités for visual effect, to replace the traditional "glass dish" of sliced carrots, celery and olives.

As we learned that evening, the drinks served at cocktail parties should be direct and unembellished, and the food served should follow suit. First, cocktail foods should be easily identifiable, served on an appealing, uncluttered tray. Gone forever are the trays and trays piled high with mysterious rounds of bread covered with squiggles of mayonnaise, anchovy pastes, jellies and dyed caviar. At a large cocktail party, six or seven varieties of food should be offered; some hot, some cold. We recommend a platter of crustaceans, culls (baby potatoes) filled with caviar, slices of peeled cucumber filled with marinated scallops or crab, a variety of vegetable sorbets set in a cucumber "shell" or smoked salmon on buttered black bread with a fleck of dill. If it is possible to hire a staff, take the preferable route of passing foods on trays. Refurbish the trays frequently to keep the food attractive and fresh looking. If a table must be set up, the following suggestions for food may help. Set out a board piled high with rounds of beef or veal tartare and their appropriate condiments. Thin slices of salmon hold up well if left out for only awhile. A ham may be set out along with a basket filled with sliced hard sausages and salamis. The basket of crudités can be passed or placed on a table. And remember, cheese is *not* a cocktail food; it should be served within a meal, not before.

Large numbers of guests at a cocktail party demand more help. If, for example, you are entertaining a hundred people, one bartender cannot handle this number, nor one waiter. As a minimum, calculate one waiter and one bartender for every fifty guests. A bar should be set up in hall or foyer, where the guests enter. Another should be set up in a library or somewhere distant from the entrance. These bars should always be covered with a white cloth reaching to the floor to block the view of set-ups, extra liquor bottles and ice stored below.

Serving white wine at cocktail parties has been a trend for quite a few years, but this wine, when drunk in quantities, is so acidic that people are now requesting red wine as well. Whatever white wine you serve should be dry or only slightly fruity. Chardonnay is ideal; fuissé and fumé also work well with food, as does Vouvray. Soave is also a good choice for parties. Sweet wines will cause discomfort if drunk in quantity. A Côtes-du-Rhône is a good red wine for large gatherings. Either red or white jugged wines can be quite good (taste them first), but they are not particularly attractive in their bottles. Present them in large carafes or pitchers set in ice.

Years ago we began serving mineral waters for several reasons. These waters were less harsh than the carbonated varieties and the bottles were more attractive. A slice of lemon or lime served in the water is preferable to a "squeeze" of the fruit, which tends to overpower the water.

A final word. Although the cocktail party has replaced the "tea," it is not a meal. Whatever foods you decide to serve, remember that they are just a prelude.

COCKTAILS

LIQUOR LIST FOR A TWO-HOUR COCKTAIL PARTY FOR 25 GUESTS

2 Quarts	Vodka	1 Fifth	Campari	2 Quarts	Coke
1 Quart	Gin	1 Fifth	Dubonnet	4 Quarts	Mineral Water
1 Quart	Light Rum	1 Fifth	Dry Sherry	Lemon peels and lime sections	
2 Quarts	Scotch	6 Bottles	Dry White Wine	35 pounds of ice	
1 Quart	Bourbon	2 Bottles	Red Wine	75 glasses—figure 3 drinks	
1 Fifth	Canadian or	4 Quarts	Club Soda	per guest	
	Rye Whisky	4 Quarts	Tonic Water		
1 Fifth	Dry Vermouth	2 Quarts	Ginger Ale		

For parties of 50, double this list except for the Vermouth, Campari, Dubonnet and Sherry.

For parties of 75, double the Vermouth, Campari, Dubonnet and Sherry, and triple the remaining items.

CRUDITÉS

When composing a basket of crudités, fill the basket to the brim with rolled paper and cover with a white cloth napkin. Choose the freshest, most attractive vegetables at your market. If there is a large choice, buy the vegetables in small quantities.

Suggested vegetable assortment: Radishes with their leaves; scallions; zucchini and squash that have been cut into long strips; cucumbers that have been peeled and seeded and cut into strips; white turnips and red and orange beets cut into tissue-paper-thin rounds; all varieties of cherry and miniature tomatoes; separated leaves of endive; hearts of celery; sliced fennel bulbs; and inner romaine leaves. All can be prepared and served raw.

Cauliflower and broccoli florets, string beans, wax beans and Brussels sprouts are best when blanched in hot water for a couple of minutes, then rinsed in cold water and drained.

Attractively served with Crudités Sauce, all or some of these cool, crisp vegetables make a pleasant accompaniment with drinks.

Hard and soft salamis and sausages presented in a beautiful basket make excellent cocktail food. *Opposite:* The well-stocked tray bar.

CRUDITÉS SAUCE

INGREDIENTS

1 pint cottage cheese
2 tablespoons tarragon-flavored wine vinegar
Coarse salt, to taste
Freshly milled black pepper
2 tablespoons packed fresh basil, julienne sliced
1 tablespoon packed mint leaves, julienne sliced
3 tablespoons chopped parsley
2 scallions, chopped fine

TOOLS

Food processor or blender

METHOD

Purée the cottage cheese, vinegar, salt and pepper in a food processor or blender until velvety smooth. Add the herbs and scallions and mix for a second; flecks of green should show through the cheese.

Serves 25

ROQUEFORT GRAPES

INGREDIENTS

½ pound Roquefort cheese, at room temperature
½ pound cream cheese (preferably not the gum-base variety), at room temperature
¼ pound pistachios
1 bunch (about 1 pound) small, seedless green grapes, chilled

TOOLS

Electric mixer with paddle attachment
Food processor

METHOD

Thoroughly blend the Roquefort and cream cheese with an electric mixer. Wrap the cheese in waxed paper and refrigerate for 2 hours.

In the food processor, chop the nuts finely by turning the machine on and off two or three times. Reserve.
Remove the grapes from their stems.
Flatten a small amount of the cheese mixture in the palm of your hand. Place a grape in the center of the mixture and roll the grape and cheese between both palms until the grape is entirely coated; transfer to a deep pan lined with waxed paper. Wrap each grape with the cheese mixture, then refrigerate for 3 hours until firm. After 3 hours roll the grapes in the chopped pistachios to cover completely.
Arrange the grapes in a bunch on a tray. Tuck some vine leaves or lemon leaves under the top of the bunch; refrigerate again until ready to serve.

Serves 25

VEAL TARTARE

INGREDIENTS

6 tablespoons unsalted butter
1 teaspoon chopped fresh rosemary
1 loaf French bread, thinly sliced
¼ cup finely minced shallots
1 pound lean white veal, finely ground at the time of preparation
Kosher salt and freshly milled pepper, to taste
¼ cup chopped parsley

METHOD

Preheat the oven to 300°
Cream 4 tablespoons of the butter and fold in the rosemary.

Lightly butter the bread, reconstructing the loaf as you go along; wrap in foil and reserve.
Sauté the shallots in the remaining 2 tablespoons of butter over low heat until wilted; reserve on the warm part of the stove.
Heat the bread in the oven for 10 minutes then reduce the oven temperature to warm.
Mix the ground veal with the shallots and season with salt and pepper.
Using the back of a fork to press and line the meat, spread about 1 tablespoon of the veal mixture on each slice of warm bread. Dust with chopped parsley and serve.

Serves 25

The simple, unmanned bar.

RATATOUILLE TARTLETS

INGREDIENTS

Savory pastry (see Appendix, page 247), halve the
    recipe
Approximately 2 quarts ratatouille, (see page 232)
¼ cup finely chopped parsley

METHOD

Make 72 tartlet shells from the savory pastry.
When you are ready to serve, place a heaping
teaspoon of ratatouille into each tartlet shell. Do not
fill the shells ahead of time or the pastry will become
soggy. Dust with the parsley.

Yield: 72 tartlets

POTATOES AND CAVIAR

INGREDIENTS

50 tiny red or new potatoes (culls are ideal)
Vegetable oil
Fresh caviar (7 ounces or more depending
    on your generosity)
Sour cream
¼ cup chopped chives

TOOLS

Baking sheet

METHOD

Preheat the oven to 375°.
Wash the potatoes and dry thoroughly; coat them
    very lightly with oil.
Place the potatoes on a baking sheet and bake until
    done. (You will probably have to bake the potatoes
    in two or three batches.)
Pierce the top side of the potato with a paring knife
    and pinch as you would a large baked potato. Fill
    the opening with the caviar and top with a tiny
    spoonful of sour cream and a sprinkling of the
    chives. Serve immediately.

Serves 25

DINNER

"TO DINE" suggests the art of eating. Although dining may be considered a minor art, the hours devoted to it consume a good part of our lives. Both host or hostess and guests should derive pleasure from the efforts made for a dinner party.

This chapter conveys the essence of fine entertaining. Each dinner menu and its accompanying photographs has been designed to show you a wide range of entertainment possibilities in various surroundings. As I've said before, there are no hard and fast rules for giving dinners: what was once considered "right" has long been suspended. You, the host or hostess, create what is "right" by bringing to each dinner your own personal style.

After doing thousands of dinners, I've come to realize that the main attention—besides serving wonderful food—should be directed toward preventing chaos. For us, a framework of steps has emerged over the years which may help you, particularly in giving the elaborate dinner parties that so confound so many hosts and hostesses.

When giving a dinner, you set a date, write or call to invite, plan a menu, choose wines and liquors, and—if the party is large—you hire a maid, bartender and butler, or a person who performs all three functions. If you intend to perform all these roles yourself, it is essential to organize in advance so that you can spend as much time as possible enjoying your guests. Nothing is more unpleasant than plowing through a meal, slaving over a battery of boiling and steaming pots, rushing through each course to attend to the next, only to find yourself at midnight facing a pile of dirty dishes.

This does not necessarily mean that you have only two alternatives, either hiring help or entertaining less. For example, I have a friend who demonstrates real imagination in entertaining: she sets her entire dinner on a sideboard in her dining room and after each course picks up the used plates and silver and puts them in a large wicker basket lined with a heavy plastic bag. By the end of the meal, everything has been stacked in the basket. The basket is left for the following day.

On the morning of the dinner, silver should be polished and set out. When individual services are used, all the necessary utensils should be on the table from the beginning of the meal. For instance if your first and second courses require knife and fork, place two knives and two forks at each setting, a complete set for each course. A dessert fork and spoon are placed above the plate to facilitate the flow of the meal. Choose the dishes you wish to use for each course and set them out as well.

Use clear glasses only—to show off the color of the wine—and make sure there is a glass for each type of wine to be served. Plates should be large enough to arrange the food for visual effect; napkins large and plain, of good linen or cotton (synthetic material is unpleasant to touch and less absorbent).

Use soft lighting to illuminate the room, preferably candlelight, although it should not be so dim that the guests must strain to see the food on their plates. Table decorations or flowers should be low in height so that the guests don't have to crane their necks in order to conduct a conversation across the table.

When bread is served, we prefer to place a roll on the guest's napkin or pass breads in a cloth-lined basket, rather than using a bread and butter plate and knife. By removing this extra plate, we give the table the appearance of extra space. Set a block of butter on a garden leaf placed on a small plate on the table.

Before the dinner, arrange a tray of coffee cups, spoons, sugar and a creamer. Use a simple filter-type coffee maker, so that boiling water is all that remains to be done at dinner's end. Since there are always a few requests for tea and decaffeinated coffee, those too should be available.

If you intend to serve liqueurs after dinner, arrange the bottles and glasses on a tray. Put the clear fruit liquors—such as *poire*, *framboise*, or *kirsch*—in the refrigerator before dinner, so that they will be ice cold when served. We like to put the glasses in the freezer, too; not only do they look more attractive frosted, but the liquors remain cold and syrupy much longer after they are poured.

Decide on your dinner menu about a week before the party, but stay flexible. You might find a special, seasonal discovery the day you go to the market. Wines should be chosen to complement the food. The rule of thumb is a white wine with the first course, a red with the main course, and champagne with dessert. Although many liquor stores suggest seven glasses of wine to the bottle, we count five or six and six for champagne. The average consumption of wine at a dinner is a half-bottle per person exclusive of champagne.

A dinner—formal or informal, inside or outside, early supper or late late meal—is the pause at the end of a long day. It should provide a few hours of ease for you and your guests.

GLORIOUS

MENU

Poached Oysters and Scallops with
Truffle, Saffron and Mustard*

Medallions of Veal, Lamb and
Sweetbreads with Basil Sauce and
Vegetables*

Dandelion Salad*

Praline Soufflé with
Raspberry Sauce*

Espresso

·

Puligny-Montrachet · Château
Pétrus · Vintage Champagne

Serves Six

The plate as palette.

Many times we are called in to do a dinner for a client and we are led into a very plain dining room or a home "office" in an apartment, informed that this is the location of the planned dinner. As a result, our job involves more than just the food. We try to help the hostess pull together some "arrangement" of her varied plates and glasses, helping her transform whatever she has into an exquisite set for the meal. When the setting is relatively plain, even greater emphasis must be placed on the flowers, the lighting and on the menu.

This particular dining room served a dual function: it was an office and a dining room as well. We covered a round folding table with a felt cloth (to soften the hard surface), then covered it again with a cloth that reached to the floor (to hide the table legs). We borrowed a soup tureen from the china set and filled it with primroses. Since this was a festive spring dinner, the primroses—those hearty flowers that bloom before crocuses—were ideal accents to the reds, pinks and yellows in the china. The votive candles illuminated the glasses, carafes and silver, and the table became the focus of attention in the room.

The recipes for this dinner may seem more difficult than many appearing in this book, but by shopping and preparing in advance, you can present a glorious meal with a certain ease. Since the main course is arranged in the kitchen, the passing of platters is eliminated and service is minimal. Be sure the plates are hot.

The first course is neither a soup nor a sauce, but a creamy bath for the mélange of vegetables, oysters, scallops and truffles. Flecks of saffron brighten the whiteness of the dish and the seeds in the mustard lend sharpness.

The variety of meats—medallions of lamb, veal and sweetbreads quickly sautéed in a large skillet—constitute a sophisticated "mixed grill." Cooking the brown sauce with fresh basil adds a subtle but notable lift. Shaping the vegetables—in this case turnips, carrots and cucumbers—needs practice. When done successfully, the shaped vegetables enhance the entire plate.

Serve a rough and gutsy salad of dandelions to awaken the palate after the two earlier delicate courses. The dandelion weed is at its best in early spring; the tiny buds bounce off the tongue like unbrined capers. If you pluck the dandelions from your lawn, do so before they have flowered and the leaves have turned bitter. If you prefer to serve another salad that continues the subtle flavors of the earlier courses, serve boursault on a leaf of romaine or a triple crème with Bibb.

For dessert, serve the "nut" soufflé with raspberry sauce and fresh raspberries, if they're available.

Start this glorious meal with poached oysters and scallops with a truffle, saffron and mustard.

POACHED OYSTERS AND SCALLOPS WITH TRUFFLE, SAFFRON AND MUSTARD

INGREDIENTS

1 pint (2 cups) heavy cream
1 medium carrot, cut into 2-inch julienne (about
1 cup)
1 leek, cut into 2-inch julienne and thoroughly washed
(about 1 cup)
12 plump oysters, shucked, with their juices
12 sea scallops
Dash of cayenne
¼ teaspoon saffron
1 truffle
1 tablespoon French mustard with seeds

TOOLS

2 1½-quart saucepans
2 oven-proof casseroles

METHOD

Preheat the oven to 250°.

In a saucepan, reduce the heavy cream to 1 cup over
medium heat.

Meanwhile, bring 3 cups of water to a boil. (Use the
same water for blanching the vegetables and
poaching the mollusks.)

Blanch the carrots and drain thoroughly, reserving the
cooking liquid. Rinse briefly under cold running
water. Cover the carrots and keep them warm in
an oven-proof casserole.

Bring the reserved liquid to a boil again and repeat
the process with the leeks. Add to the casserole with
the carrots.

In the same liquid, poach the oysters with their juices
for 1 minute. Reserve in a separate oven-proof
casserole and partially cover.

184

In the same liquid, repeat the process with the scallops. Reserve the scallops with the oysters.

Over high heat, reduce the liquid by half and strain it into a clean saucepan.

Strain in the heavy cream. Add the cayenne and saffron. Keep the mixture warm over low heat and whisk it occasionally.

Place the two casseroles in the oven for 5 minutes.

Slice 6 thin rounds from the truffle and set aside.

Divide the vegetables into six warmed shallow soup plates and arrange the oysters and scallops in the plates.

Strain the liquid from oysters and scallops into the cream mixture.

Swirl the mustard into the cream mixture (this is neither a soup nor a sauce, but a rich, creamy bath).

Pour the cream mixture into the soup plates, add a truffle slice to each plate and serve.

NOTE

If you plan to prepare the entire menu as given, we suggest you prepare the vegetables for this course in advance and reheat them just before serving.

Serves 6

MEDALLIONS OF VEAL, LAMB AND SWEETBREADS WITH BASIL SAUCE AND VEGETABLES

INGREDIENTS

Half of 1 pair of sweetbreads
2 teaspoons salt
½ small loin of veal (about 2 pounds), boned and trimmed
1 loin of lamb (about 2 pounds), boned and trimmed
½ bunch carrots, peeled
3 medium white turnips
2 to 3 large cucumbers, peeled and seeded
2 cups brown sauce (see Appendix, page 247)
1 tablespoon finely chopped basil
Salt and freshly milled black pepper
½ cup clarified butter (see Appendix, page 245)

TOOLS

Sauté pans
Holding pans

METHOD

Wash the sweetbreads and cover with ice water; let them stand for 45 minutes, then drain and place in a pot of simmering salted water to cover. Simmer the sweetbreads for 10 minutes, then drain and cool in cold running water. Carefully remove the outer membrane and any excess fatty tissue and refrigerate.

Cut the veal into six 1½-inch-thick slices. Use the remaining veal for another dish.

Tie each medallion around its circumference with kitchen string; refrigerate.

Repeat the same process with the lamb; refrigerate.

Pare the carrots, turnips and cucumbers into 1½- to 2-inch olive shapes, making 12 of each.

Cook the carrots and turnips separately in lightly salted boiling water until almost tender. Refrigerate in cold water.

Refrigerate the cucumbers.

This recipe may be prepared up to this point in advance.

When you are ready to continue cooking, bring the meats and vegetables to room temperature.

Preheat the oven to 300°.

Bring the brown sauce to a simmer and reduce by half. Add the basil and keep the sauce warm over low heat.

Cut the sweetbreads into six 1- to 1½-inch slices. Season with salt and pepper.

Lightly coat a medium-sized skillet with ¼ cup of the clarified butter. Over high heat, brown the veal on

continued

Primroses are an accent to the reds, pinks and yellows in the china.

185

both sides. Remove the veal to another pan and keep warm in the oven.

Brown the lamb lightly on both sides and reserve with the veal.

Add more of the clarified butter to the skillet. Sauté the sweetbreads lightly and reserve them with the lamb and veal.

Meanwhile, sauté all of the vegetables in a separate skillet with the remaining clarified butter. When the cucumbers are translucent, all the vegetables will be heated through.

Arrange the veal, lamb, lightly sautéed sweetbreads and vegetables on heated plates and strain a little of the basil sauce over each.

NOTE

The veal should be pink when served and the lamb should be served rare.

Serves 6

DANDELION SALAD

INGREDIENTS

Fresh, young dandelion greens, with roots and buds included
¼ loaf French bread, halved lengthwise
1 clove garlic, peeled and crushed
About 2 tablespoons olive oil
1 egg, hard boiled
Half a kippered herring
1 teaspoon Dijon-style mustard
About ⅓ cup vinaigrette (see Appendix, page 245)

METHOD

Preheat the oven to 400°.

Thoroughly wash the dandelion greens. Remove the roots, leaving the greens in full clusters. Wash the greens again, drain, dry and refrigerate.

Rub the bread with the garlic and brush it with the olive oil.

Force the white of the egg through a coarse strainer into a bowl and then the yolk into a separate bowl.

Bake the kippered herring for 8 minutes and remove from the oven. Increase the oven temperature to broil.

Remove the skin from the herring and carefully pull the flesh from the bones. Reserve the herring and keep warm.

Broil the bread until it is golden brown and cut it into large croutons.

Whisk the mustard into the vinaigrette.

Combine all the ingredients except the croutons and toss well. Divide the salad among the plates and sprinkle with the croutons.

Serves 6

PRALINE SOUFFLÉ WITH RASPBERRY SAUCE

INGREDIENTS

Praline
Vegetable oil for the cookie sheet
½ cup sugar
½ cup lightly chopped walnuts *or* chopped pecans

Soufflé
Unsalted butter to grease the soufflé dish
Sugar to dust the soufflé dish
1 ¼ cups egg whites (about 8 whites), at room temperature
Pinch of salt
⅓ cup superfine sugar
⅛ teaspoon cream of tartar
1 pint (2 cups) heavy cream, whipped
Raspberry sauce (see Appendix, page 250)
½ pint fresh raspberries

TOOLS

Cookie sheet
Food processor
2-quart soufflé dish
Electric mixer with balloon whisk attachment
Roasting pan to hold the soufflé dish for the water bath
Pastry bag with star tube

METHOD

To prepare the praline:
Brush the cookie sheet with oil and wipe off any excess with a paper towel. Heat the sugar with ¼ cup cold water in a heavy saucepan over medium heat, stirring with a wooden spoon only until the sugar is dissolved. When the sugar begins to turn a golden color, rotate the saucepan to ensure that the color is uniform. Caramel burns very quickly so watch it carefully. When it turns amber, fold in the walnuts and immediately pour a thin layer of the mixture onto the cookie sheet. Cool completely.

Break up the praline and blend in a food processor in two or three batches until it is reduced to a sandy powder. There should be about 1¼ cups. Reserve ½ cup of the praline powder; store the remainder in a sealed container. It will keep for weeks.

To prepare the soufflé:
Preheat the oven to 350°.
Butter and sugar the soufflé dish.
Using the electric mixer, beat the egg whites with a pinch of salt until frothy.
Gradually beat in the sugar until the whites form stiff peaks, then add the cream of tartar.
Fold in the reserved praline powder and pour the mixture into the soufflé dish.
Place the dish in a roasting pan on the middle shelf of

the oven and pour boiling water into the pan until it reaches half way up the sides of the dish.

Bake for 40 minutes or until a knife blade inserted into the middle of the soufflé comes out clean. Remove the soufflé dish from the water bath and place it on a cooling rack. Run a sharp paring knife carefully around the sides of the soufflé to loosen the outside edges. The soufflé will collapse as it cools.

When the soufflé is cool, place a serving platter upside-down over the dish and invert the soufflé. Leave the soufflé dish in place until you are ready to assemble the dessert.

Spoon the whipped cream into a pastry bag fitted with a star tube. Remove the dish and pipe the cream around the "sides" of the soufflé to form a border high enough to hold a light coating of raspberry sauce on top. Pour in the raspberry sauce and scatter the fresh raspberries around the plate.

Serve the soufflé with the remaining sauce on the side.

NOTE

This dessert may be made as much as three hours before dinner. Do not refrigerate.

Serves 6

Two Tables of Six

MENU

Hot Sole Mousse with Shrimp
and Truffle Sauce*

Roast Rack of Spring Lamb*
Vegetable Purées*
Noodles*

Orange Brulée with Julienne of
Orange*

Espresso

·

Meursault · A fine Médoc
Nonvintage Champagne

Serves Twelve

Here is a party where we created the maximum effect by setting up two tables for six people rather than one for twelve. Glass *bibelots*, treasures of the hostess, surround the dozens of tulips and reflect the soft light given off by the two sets of candles. Wine carafes are placed on both tables and each table is set as a mirror image of the other. The room is actually small and the tables close together. But with the flowers and *bibelots* we created a deceptive visual extravagance—a *trompe-l'oeil*. The guests enjoyed a sense of grandeur, while the room remained intimate. The menu became part of the mirror trick, too. Here we repeated the reds, oranges and yellows of the table setting.

The fish mousse is made in two loaf pans, each turned out and sauced on its own platter. While making the mousse is not difficult, a good deal of effort is required to give this dish its unique appearance.

Preparing the rack of lamb and vegetables is simple. Serve the vegetables and noodles in individual bowls set on both meat platters. This facilitates serving and guarantees that the meat will not be followed by tepid vegetables. You should have extra help in order to serve the two courses simultaneously.

Finally, the success of the orange dessert lies more in preparation than in skillful cooking.

HOT SOLE MOUSSE WITH SHRIMP AND TRUFFLE SAUCE

INGREDIENTS

Mousse
Butter for greasing the loaf pan
2½ pounds fillet of sole
5 eggs
Salt and freshly milled black pepper, to taste
A few gratings of nutmeg
1 quart (4 cups) heavy cream

Sauce
6 tablespoons unsalted butter
1 cup finely chopped onions
1 cup finely chopped celery, inner stalks only
1 cup finely chopped carrots
1 pound tomatoes, peeled, seeded and puréed
   with their juice
A few leaves fresh tarragon
½ cup fish stock (see Appendix, page 246)
½ cup white wine
¼ pound mushrooms, thinly sliced
12 small shrimp, in their shells
½ cup *crème fraîche* (see Appendix, page 245)

Spinach
2½ pounds spinach, trimmed and washed
5 tablespoons clarified butter (see Appendix, page 245)
2 large shallots, finely minced
½ cup finely chopped parsley

Accompaniment
A few fresh tarragon leaves
1 truffle, thinly sliced

TOOLS

Food processor *or* meat grinder
Electric mixer with paddle attachment
2 large platters
2 1½-quart loaf pans, preferably porcelain or enamel
Roasting pan large enough to hold both loaf pans

METHOD

To prepare the mousse:
Butter both loaf pans.
Cut the sole into cubes and purée in a food processor

continued

189

The sole mousse—two platters of ivories, corals and pinks.

or pass the cubes through the fine blade of a meat grinder (if the fish is stringy, pass the purée through a drum or other fine sieve).

Spoon the purée into the bowl of an electric mixer. One at a time, fold in the eggs. Add the salt, pepper and nutmeg.

Gradually add the cream and blend thoroughly.

Divide the mousse between the loaf pans and cover tightly with foil.

The mousse can be prepared up to this point in advance and refrigerated. Be sure to remove the mousse from the refrigerator 2 hours before baking.

Preheat the oven to 350°.

Place the loaf pans in a roasting pan on the middle shelf of the oven and pour in boiling water until it reaches half way up the sides of the loaf pans. Bake 30 to 40 minutes or until the mousse recedes slightly from the sides or a knife blade inserted in the middle of the mousse comes out clean.

To prepare the sauce:

Melt 4 tablespoons of the butter in a sauté pan and cook the onions, celery and carrots until soft but not brown.

Add the tomato purée, tarragon, fish stock and white wine. Simmer for 30 minutes.

Purée the mixture and strain through a fine sieve. Return the sauce to the pan and keep it warm over low heat.

Melt the remaining 2 tablespoons of butter and sauté the mushrooms briefly. Remove the mushrooms with a slotted spoon. Reserve and keep warm.

Using the same pan set over high heat, sauté the shrimp in their shells until they turn pink. Set the shrimp aside and keep warm. Add the pan juices to the sauce.

To prepare the spinach:

Bring a large pot of lightly salted water to a boil. Submerge the spinach in the water and drain immediately; allow to cool in a colander.

Heat the butter in a large skillet and sauté the shallots until wilted. Add the spinach and heat through. Fold in the parsley.

To assemble the platters:

Run a sharp knife around the edges of the two mousse molds and turn the mousse out onto warmed platters. Soak up any liquid with a paper towel.

Finish the sauce by stirring in the *crème fraîche* and pour the sauce on top and to one side of each mousse. Spoon the spinach onto the other side of each mousse.

Arrange a few tarragon leaves, the mushrooms, the shrimp and truffle slices over and around the mousse and serve immediately.

Serves 12

ROAST RACK OF SPRING LAMB

INGREDIENTS

2 cups fine dried bread crumbs
1 cup chopped parsley
2 cloves garlic, finely minced
1 tablespoon chopped fresh rosemary
¼ cup olive oil, plus a few tablespoons for basting
2 double racks of lamb, trimmed
Kosher salt and freshly milled black pepper
2 cups brown sauce, reduced to half, optional (see Appendix, page 247)

TOOLS

2 roasting pans

METHOD

Preheat the oven to 450°.
Mix the bread crumbs, parsley, garlic and rosemary with ¼ cup of the olive oil.
Brush each rack of lamb with olive oil. Season with salt and pepper.
Spread the bread crumb mixture evenly over the meaty part of each rack and place the racks, meat side up, in the roasting pans.
Roast for 10 minutes; reduce the heat to 400° and roast 10 minutes more.
Remove the racks from the oven and place them under the broiler to give the crust extra color. Let the meat rest for 5 to 7 minutes before carving.
Serve the lamb with the brown sauce, if you like.

Serves 12

VEGETABLE PURÉES

INGREDIENTS

¾ pound string beans, stem end removed and cut in half
¾ pound peas, shelled
1½ pounds baby carrots, cleaned and peeled
4 tablespoons unsalted butter
Salt and freshly milled white pepper, to taste

TOOLS

Food processor

METHOD

Cook the vegetables separately in lightly salted boiling water until tender.
Purée the vegetables in separate batches:
　　Add one tablespoon of butter to the beans and purée in a food processor.
　　Add one tablespoon of butter to the peas and purée.
　　Add two tablespoons of butter to the carrots and purée.
Mix the bean and pea purées together and serve along with the carrot purée in heated bowls.

Serves 12

NOODLES

INGREDIENTS

1 pound fresh or dried noodles
¾ cup clarified butter (see Appendix, page 245)
Salt and freshly milled black pepper, to taste

METHOD

Cook the noodles in a large quantity of salted boiling water. Drain and toss with the clarified butter.
Season with salt and pepper; serve in a heated bowl.

Serves 12

ORANGE BRULÉE WITH JULIENNE OF ORANGE

INGREDIENTS

8 large navel oranges, peeled (zest reserved for
orange zest grenadine) and pith removed

Grand Marnier Sauce
12 egg yolks
1 cup sugar
¼ cup Grand Marnier
1 quart (4 cups) heavy cream, scalded

¼ cup orange zest grenadine (see Appendix,
page 250)
¼ cup chopped pistachios

TOOLS

Double boiler *or* stainless-steel or copper bowl that will
fit over a pot
12 oven-proof shallow plates or 2 oval tin-lined copper
pans 12½ x 9 x 1½"

METHOD

Cutting between the membranes, carefully section
each orange; refrigerate.

To prepare the Grand Marnier sauce:
Beat the egg yolks until smooth and lemon-colored.

Fold in the sugar.
Place the yolk mixture in the top of a double boiler
over a bath of simmering water and whisk, gradually adding the Grand Marnier. As the mixture begins
to thicken, gradually add the cream.
When the mixture coats the whisk or a wooden
spoon, remove from the heat and reserve.

Equally divide the orange sections among the shallow
plates or pans. Pour the sauce around the oranges,
not on top of them.
Sprinkle with the orange zest grenadine.
Place each plate or pan under the broiler for 15
seconds or long enough for the cream to glaze.
Sprinkle with the pistachios and serve.

NOTES

The orange zest grenadine may be made with the
oranges a day in advance.
In this case, peel only the zest from the oranges and
leave the skin and pith on and refrigerate to keep the
oranges from drying out.

Serves 12

GAMESMANSHIP

MENU

Purée of Yellow Split Pea Soup*

Apple-Smoked Game Hens with
Apricot Glaze*
Warm Potato Salad*
Sautéed Apples*
Pickled Cherries*

Chicory with Roquefort and Walnuts
Vinaigrette

Raspberries
Crystallized Ginger

Coffee

·

Magnums of Château de la Chaize
Brouilly · Magnums of
Nonvintage Champagne

Serves Sixteen

The prospect of eighteen or twenty guests arriving for dinner *is* a dread, and the only path to survival lies in flexibility. This menu was devised for the woman who loves to entertain but hates to cook. She enjoys bringing together large groups of friends but hasn't a dining room large enough to seat all her guests.

The buffet dinner has become synonymous with eating on laps. It needn't be. If you intend to have a large buffet, provide some surface for each guest in order to spare him or her the frustrations of balancing plate, knife and fork, napkin and glass while eating. Set up improvised dining tables around the house, in the library, den or even in the front hall if it is large enough.

For ease of movement, place the soup course on the tables before the guests are called to dinner. (As an alternative, each table might have its own tureen from which the guests can serve themselves.) As the tables are being cleared of the soup course, invite the guests to serve themselves the entrée.

The game hens—mail order items—are brushed with a bourbon and apricot glaze. The potato salad is served warm with a vinaigrette. The pickled cherries may be put up days, weeks or even months ahead. Only the sautéed apples are prepared at the last minute. Since this is a rich dinner, the chicory salad with roquefort and walnuts is refreshing.

Set a magnum of wine on each table, with extra bottles of iced wine placed on the buffet table for guests to carry to their individual tables when needed.

The dessert is finger food—berries and crystallized ginger. Bowls of each may be put on the dining tables, or you may prefer to serve the dessert in another room along with the coffee.

The menu for this large group appears complicated, but its appearance is deceptive. The foods actually require little preparation and little time to cook. Instead, the hostess lavished her efforts and time arranging the wildflower bouquets she had gathered from her backyard field.

PURÉE OF YELLOW SPLIT PEA SOUP

INGREDIENTS

A "leftover" smoked ham bone, trimmed of most of
    the fat (reserve the choicest bits of ham for slicing
    into julienne and sprinkling on the soup)
2 pounds yellow split peas
1 medium onion, chopped (about 2 cups)
3 cups chopped celery, including some leaves
1 clove garlic, peeled and halved
5 whole cloves
Salt and freshly milled black pepper, to taste
Heavy cream, to thin the soup
Dijon-style mustard (optional)

TOOLS

6- to 8-quart stockpot
Food processor

METHOD

Place all of the ingredients except the salt, pepper,
    cream and mustard in a stockpot. Cover with
    approximately 3½ quarts of water and bring to
    a simmer over medium heat and cover. Cook for
    1½ hours, stirring occasionally to prevent the soup
    from sticking. Season with the salt and pepper.
Continue cooking until the meat falls off the bone and
    the peas are soft and mushy. Remove the bone
    from the pot.
Working in batches, purée the soup in a food proces-
    sor; strain it into a clean pot and keep warm.
Pour in the heavy cream and stir until the soup
    reaches the desired consistency.
Serve with the reserved ham julienne and offer the
    mustard to stir into the soup if desired.

Serves 16

APPLE-SMOKED GAME HENS WITH APRICOT GLAZE

INGREDIENTS

16 apple-smoked game hens (1- to 1¼-pounds each),
    at room temperature
1 cup apricot jam
⅓ cup good-quality bourbon

TOOLS

2 roasting pans

METHOD

Preheat the oven to 275°.
Arrange the hens side by side in the roasting pans and

bake for 10 minutes.
Warm the apricot jam in a saucepan over low heat.
    Pour in the bourbon and stir until the mixture is
    thoroughly blended.
Brush the hens with the apricot mixture, bake for 10
    minutes and brush them again.
Bake for 5 minutes more.
To serve, stack the hens in a large crock.

NOTE

If apple-smoked game hens are not available, substitute hickory-smoked game hens.

Serves 16

WARM POTATO SALAD

INGREDIENTS

5 pounds small new potatoes or red potatoes
1 pound slab bacon, sliced and cubed
½ cup light red wine vinegar
1 tablespoon Dijon-style mustard
Salt and freshly milled black pepper, to taste
⅓ cup chopped cilantro or parsley
2 tablespoons chopped chives

METHOD

Preheat the oven to 225°.
Boil the potatoes in their skins in lightly salted boiling
    water until tender. Drain.
Cut the potatoes into ¼-inch slices.
Line a bowl with a clean kitchen towel. Put the

potato slices in the bowl and cover with another
    towel.
Place the potatoes in a warm oven, just until heated
    through.
Render the cubed bacon until crisp and golden brown.
    Remove with a slotted spoon and drain on paper
    towels.
Strain the rendered fat and reserve 1 cup.
In a saucepan, heat the bacon fat and whisk in the
    vinegar and mustard. Do not boil.
To assemble the salad, put the warm potatoes in a
    serving bowl and add salt and pepper and cilantro
    and chives.
Pour the vinegar and oil mixture over the salad and
    toss before serving.

Serves 16

Dinner is announced. *Opposite:* Desserts and coffee are served in an adjoining room to permit the guests to circulate.

SAUTÉED APPLES

INGREDIENTS

8 large Granny Smith or other tart apples
¼ cup clarified butter (see Appendix, page 245)
Salt, to taste

TOOLS

Large nonstick sauté pan

METHOD

Peel and core the apples and cut them into ¼-inch
    slices.
Coat the sauté pan with clarified butter. Gently sauté
    the apples over low heat until they wilt.
Salt the apples lightly and serve in a warm bowl.

NOTE

If you wish to peel and core the apples ahead of time,
toss them with freshly squeezed lemon juice and
cover them tightly to prevent discoloration.

Serves 16

PICKLED CHERRIES

INGREDIENTS

2 quarts fresh Bing cherries
Imported cider vinegar
1 cinnamon stick
5 black peppercorns
1 teaspoon sugar

TOOLS

5-quart pot
2 1-quart sterilized canning jars

METHOD

In the pot, cover the cherries with equal amounts
    of water and vinegar. Add the remaining ingredients.
Bring the mixture to a simmer and poach the cherries
    for 8 to 10 minutes depending on size. Allow to
    cool.
Pour the cherries and the juice into the canning jars
    and refrigerate.

NOTE

Pickled cherries complement game dishes as well as
most cold meats.

Yield: 2 quarts

PEASANT GLAMOUR

The *risotto*, opposite, is served with *porcini*, fragrant wild mushrooms from the Piedmont region of Italy.

There is something to be said for a menu that has little to do with its setting. Dress the table in your finest heirlooms and let the plain fare contrast.

Rice, to most nations, is just rice. The Italians give it soul. Originally a Milanese dish, *risotto* is a cousin of *paella*, the Spanish rice dish seasoned with saffron. *Risotto* is a popular alternative to pasta and, like pasta, may be served in various ways. *Risotto* may be presented with vegetables (*primavera*), with seafood, with chicken or chicken livers, with asparagus tips or wild mushrooms. In Florence, *risotto* is sometimes served with a sprinkling of rose petals and a fully opened blossom on top. A white truffle shaved over *risotto* is the noblest of presentations.

In Milan, *risotto* is customarily served with *osso buco*, but we prefer to serve it alone as a first course (with enough for a second passing). The Milanese eat *risotto* with a spoon. However you choose to eat it, its texture should be slightly moist (from being cooked in stock) and very creamy (from the addition of grated cheese). Each grain should be distinct; its appearance, shiny and gilded.

The wild mushrooms we chose for the *risotto* are known as *porcini*. They are usually thinly sliced and mixed into the *risotto*, but these were so small and beautiful that, to appreciate their full flavor, we chose to leave them whole and sauté them.

Osso buco is another Milanese dish. It is composed of the veal shank, which includes the meat, the bone and the marrow. The Italian *osso buco* is cooked in a covered casserole, a method that allows the meat to retain its essential flavor and moisture. *Osso buco* is cooked with vegetables, which are then puréed and incorporated into the sauce to add flavor and body.

Gremolata, a confetti-like mixture, sometimes includes anchovies, rosemary and sage, usually includes parsley and garlic, and always includes lemon peel. We like to add orange peel to balance the bitter lemon and to add another color.

The salad is a combination of crisp and slightly bitter *radicchio* and tender, sweet *mâche*. These greens are not native to this country, but are flown in from Italy and France and are available during the winter months. They need only a sprinkling of lemon juice or good wine vinegar, some milled pepper and salt, and olive oil (no mustard or herbs). The salad adds colors to an otherwise gold and brown meal.

In Italy dessert sweets usually do not follow a meal. Rather, Italians prefer desserts with a midafternoon coffee. Figs are the most authentic Italian fruit. The cookies here are store bought, but not the usual fare: *amaretti* come in pairs, wrapped in printed tissue paper like little prizes. They are.

RISOTTO WITH PORCINI

INGREDIENTS

2 quarts chicken stock (see Appendix, page 246)
8 tablespoons (1 stick) unsalted butter
½ cup minced onions
2 cups Arborio rice (see Notes)
8 to 10 small fresh or dried juniper berries, crushed
Pinch of saffron
½ cup grated Parmesan cheese
Salt and freshly milled black pepper, to taste
1 pound small *porcini* mushrooms, cleaned with
    paper towels and sliced if large (see Notes)
¼ cup clarified butter (see Appendix, page 245)

TOOLS

3-quart heavy enamel *or* stainless-steel saucepan
½-cup ladle

METHOD

Bring the stock to a boil and keep hot.
In the 3-quart saucepan melt the butter over medium
    heat. Sauté the onions until they become translu-
    cent; do not brown.
Add the rice and coat it thoroughly with the butter-
    onion mixture, stirring constantly with a wooden
    spoon.

When the rice has cooked a minute or two, ladle in
    about a half cup of the stock and continue to stir
    until the stock has been absorbed.
Add another ½ cup of stock and continue this process
    until all the stock is used up.
The cooking time for *risotto* is about 25 minutes.
When the *risotto* is nearly cooked (it should be slightly
    resistant to the bite) mix in the juniper berries. Add
    the saffron, Parmesan, salt and pepper and stir.
While the *risotto* is cooking, sauté the *porcini* in the
    clarified butter until wilted.
Serve the *risotto* with the *porcini* on warmed plates.
    Offer extra grated cheese for the *risotto*.

NOTES

Arborio Italian rice has a chewier, plumper, tastier
grain than other varieties. The dish should be made
with this type of rice.

Imported fresh *porcini* are available at some fancy
food emporiums during the fall. Dried *porcini* may
also be used in this recipe although they don't have
the flavor of fresh ones.

Serves 6

The fig, the coffee with cardamom, and an amaretto cookie.

OSSO BUCO GREMOLATA

INGREDIENTS

2 veal shanks, the meaty part cut into 2½- to 3-inch
    pieces
½ cup flour
1 teaspoon salt
½ teaspoon freshly milled pepper
3 tablespoons unsalted butter
3 tablespoons virgin olive oil
1 cup finely chopped carrots
1 cup finely chopped onions
1 cup finely chopped celery
1 cup peeled, seeded and chopped tomatoes
    (about 1 pound), with the juice reserved
1 cup chicken stock (see Appendix, page 246)
1 cup dry white wine
2 bay leaves
3 sprigs parsley
1 cup brown sauce, reduced to 1/3 cup, optional (see
    Appendix, page 247)

Gremolata

1 tablespoon finely chopped orange zest
1 tablespoon finely chopped lemon zest
1 tablespoon finely minced garlic
1 tablespoon finely chopped parsley

TOOLS

Heavy skillet
Large earthenware casserole
Food processor

METHOD

Preheat the oven to 250°.
Tie the meaty veal pieces with kitchen string. (Save
    the upper and lower less-meaty parts for stock.)
Mix the flour, salt and pepper together and lightly
    dredge the veal shanks in the mixture.
Melt the butter with the oil in the skillet over medium
    heat. Brown the shanks and place them side by
    side in the casserole.
Sauté the carrots, onions and celery in the remaining
    butter and oil for about 10 minutes, scraping up the
    browned particles that adhere to the pan.
Add the tomatoes and their juice, the stock and wine.
    Simmer for 5 minutes and pour the mixture into the
    casserole.
Add the bay leaves and parsley. Cover and bake for 1
    hour.
Meanwhile, combine the gremolata ingredients and
    reserve.
Remove the shanks from the casserole. Strain the
    sauce and reserve.
Discard the bay leaves and purée the vegetable pulp
    in a food processor. Mix the purée with the sauce.

(For a richer sauce, you may add the reduced
    brown sauce at this point.)
Add 1 tablespoon of the gremolata to the mixture.
Return the veal to the casserole and cover with the
    sauce.
Cover the casserole, reduce the oven temperature to
    150° and cook for 30 minutes. If serving *risotto*, this
    is the time to start it.
To assemble the dish, remove the meat, cut off the
    string and serve on warmed plates with a little sauce
    and a sprinkling of the gremolata.

Serves 6

Hearty *osso buco.*

COLD NIGHT

For the midwinter dinner on a cold night, huddle near the kitchen range. The main dish is *choucroute*, one of those great winter dishes that originated in Alsace, the region of the goose, the pig and the cabbage. It's ideal for serving a crowd.

Although the base of *choucroute* is sauerkraut, sauerkraut is not *choucroute*. The base of this *choucroute* is stock, Alsatian wine, juniper berries, *bouquet garni* and goose fat. The ingredients of this dish depend on the cook's preferences, and may include duck or pheasant or goose and garlic sausage. You might turn eastward for inspiration and add German wursts, sausages and smoked ham and pork. Any combination of sausages, sliced hams, smoked pork loin or spareribs or apple-smoked chicken will augment the flavors of this dish. You might consider another combination: partially roasted loin of pork, finished off in the *choucroute*, with garlic sausage added. And still another combination is the addition of mildly cured ham, sliced and layered on top of the *choucroute* (cover the casserole and heat it in the oven for ten minutes or until the ham wilts and is thoroughly heated). For a stronger juniper flavor, add a splash of gin to the *choucroute*.

This recipe serves eighteen. Because the preparation of *choucroute* is an all-day undertaking, produce the required amount for your guests and set aside the rest for another meal.

There is nothing more traditional for a winter night's dessert than a baked apple. We have glamorized our apple by pouring a little caramel over the top and serving it with unsweetened whipped cream.

MENU

Shucked Oysters and Little Necks

Choucroute with Braised Pheasant*

Caramelized Baked Apples*

Espresso

·

Imported Beer
Léon Beyer Gewürztraminer

Serves Twelve

Raw oysters and clams are offered with drinks. *Overleaf: Choucroute* makes a great kitchen dinner on a cold night. Here guests sit around the range and help themselves.

CHOUCROUTE WITH BRAISED PHEASANT

INGREDIENTS

8 pounds fresh sauerkraut
5 to 6 ounces goose fat
5 cups finely chopped onions (about 3 large onions)
3 to 4 large cloves garlic, finely chopped
2 large Granny Smith apples, peeled, cored and
   roughly chopped
2½ cups finely chopped carrots (about 4 to 5 medium
   carrots)
1½ to 2 quarts chicken stock (see Appendix,
   page 246)
½ cup aromatic gin
1 bottle Riesling from Alsace
1 *bouquet garni* (8 parsley sprigs, 3 carrot tops, 2 bay
   leaves, 12 peppercorns, crushed, and 18 juniper
   berries, crushed, all tied in a damp cheesecloth)
2 pounds lean salt pork or smoked bacon
2 large pheasants or 2 ducks (4 to 5 pounds each)
Salt and freshly milled black pepper, to taste
Vegetable oil
4 pounds garlic sausage

TOOLS

Stockpot *or* brazier
10- to 12-quart casserole

METHOD

To prepare the sauerkraut:

Place the sauerkraut in a large stockpot and fill with
   cold water.
Swirl the sauerkraut to rinse thoroughly and drain in a
   colander. Repeat this process two more times.
Set the stockpot in the sink. Place the colander of
   sauerkraut in it and fill the pot with cold water.
   Rinse under a steady stream of cold water for 1
   hour.
Drain and wring out the sauerkraut by the handful,
   pressing out as much moisture as possible. Fluff the
   sauerkraut strands and reserve.
Melt the goose fat in the stockpot and add the onions
   and garlic. Simmer until the onions wilt; do not
   brown.
Stir in the apples and carrots; add the sauerkraut and
   toss the mixture.
Pour in the stock, gin and at least half of the wine.
   (Add more wine if the sauerkraut is not very moist.)
Preheat the oven to 325°.
Bring the sauerkraut to a boil over medium heat and
   stir to prevent sticking.

Transfer half of the sauerkraut mixture to the casserole.
   Add the *bouquet garni* and the salt pork and
   cover with the remaining sauerkraut.
Cover the casserole and bake for 3 hours, tossing the
   mixture every hour. Cool and refrigerate overnight.

To prepare the pheasant:

Preheat the oven to 425°.
Salt and pepper the cavities; brush the birds with oil.
Roast the bird for 30 minutes (the flesh will be pink
   and the birds partially cooked). Cool and follow the
   cutting method on page 222.
The pheasant may be prepared the same day as you
   prepare the sauerkraut or the day you plan to
   complete the recipe.

To serve, remove the sauerkraut and birds from the
   refrigerator at least an hour before proceeding.
Preheat the oven to 275°.
Place all the ingredients from the casserole into a
   large pot and bring to a boil over moderate heat.
   Remove the *bouquet garni.*
Layer the hot sauerkraut, pork fat and pheasant in the
   casserole. Cover the casserole and bake for 1½
   hours.
Meanwhile, pierce the sausage casings with a sharp
   fork or paring knife.
Place the sausages in a pot of cold water. Bring the
   water to a boil and simmer the sausages for 45
   minutes.
When cooked, remove the casings, slice the sausages
   and serve with the sauerkraut and pheasant.
Accompany the choucroute with parsleyed boiled
   potatoes, rye and pumpernickel breads and a
   variety of strong mustards.

NOTES

This recipe actually feeds 18 people, but because it
takes the better part of a day to prepare, we suggest
that you set some of it aside for another meal. The
"riper" the choucroute, the better.

Add more meats to it if you wish. (A partially roasted
loin of pork finished in the sauerkraut is delicious.)
Choucroute has many variations. Smoked pork chops,
smoked spareribs and apple-smoked chicken, mild,
sweet cured ham and small frankfurters provide a
lavish—if not slightly Germanic—touch.

Serves 12

CARAMELIZED BAKED APPLES

INGREDIENTS

12 medium apples (Rome, Cortland or Idared)
Apple cider
1 cup sugar
1 pint (2 cups) heavy cream, whipped

TOOLS

1 or 2 oven-proof dishes for the apples

METHOD

Preheat the oven to 375°.
Core the apples and peel off an inch of skin around
   each end.
Set the apples in an oven-proof dish and pour ⅛ inch
   of cider around the apples. Bake for 20 minutes or
until tender. When cooked, place them on individual
   dishes or a platter.

To prepare the caramel:

Heat the sugar with ½ cup of cold water in an
   enameled saucepan over medium heat. Stir with a
   wooden spoon only until the sugar has dissolved.
   When the sugar begins to turn a golden caramel,
   rotate the saucepan to even the color. Caramel
   burns very quickly; watch it carefully. When the
   color is amber, it is done.
Immediately pour some of the caramel over each
   apple. Serve with unsweetened whipped cream.

Serves 12

A brass coal bucket filled with chilled wine and beer.

FOURSOME

There comes the meal when just a "bird-and-bottle" is ideal. One of the easiest and most satisfying dinners includes the basic roasted chicken, for which the only "art" involved is your attention: to preserve the essence, tenderness and juiciness of the bird, you must baste it often. Stuff the bird with tarragon leaves, an herb that perfumes the flesh and raises the chicken out of the ordinary. When the chicken is cooked, deglaze the pan with a little stock and white wine, and your "sauce" is made.

For added interest, lightly sauté some papaya slices in butter and serve them with the vegetables. The pearly black seeds of the papaya, flamed in Cognac, make a natural relish.

For dessert, we create a strawberry soufflé with a base of berry purée instead of a roux; beer foam is added to give it the lift.

This is a simple dinner menu in every respect. You might add a salad and cheese course to supplement the meal and to give your guests reason to linger at the table.

MENU

Simple Roast Chicken*

Icicle Radishes, Carrots, Snow Peas and Papaya*

Green Salad
L'Ami du Chambertin
French Bread

Strawberry Soufflé
with Raspberry Sauce*

Espresso

.

Gevrey-Chambertin

Serves Four

A rainbow of vegetables—snow peas, carrots, and white icicle radishes with papaya—surrounds the simple chicken.

SIMPLE ROAST CHICKEN

INGREDIENTS

A 4- to 4½-pound chicken
Salt and freshly milled black pepper
4 sprigs fresh tarragon
1 cup dry white wine
½ cup chicken stock (see Appendix, page 246)
1 tablespoon unsalted butter

TOOLS

Roasting pan and rack

METHOD

Preheat the oven to 400°.
Remove the fat from the cavity of the chicken and salt
and pepper the cavity.
Place the tarragon in the cavity and truss the bird. Rub
the bird with salt and pepper.
Set the chicken on a rack in a roasting pan and place
in the oven. Immediately reduce the heat to 350°.

Roast the bird, basting frequently, for 1½ hours, or
until the skin is golden brown and the leg juices run
clear when pierced.
Transfer the bird to a warm pan or platter.
Spoon any excess fat out of the roasting pan. Add the
wine and stock and deglaze over high heat,
scraping up any brown particles that adhere to the
pan. When the sauce is reduced by half, strain it into
a warm sauce bowl and swirl in the butter.
Surround the bird with the vegetables and papaya
included in the menu and serve.

NOTE

A whole lemon or small orange pricked with a fork
may be substituted for the tarragon.

Serves 4

ICICLE RADISHES, CARROTS, SNOW PEAS AND PAPAYA

INGREDIENTS

1 bunch white icicle radishes, peeled
1 bunch baby carrots, peeled
½ pound snow peas
Unsalted butter
1 papaya, peeled, halved, and sliced thin with the
seeds removed
1 tablespoon Cognac

METHOD

Blanch the radishes in lightly salted boiling water for
about 3 minutes. Drain, set aside, and keep warm.
Boil the carrots in lightly salted water until tender,
drain, set aside and keep warm.

Boil the snow peas in lightly salted water for about 1
minute, drain, set aside and keep warm.
Briefly sauté the vegetables individually in butter and
remove to a heated platter.
Sauté the papaya briefly in butter and remove the fruit
to the warmed platter with the vegetables.
Toss the papaya seeds into the sauté pan and briefly
stir them over high heat. Add the Cognac and
ignite it.
As soon as the flame dies, sprinkle the seeds over the
papaya slices and serve with the roast chicken.

Serves 4

STRAWBERRY SOUFFLÉ WITH RASPBERRY SAUCE

INGREDIENTS

1 teaspoon unsalted butter to grease the soufflé dish
Granulated sugar to dust the soufflé dish
1 pint fresh strawberries
7 egg whites, at room temperature
Pinch of salt
½ cup confectioners' sugar
3 to 4 tablespoons beer foam

Sauce

½ cup raspberry sauce (see Appendix, page 250)
½ cup seeded strawberry purée
⅓ cup superfine sugar

TOOLS

1½-quart soufflé dish
Aluminum foil for a collar
Food processor
Electric mixer

METHOD

Preheat the oven to 350°. Butter the soufflé dish and
dust it with the granulated sugar.

Butter and sugar a foil collar and pin it around the
dish; it should reach 2 inches above the rim of the
dish.

Purée the strawberries in a food processor. Strain
through a fine sieve to remove all of the seeds.

Using an electric mixer, whip the egg whites with a
pinch of salt. Gradually add the confectioners' sugar
and continue beating until the whites form stiff
glossy peaks.

Thoroughly blend a large heaping spoonful of the egg
whites into 1 cup of the strawberry purée. Reserve
the remaining purée for the sauce.

Fold the remaining whites and the beer foam into the
strawberry mixture. Do not overblend.

Turn the mixture into the soufflé dish and bake 20 to
25 minutes or until the top is golden brown.

Combine the sauce ingredients and mix thoroughly.

Serve the soufflé immediately on warmed plates, accompanied by the sauce.

NOTE

You may wish to serve the soufflé with a plain
raspberry sauce.

Serves 4

Hot strawberry soufflé.

ABBONDANZA

Almost every country offers, in one form or another, a boiled dinner. On a cold winter's night such a meal can be second to none. The Irish have their corned beef and cabbage; the French, a concoction called *pot-au-feu*; the Germans boil everything; and although the traditional English dinner is roasted, it tends to *taste* boiled. The Northern Italians, however, make a version of this dinner called *bollito misto* that truly sings.

This boiled dinner is a feast of meats and root vegetables, its combinations determined by your fancy. The meats include inexpensive cuts of beef, chicken and a good fresh garlic sausage. Since this humble platter is intended to appear regal, shins, shanks, brisket or similar cuts of good veal can be used. Beef tongue or fresh lamb's tongue can also be added, but I prefer small veal tongues.

The process of adding the meats to the pot, one after the other, and then cooking the vegetables separately—but in the same broth—results in a rich, aromatic and delicious "soup."

Spread the marrow on buttered toast and sprinkle it with a little milled pepper and rock salt. Marrow is a real treat, so always serve an extra platter of these "bones" for those who truly love it.

By placing the fruits in glass beakers, you can show them off like big jewels. Or you might try setting up the various fruits on a large platter, served like the *bollito* itself. Cook the fruits the day you plan to serve them and don't refrigerate them. Even though poached fruits happen to be wonderful with hot zabaglione sauce, with this heavy menu you would be wise to omit the sauce. If you'd like a more elaborate dessert, serve a plain orange-flavored cake with the fruit.

BOLLITO MISTO

INGREDIENTS

Basic Stock

A 7-pound beef shin bone. Ask your butcher to cut off the upper and lower portions (about 3 pounds) of the shin bone. Use these portions for the stock and the center portion (about 4 pounds) for the *bollito* itself.

2 pounds beef rib bones

1 veal knuckle, cut into 3 or 4 pieces

1 bunch celery, chopped

4 large carrots, chopped with tops reserved

2 large onions, quartered

3 cloves garlic

10 peppercorns

10 sprigs parsley

3 bay leaves

2 sprigs fresh thyme or 1 teaspoon dried thyme

1 sprig rosemary or 2 teaspoons dried rosemary

1 onion, halved and baked in a 475° oven for 30 minutes

Salsa Verde

1 slice French, Italian or semolina bread

¼ cup Balsamic vinegar

1 large clove garlic, minced

6 anchovy fillets, drained and patted dry

2 cups chopped parsley

continued

2 tablespoons capers, drained
¾ cup virgin olive oil
Salt and freshly milled black pepper, to taste
1 egg, hard boiled

Meats and Vegetables
2 large carrots
20 marrow bones, cut into 2- to 3- inch lengths
2 chickens (about 4 pounds each) or 1 large capon, trussed
20 small white onions
5 medium white turnips, quartered, with tops removed
20 small leeks, white part only
20 baby carrots, peeled
4 to 5 small parsnips, peeled and quartered lengthwise
4 small calf tongues
4 pounds garlic sausage
20 small potatoes, peeled and pared into 1½-inch olive shapes
20 leaves Savoy cabbage

TOOLS

For the basic stock
A 4- to 5-gallon stockpot

For the salsa verde
Food processor
Sieve

For the bollito misto
2 4- to 5-gallon stockpots
Cheesecloth
Large strainer

METHOD

To prepare the stock:
Place all of the ingredients, except the burnished onion, in the stockpot and add water to cover.

Bring the water to a boil and continue to boil for 20 minutes (this method prevents the stock from becoming cloudy).

Skim the stock. Add the burnished onion and simmer the stock for 1½ hours more, skimming from time to time.

Strain and reserve. (This recipe may be prepared up to this point a day in advance.)

To prepare the salsa verde:
Soak the bread in the vinegar and squeeze out the excess vinegar.

In a food processor, purée all the ingredients, except the egg, turning the machine on and off two or three times to process. Refrigerate the sauce.

Shortly before serving, sieve the egg white and yolk · separately and sprinkle them over the sauce.

To prepare the meats and vegetables:
Tie a carrot disc to each end of each marrow bone. Place the bones and carrots in a double layer of cheesecloth and tie the sack closed with string, leaving one end long enough to attach to a handle of the pot.

Tie string to the center portion of the reserved beef shin and to the chickens, leaving the ends long enough to attach to a handle of the pot.

With a paring knife, cut a small "X" in the root end of each white onion. Blanch the onions in boiling water for 1½ minutes. Peel off the skins and tie the onions in a cheesecloth sack, leaving one end of the string long enough to attach to a handle of the pot.

Tie the turnips, leeks, carrots and parsnips in individual cheesecloth sacks as above.

To prepare the bollito misto:
Bring the reserved stock to a boil, add the meaty beef shin and boil for 20 minutes. Skim the stock and reduce the heat to a moderate simmer. (Skimming the stock each time meat is added ensures a clear soup.)

Add the calf tongues. Cook for 1½ hours and remove from the stock to cool. Continue simmering the stock and beef shin.

When the tongues are cool enough to handle, remove the outer skin (it will slide off easily). Pare away any gristle and fat and return the tongue to the stockpot.

Set the chickens in the pot, remembering to tie the end of the string to the pot handle. Cook for about 45 minutes.

Meanwhile, pierce the sausages with a fork or paring knife and simmer them in a pot of water for 30 to 45 minutes, depending on their size. Set aside and keep warm.

While the sausages are cooking, add the sacks of vegetables to the stockpot; tie the ends of the strings to the pot handle.

Add the potatoes to the stockpot, if it is large enough to hold them. If not, boil them separately.

Remove the parsnips after 15 minutes; simply untie the string from the pot handle and pull the sack of vegetables out of the pot. Set aside in a large pot, cover and keep warm.

Test the other vegetables for tenderness with a long needle or sharp kitchen fork. When tender, remove them from the pot and set aside with the parsnips. Add a few large spoonfuls of the soup to keep the vegetables moist.

When the chickens are tender, remove them to a separate pot. Add a few large spoonfuls of soup; cover and keep warm.

continued

A plate of soup with marrow bone begins the meal. The bread awaits the marrow.

For two, or twenty, the *bollito misto*.

Add the marrow bones to the stock and simmer 15 to 20 minutes.

Meanwhile, blanch the cabbage leaves, a few at a time, in lightly salted boiling water for about 1 minute. Remove the leaves, taking care not to tear them, and plunge them into cold water. Drain on paper towels.

Roll and fold the leaves into small packets and reserve them in a pan with a few large spoonfuls of the soup. Cover and keep warm.

To assemble and serve the bollito misto:

Serve a marrow bone with a ladle or two of the broth in each soup plate as the first course. We suggest ending this course by spreading the marrow on a piece of toasted French, Italian or semolina bread spread with sweet butter, rock salt and pepper.

During this time, the bagged vegetables and the chicken may be returned to the stockpot to keep them moist.

To assemble the entrée, warm a large platter and set the shin in the center of the platter. Surround it with the chicken and the tongues. Unbag the vegetables and arrange them around the meats. Tuck the cabbage packets around the vegetables and add the potatoes. Peel and slice the sausages and place them near the edge of the platter.

Ladle some soup over the platter and serve the *bollito misto* with more toasted bread; the *salsa verde*, rock salt and Mostarda fruits.

NOTES

Although time consuming, this is an easy meal to prepare. It *is* a show-stopper!

If you prefer having two dinner parties for ten, prepare half the vegetables the first evening and the other half the second evening. Veal shin, beef tongue, oxtail, turkey, brisket and chuck are meats you may prefer to use in place of those listed.

Serves 20

Required accompaniments: Mostarda fruits and . . .

. . . salsa verde . . . .

Poached fruits for dessert.

POACHED FRUITS

INGREDIENTS

1 large ripe pineapple
Sugar (the amount depends upon the sweetness of the fruit.
1 bunch seedless green grapes, washed and left on their stems
2 dozen small Italian plums, halved and pitted
12 red plums
8 nectarines, sliced with their skins intact
1 pint red raspberries
12 green figs
½ cup green Chartreuse
8 pears

TOOLS

Asparagus steamer, if available *or* tall, narrow pot

METHOD
Pineapple

Peel the pineapple completely with a sharp knife; do not remove the leaves. Set the pineapple in a tall narrow pot (an asparagus steamer, if you have one).
Add 2 cups of sugar and enough cold water to just cover the fruit, leaving the leaves out of the water. Poach for about 15 minutes. (Use a long needle to test the tenderness of this fruit.)

Grapes

Cover the grapes with cold water and stir in 1½ to 2 cups of sugar. Poach for 10 minutes.

Italian Plums

Toss with about ¾ cup of sugar and sauté over low heat until limp.

Red Plums and Nectarines

Follow the directions for the Italian Plums.

Raspberries

Toss the raspberries with ½ cup of sugar and sauté them over low heat for 5 minutes, or until they start to give off some of their juices.

Figs

Place the figs in a shallow pan, small enough to hold them snugly.
Add the Chartreuse, 1 cup of sugar and cover with cold water. Top with a round of waxed paper to fit the pan.
Bring to a simmer over moderate heat and poach the figs until tender.

Pears

Follow the directions given for the Poached Pears on page 238.

NOTES

Present the fruits in glass beakers of varying sizes. Any leftover fruit may be cut into smaller pieces. Combine their syrups and simmer to reduce to 2 to 3 cups. Pour the syrup over the fruits, cover tightly and refrigerate. They will keep for a couple of weeks if tightly covered.

Serves 10

LOFT SUPPER

This meal doubles as an early supper or a late late supper, a one-dish dinner ideal for serving in an artist's working studio equipped for minimal entertaining. The entire meal may be presented in bowls and tureens, eaten with large bowl-like spoons and with your fingers.

This meal is a *bourride*, a variation of *bouillabaisse*, that wonderful French invention that rests in some middle kingdom between a fish soup and stew. *Bouillabaisse* contains a fish stock base, but tomato and saffron are what give it its wonderful crimson color. By contrast, *bourride* is *garlic based* and the fish stock is blended with egg yolks to make it golden and creamy.

Aïoli always accompanies *bourride*. Known as the butter of Provence, this mayonnaise with macerated garlic is served with hot or cold vegetables and is excellent with fish.

When buying fish fillets, make sure they are firm and pearly. When buying whole fish, be sure the eyes are bright and clear, the gills red and the skin lustrous. Fish should never smell "fishy." (A warning: flounder and sole are a bit too delicate in texture for this dish.)

Present a tray of various aged chèvre cheeses—about six, ranging from soft and creamy to very hard—and a salad if you like. Plain oranges for dessert refresh the palate, but if you find this too simple, remove their skins, slice them and serve them cold, sprinkled with freshly grated coconut and a little cold *kirsch*.

MENU

Bourride with Aïoli*

Oranges

Espresso

•

Cuvée "Louis Metaireau" Muscadet

Serves Eight to Ten

The *bourride*: a one-course dinner served in two stages.

The *bourride:* stage two.

BOURRIDE WITH AÏOLI

INGREDIENTS

Aïoli
2 tablespoons dried bread crumbs
2 tablespoons white wine vinegar
4 egg yolks
8 to 10 cloves garlic, finely minced
Salt and freshly milled white pepper, to taste
2 cups virgin olive oil

3 quarts plus 1 cup fish stock (see Appendix,
 page 246)
1 cup dry white wine
2 cups chopped fennel leaves and stalks
2 large strips of lemon zest
2 fennel bulbs, halved and cut again into thirds
3 cups chicken stock (see Appendix, page 246)
Unsalted butter
24 small red potatoes or new potatoes
6 to 12 baby artichokes or substitute 2 to 3
 large artichokes, cut into eighths
1 lemon, halved
¼ cup olive oil
1 loaf French bread

3½ pounds fish fillets—a combination of haddock,
 scrod or striped bass (if using bass, leave the skin on)
8 to 10 egg yolks

TOOLS

Food processor
Stockpot
Sauté pan
Electric mixer

METHOD

To prepare the aïoli:
Mix the bread crumbs with the vinegar and wring out
 the liquid in a paper towel.
In a food processor, purée the bread crumb mixture,
 egg yolks, minced garlic and salt and pepper until
 velvety smooth.
Slowly pour in the oil, blending until you have a
 creamy mayonnaise. (You may add lemon juice to
 taste if you prefer a tarter mayonnaise.) Reserve.

In a stockpot, combine the fish stock, white wine, chopped fennel and lemon zest. Bring to a simmer over medium heat and simmer for 15 minutes. Strain. (This recipe may be prepared up to this point as much as a day in advance. Simply refrigerate the *aïoli* and soup until you wish to proceed.)

To prepare the vegetables:

Place the cut fennel bulbs in a sauté pan and cover with the chicken stock. Fit the pan with a buttered round of waxed paper. Bring the liquid to a simmer and cook the fennel until tender. Set aside.

Boil the potatoes in lightly salted water, drain and place in a bowl lined with a kitchen towel. Cover them with another towel and place in a warm oven.

Halve the small artichokes and rub them with the lemon. Remove and discard the chokes.

Sauté the artichokes in the oil. (If using the large artichoke wedges, trim the leaves with scissors, rub the wedges with lemon, remove and discard the choke. Instead of sautéing them, cook the wedges in lightly salted boiling water with lemon juice.) Set aside.

Preheat the oven to 325°.

Prepare the croutons by cutting the bread into ½-inch slices. Place them on a cookie sheet and bake for 15 to 20 minutes or until golden brown; reserve.

Poach the fish fillets in lightly salted water for about 4 minutes. Remove the fish with a slotted spoon to an oven-proof dish and keep warm in a low oven.

Beat the egg yolks with the electric mixer until smooth and lemon colored.

Reheat the stock and, one ladle at a time, add it to the egg mixture, whisking constantly. Return the mixture to the stockpot set over low heat. Blend in half of the *aïoli* and simmer, about 5 minutes, until the soup thickens, stirring from time to time.

Pour the *bourride* through a fine sieve into a heated tureen and serve with the warm croutons and the remaining *aïoli*.

Serve the fish and vegetables with the soup or serve the soup as a first course followed by the fish and vegetables. However you serve it, eat it all out of a soup dish.

NOTES

If you have a passion for garlic, and fresh fish is not available, substitute rich chicken broth for the fish stock and poached chicken for the fish fillets.

Choose vegetables that complement chicken, such as leeks, carrots and string beans. The result will be a kind of Provençal Waterzooie if not an agreeable mock *bourride*.

Serves 8 to 10

Country Sit-Down

The summer house where we prepared this meal retains an air of informality, although it is not a cottage. Summer house china is usually a mixture of odd sets that have been accumulated over the years. We counted enough china to cover a three-course dinner for four to six people by matching plates for each course.

In designing the menu, we were able to take advantage of local produce. Corn and cauliflower were at the height of their seasons and the Long Island ducks were raised nearby.

The first course represents an elegant disguise for leftover cooked corn. It distinguishes itself by demanding immediate attention as soon as it is brought to the table. Because this soufflé falls like most, it should be presented when the guests are seated, for full effect.

The duck requires a good deal of effort and time. You may prefer to start early in the morning and complete the preparation just before dinner. Long Island ducks, in particular, have more fat and bones than meat. By partially boning the birds and trimming away the fat, this duck dish has little excess fat when served.

The usually bland cauliflower is served under a sprinkling of Niçoise olives, pimientos and scallions and is dressed with vinaigrette. This warm vegetable salad is spicy enough to rival the strong duck flavors.

Raspberries—in any form—are an extravagance, but catching the last harvest was an irresistible "economy."

MENU

Corn Soufflé*

Long Island Duck with Olives and Pistachios*
Cauliflower Niçoise*

Red Raspberry Tart*

Espresso

•

Mâcon Villages · Aloxe-Corton

Serves Four

Corn soufflé, opposite, is an excellent first course, followed by any type of roasted fowl. This Long Island duck recipe is time consuming, but well worth the effort.

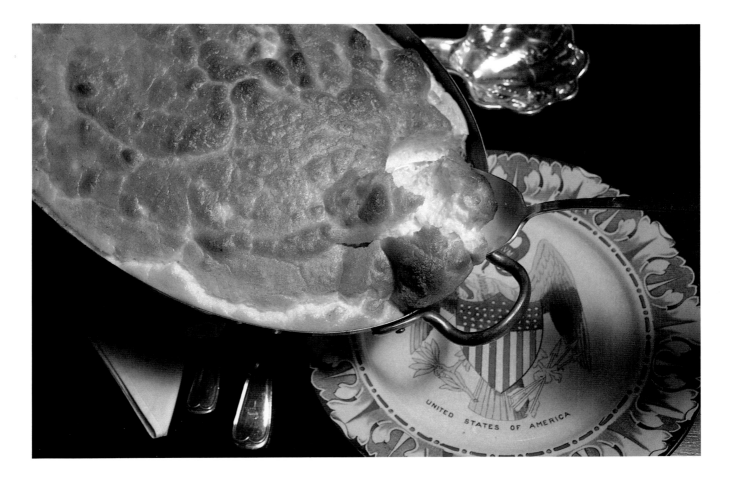

CORN SOUFFLÉ

INGREDIENTS

Butter and flour for the soufflé pan
3 cups cooked fresh corn kernels (from about 6 ears)
3 tablespoons unsalted butter
3 tablespoons flour
1 cup warm milk
1 cup warm heavy cream
Salt and freshly milled black pepper, to taste
5 eggs, separated

TOOLS

Food processor
A 9 x 13 x 2" tin-lined copper soufflé pan or casserole
Electric mixer with balloon whisk attachment

METHOD

Preheat the oven to 400°.

Butter and flour the soufflé pan.

Place the corn in a food processor and turn the machine on and off two or three times until the kernels are lightly crushed and a milky liquid appears; reserve.

Heat the butter in a saucepan. When the foam subsides, remove from the heat and whisk in the flour. When the paste is smooth, return to the heat and whisk in the warm milk.

Cook, whisking constantly, until the mixture is thick and glossy. Whisk in the warm cream.

Remove from the heat, fold in the crushed corn purée and its liquid; season with salt and pepper and reserve.

Using an electric mixer, beat the egg yolks for about 5 minutes or until lemon colored and thick.

In a separate bowl, beat the egg whites with a pinch of salt until they form stiff peaks.

Mix the yolks into the corn mixture and blend in a large spoonful of the egg whites. Gently fold the remaining whites into the mixture. Do not overblend; puffs of white should be visible.

Pour the mixture into the prepared pan and bake on the lowest rack for 12 to 15 minutes or until lightly puffed and golden brown.

Serve immediately on warmed plates.

NOTE

To cook fresh corn on the cob, place it in lightly salted boiling water to which half a quart of milk has been added. Turn off the heat immediately and let stand for 5 minutes.

Serves 4

LONG ISLAND DUCK WITH OLIVES AND PISTACHIOS

INGREDIENTS

2 Long Island ducks (4½ to 5 pounds each)
Salt and pepper, to taste
1 Granny Smith apple, halved
¼ cup olive oil
1 quart brown sauce (see Appendix, page 247)
1½ teaspoons arrowroot
¼ cup dry vermouth
24 large green California-type olives, drained
¼ cup chopped pistachios

TOOLS

Large roasting pan and rack
Poultry shears
Baking sheet that will fit under your broiler

METHOD

Preheat the oven to 400°.

Wash the ducks and pat them dry. Remove any internal excess fat and salt and pepper the cavities.

Place an apple half in each cavity and liberally coat each duck with the oil. (There is no need to truss the birds.)

Place the ducks on a rack in a roasting pan and roast for 25 to 30 minutes. The ducks will not be completely cooked. (Their juice will be bloody.) Allow the ducks to cool for 30 minutes.

Using poultry shears, cut the ducks in half lengthwise, breast side first; cut away the backbone. Remove the wing tips and leg tips with a cleaver. Reserve all of the bones.

Remove the upper wing bone from the breast portion.

Remove the thighs and legs from the frames with a sharp boning knife. Cut the legs from the thighs.

Taking care not to tear the flesh, cut the breast meat from the frame. Remove any protruding breast bones. Do not bone the legs and thighs.

Trim off any excess skin that does not cover the flesh. If the ducks are excessively fatty, use a sharp paring knife to scrape away as much fat as possible without tearing the skin.

Arrange the duck pieces, skin side up, on a baking sheet. Cover and refrigerate. The duck may be prepared in advance up to this point.

Heat the brown sauce. Add half of the bones to the sauce; save the remaining bones for another stock. Simmer over low heat until the sauce is reduced by a third. Strain the sauce and refrigerate. The sauce may be prepared in advance up to this point.

Remove the duck pieces from the refrigerator 1 hour before finishing the dish.

Preheat the oven to 375°.

Remove the sauce from the refrigerator and skim off the congealed fat. Heat the sauce.

Dissolve the arrowroot in the vermouth (or in ¼ cup of the red or white wine you plan to serve with dinner). Whisk the arrowroot mixture into the sauce. Add the olives and keep the sauce warm.

Reheat the duck for 5 minutes.

Adjust the oven temperature to broil and place the duck under the broiler until browned and crisp.

Transfer the duck pieces to a heated platter, cover with the sauce and olives and dust with the pistachios.

NOTES

The breast is the choicer meat. The legs are included to feed only the truly hungry. Because this is a very rich dish, a little will go a long way.

Borscht made with a duck stock base is an exceptional soup.

Serves 4

CAULIFLOWER NIÇOISE

INGREDIENTS

2 small heads cauliflower
1 quart milk
Salt, to taste

Niçoise Sauce

2 tablespoons red wine vinegar
4 tablespoons olive oil
Salt and freshly milled pepper, to taste
2 tablespoons pitted, chopped black Niçoise olives
1 tablespoon minced pimiento, patted dry
3 scallions (including some of the green), sliced
　　lengthwise and chopped
Juice of ½ lemon
1 tablespoon finely chopped parsley, for
　　accompaniment

TOOLS

A steep-sided bowl small enough to snugly hold the
　　florets and cauliflower julienne

METHOD

Cut the cauliflower into medium florets. Cut the large
　　stems into julienne.
In a saucepan, bring 3 to 4 quarts of water and the
　　milk to a boil. Add the salt and the cauliflower
　　pieces. Cook about 7 minutes or until tender. Do
　　not overcook.

Drain the cauliflower in a colander; cool under cold
　　running water and drain again.
Set the florets, one by one, stem side up in a bowl until
　　the bowl is full. Use the smaller pieces to fill the
　　center and the julienne to reconstruct what will
　　resemble a large head of cauliflower when
　　turned out.
Set a heavy plate over the bowl and press down.
　　Invert the plate and bowl and set on top of a pot of
　　simmering water for 10 minutes or until warm.

Meanwhile, prepare the sauce:

Combine the vinegar and olive oil. Season with salt
　　and pepper. Add the olives, pimiento, scallions and
　　lemon juice; whisk together and reserve.

When the cauliflower is thoroughly warm, invert the
　　plate and bowl and replace the plate with a
　　serving dish. Invert once again and unmold.
Pour the sauce over the cauliflower and sprinkle with
　　the parsley.

NOTES

The Cauliflower Niçoise should not be cooked whole.
By reconstructing the cauliflower shape, your guests
will not struggle when serving themselves.

Serves 4

RED RASPBERRY TART

INGREDIENTS

Pâte brisée (see Appendix, page 248)
Pastry cream (see Appendix, page 251)
Framboise or other complementary *eau de vie* for the
    pastry cream
2 pints fresh raspberries
Apricot glaze (see Appendix, page 249)

TOOLS

12-inch fluted, loose-bottomed tart pan
Lightweight aluminum foil
Dried beans *or* aluminum baking weights

METHOD

Prepare the *pâte brisée* and refrigerate.
Prepare the pastry cream and refrigerate.
Preheat the oven to 425°.
Roll out the pastry dough on a lightly floured surface.
Place the dough in a tart pan, fitting it evenly over the
    bottom of the pan and pressing it against the inside
    edges. Roll over the pan with a rolling pin to trim
    excess dough. Prick the dough surface with a fork.
Cover the pastry with aluminum foil and weight with
    beans or aluminum baking weights.
Bake for 5 minutes.
Remove the beans and foil and bake 8 minutes
    more or until the pastry is lightly browned.
Remove to a rack to cool.
When cool, remove the tart pan collar. Whisk the
    chilled pastry cream and fill the shell.
Arrange the raspberries on the cream. (Do not wash
    the berries; they become soupy.)
Make the apricot glaze and lightly coat the berries
    with it.

NOTES

Assemble the tart a couple of hours before serving
dinner. It should not be refrigerated.

Serves 4

A raspberry tart.

KITCHEN

MENU

Julienne of Leeks Vinaigrette*

Cider and Beer Glazed Fresh Ham*
Herbed Mashed Potatoes
with Béchamel*
Broccoli with Lemon Butter

Baked Pears in Custard Sauce*

Espresso

·

Dopff Gewürztraminer · Beer

Serves Eight to Ten

No one has to serve or be served
at this casual gathering.

This casual dinner brings guests into the "nerve center" of any country weekend: the kitchen. Drinks are served in the kitchen and guests wander in and out while the host prepares the meal. The kitchen table is set as a sideboard, large enough to hold the entire meal plus knives and forks wrapped individually in napkins, wineglasses and plates.

Instead of flowers, a few candles and a leafy head of red cabbage plucked from the garden are placed at one end of the table.

Fresh ham is a good change from the usual cured hams. It is shaped like a ham but is the color and taste of pork. Baste the fresh ham with cider and beer to obtain a dark brown glaze and a pungent sauce. The broccoli is cooked until tender and then tossed in lemon and butter.

The mashed potatoes are an extravagant touch to the meal. Coated with béchamel sauce, the potatoes are perfumed with a variety of fresh herbs and dusted with grated Parmesan cheese. The lightly caramelized pears in the custard sauce suggest a *crème brulée* with fruit. After a cup of coffee, serve Calvados (the strong apple brandy from Normandy). It is a wonderful "digestif" for a hearty weekend meal.

JULIENNE OF LEEKS VINAIGRETTE

INGREDIENTS
18 small leeks
1 cup vinaigrette (see Appendix, page 245)

METHOD
Cut the leeks into 3-inch julienne, including some of the pale green. Rinse the julienne strips several times in cold water to rid them of sand. Set aside in a bowl of ice water.

Drain the leeks and blanch them in a large pot of lightly salted boiling water for 3 to 4 minutes. Drain, rinse in cold water and drain again thoroughly.
Toss with the vinaigrette and allow the mixture to rest for 20 minutes before serving.

Serves 8 to 10

CIDER AND BEER GLAZED FRESH HAM

INGREDIENTS
A 18- to 19-pound fresh ham
Kosher salt and freshly milled black pepper
1 cup beer
1 quart fresh apple cider (without preservatives)

TOOLS
Roasting pan with rack

METHOD
Preheat the oven to 450°.
Trim the ham of its outer skin, leaving about 4 inches around the bone area. Rub with salt and pepper.
Place the ham on a rack in a roasting pan and set it in the oven. Reduce the oven temperature to 325° and bake for 15 minutes.

Pour ½ cup of the beer over the ham and bake for 15 minutes more.
Pour the remaining ½ cup of beer over the ham and bake for 1 hour.
Pour half the cider over the ham and bake for 30 minutes, basting occasionally.
Add the remaining cider and baste every half hour until the ham is cooked. Allow about 5 hours (the ham is cooked when a meat thermometer registers 185°).
Remove the ham to a serving platter and allow it to rest for 15 minutes before carving. Drain the pan juices and skim off the fat.
Serve the sauce with the meat.

Serves 8 to 12

HERBED MASHED POTATOES WITH BÉCHAMEL

INGREDIENTS
4 pounds potatoes, peeled and quartered

Béchamel
3 tablespoons unsalted butter
3 tablespoons flour
1 cup warm milk

1 cup milk
½ cup heavy cream
8 ounces (½ pound) unsalted butter
Salt and freshly milled black pepper
¼ cup fresh herbs (use any combination of at least four: rosemary, thyme, sage, chives, parsley, winter savory or tarragon)
½ cup freshly grated Parmesan cheese

TOOLS
Oven-proof baking dish

METHOD
Boil the potatoes in lightly salted water until their centers can be pierced easily with a knife.

Meanwhile, prepare the béchamel:
Heat the butter in a saucepan. When the foam subsides, remove from the heat and whisk in the flour. When the paste is smooth, return to the heat and whisk in the warm milk. Cook, whisking constantly, until the sauce thickens. Reserve.

Drain and mash the potatoes.
In a saucepan, scald the milk and cream; add the butter. Gradually pour the mixture into the mashed potatoes, mixing well until smooth and creamy. Season with salt and pepper.

Add the fresh herbs and spoon the potatoes into an
 oven-proof baking dish.
Pour the béchamel over the potatoes (it does not
 have to cover them). Dust with the Parmesan.

Broil until the top is glazed and golden brown.

Serves 8 to 10

BAKED PEARS IN CUSTARD SAUCE

INGREDIENTS

8 to 10 ripe pears
8 to 10 tablespoons sugar
3 large egg yolks
3 cups heavy cream
2 tablespoons pear brandy

TOOLS

2 shallow 10-inch casseroles or tin-lined copper
 baking pans

METHOD

Preheat the oven to 400°

Peel the pears and halve them, leaving the stems
 attached.
Core the pears and cut a small slice off the rounded
 side to prevent them from tipping in the casserole.
Fill the well of each pear with 1 tablespoon of the
 sugar.

Arrange the pears side by side in the casseroles.
Bake on the middle shelf of the oven for 45 minutes
 to 1 hour. Meanwhile, beat the egg yolks until
 smooth and lemon colored. Whisk in the cream
 and the pear brandy. The pears are cooked when
 their edges turn a dark golden brown and the sugar
 has caramelized.
Pour the cream mixture around the cooked pears in
 the oven; do not pour the mixture on top of the
 pears. Turn the oven off and let the pears rest in the
 closed oven for 20 minutes or until the cream sets.
Remove the pears from the oven and serve from the
 casseroles.

NOTE

It is essential that the pears be ripe.

Serves 8 to 10

MIDSUMMER'S NIGHT

From early May through all of June, crates of seaweed-packed soft shell crabs abound in fish markets. These delicacies of the Chesapeake and the Carolinas can be boiled, batter fried or sautéed. We prefer an unembellished treatment. In fact, these crabs are so quickly cooked that we use the term "flash fried" to define the method. Crabs have such natural beauty that they need little enhancing to make them visually pleasing. Buy them live (select them firm and allow at least three per person). If you yearn for a sauce to accompany this streamlined fare, we suggest dipping the fried crabs into an *aïoli* (see page 218) or into a *rouille* (see pages 152–53).

The parsley, too, is "flash fried," creating a delightful crunch of fluff that dissolves on the tongue and is a delicious accompaniment for crab or any fried fish.

The Cherry Clafouti is a rustic French dessert—neither a tart nor a cake—that resembles the American cobbler. Cherries are in season and, served in this manner, replace the need for buttered biscuits or bread.

MENU

Soft Shell Crabs with Fried Parsley*

Cherry Clafouti*

Coffee

·

American Beer

Serves Four

Soft shell crabs have such natural beauty that they need little enhancement to be visually pleasing.

SOFT SHELL CRABS WITH FRIED PARSLEY

INGREDIENTS

12 small soft shell crabs
About 3 teaspoons cayenne, or less, depending
    on taste
3 quarts vegetable oil
6 to 8 bunches parsley
Salt, to taste

TOOLS

Large, heavy, deep pot with fryer basket to fit *or*
    electric deep fryer

METHOD

Ask the fishmonger to prepare the crabs for cooking.
Lightly rub cayenne between the shell and flesh
    of each crab, taking care not to tear the shell
    from the flesh.
Heat the oil in a heavy, deep pot until the tempera-
    ture reaches 375°.
Set 3 or 4 crabs in the frying basket and cook them
    45 to 60 seconds. Drain the crabs on paper
    towels and place in a warm oven.
Repeat until all the crabs are cooked, checking that
    the oil stays at 375°.
Wash and thoroughly dry the parsley.
Fry the parsley in the oil, 2 or 3 bunches at a time,
    being sure to keep the temperature at 375°. The
    parsley will cook in about 10 seconds (it is done
    as soon as the sizzling stops). Drain the parsley on
    paper towels.
Lightly toss the parsley with salt and serve it immedi-
    ately with the crabs.

NOTE

This recipe is recommended for the experienced
cook only.

Serves 4

CHERRY CLAFOUTI

INGREDIENTS

1 large egg
1 cup milk
1 teaspoon vanilla
1 cup sifted flour
Unsalted butter
2 quarts red cherries, pitted
1 tablespoon sugar
1 tablespoon crystallized ginger, cut into fine julienne
    (optional)
1 cup heavy cream

TOOLS

9 x 7 x 2½" oval heavy enameled *or* porcelain
    casserole

METHOD

Preheat the oven to 375°.
Beat the egg until frothy. Stir in the milk and vanilla
    and whisk in the flour.
Liberally butter the casserole.
Toss the cherries with the ginger and place them in
    the casserole. Pour the batter over the mixture and
    sprinkle the top with sugar.
Bake for 45 minutes or until golden brown and puffy.
Serve the clafouti hot, accompanied by a pitcher of
    heavy cream.

Serves 4 to 6

AT DUSK

MENU

Ratatouille*

Garlic and Rosemary
Roasted Capon*
Parslied Culls

Baked Chèvre*

Poached Peaches with
Red Peppercorn Sauce*

Lemon Tartlets*

Espresso

·

Chilled California Le Fleurion
Vin Rouge and Le Fleurion
Vin Blanc, Joseph Phelps
Vineyards

Serves Six

French ratatouille made with American summer vegetables. *Overleaf:* The dining room furniture is moved out-of-doors.

At the height of summer, when days are long and hot and evenings cool, it's time to bring dinner out-of-doors. If the heat of the day discourages us from eating outside, the breezes at dusk beckon us to the outdoor dinner.

If you have lawn furniture, so much the better; if not, do as the French have done for centuries: borrow tables and chairs from the house and set up your dining room in the garden.

The meal is a festival of summer bounty, beginning with ratatouille, a vegetable stew of summer squash, zucchini, eggplant and tomatoes, spiced with fresh herbs of the season. I spent most of my cooking career looking for the perfect ratatouille and came upon this treasure at a country inn in the south of France. The proprietress kindly gave me her recipe.

Ratatouille—like the winter *cassoulet*—is a seasonal dish, and takes time to prepare. We make as much of it as our kitchen pots can handle and freeze it. During the cold winter nights, the ratatouille reminds us of warmer times. In the summer we refrigerate it, then bring it to room temperature before serving.

The capon that follows the casserole is permeated with a delicate savory of rosemary and garlic. The combined garlic and rosemary create the stuffing. Once cooked and soft, the garlic cloves lose their pungent sting and take on a nutlike flavor. We roast the little field potatoes alongside the capon.

As evening approaches, we light candles and serve warm baked chèvre cheese on a lettuce leaf to ward off the chill in the air. For dessert, we serve peaches sauced in wine and caramel with soft red peppercorns. As a final touch, the guests move indoors to finish the last of the miniature lemon tartlets.

RATATOUILLE

INGREDIENTS

6 sweet red peppers (2½ pounds)
6 yellow peppers (2½ pounds)
4 to 5 medium eggplants (about 6 pounds)
8 pounds ripe tomatoes
6 large white onions (4 pounds)
1 quart virgin olive oil
8 large cloves garlic, finely minced
3 pounds small green zucchini
3 pounds small yellow zucchini
1½ teaspoons fresh thyme leaves
1 tablespoon chopped fresh mint
2 tablespoons chopped fresh rosemary leaves
1 cup packed fresh basil, chopped
½ cup chopped Italian parsley
4 bay leaves
2 cups dry white wine
Salt and freshly milled black pepper, to taste

TOOLS

Large stainless-steel *or* enamel brazier

METHOD

Scorch the red and yellow peppers until black on a
   griddle or over an open flame. When thoroughly
   charred, place them in a brown paper bag to
   steam (this will enable you to peel them more
   easily). When the peppers are cool enough to
   handle, peel off the black skins with a small paring
   knife. The flesh will retain its original color.
Cut each pepper in half; remove and discard the ribs
   and seeds. Dice the peppers and reserve with any
   excess juice.
Scorch the eggplants in the same way. When cool,
   peel them and cut into 1-inch cubes.
Blanch the tomatoes in boiling water, then plunge
   briefly into cold water. When cool, peel and seed.
   Strain the juice, reserving 2 cups.
Finely chop the onions.
In the brazier, heat 2 cups of the oil. Sauté the onions
   and garlic for 30 minutes; do not allow them to
   brown.
Cut the green and yellow zucchini into ½-inch strips
   and then into ½-inch cubes.
Coat the zucchini cubes with the remaining 2 cups of
   oil and drain in a colander. (You can save this oil for
   future cooking.)
Soak the herbs, except the bay leaves, in the wine.
When the onions have simmered for 30 minutes, add
   the tomatoes and tomato juice.
Stir and simmer for 15 minutes.
Add the peppers and their juice, the eggplants and
   zucchinis.✳ continued

Pour in the wine and herb mixture and add the bay
leaves. Mix thoroughly and simmer partially covered for 2½ to 3 hours, stirring every 20 minutes.
Season with salt and pepper.

Thoroughly drain the ratatouille in a colander or large
sieve and reserve the juice.

Set the drained ratatouille in a cool place or in an ice
water bath until cooled. Refrigerate it and the juice
for about 24 hours.

When thoroughly chilled, remove the oil from the
juice. (This oil residue may be reserved for similar
vegetables. Keep it refrigerated.)

Moisten the ratatouille with enough juice to loosen it.
The remaining juice may be heated and served as
a soup.

Serve the ratatouille cold as a first course with fresh
lemons.

NOTE

Served hot, we recommended ratatouille with
roasted or grilled lamb or veal.

Yield: Approximately 8 quarts

GARLIC AND ROSEMARY
ROASTED CAPON

INGREDIENTS

An 8- to 9-pound capon
Olive oil
2 tablespoons Kosher salt
Freshly milled black pepper
8 heads of garlic
½ pound (2 sticks) unsalted butter
1 tablespoon fresh rosemary leaves
1 medium carrot, chopped
1 medium onion
1 large celery stalk, chopped
2 cups chicken stock (see Appendix, page 246)

METHOD

Preheat the oven to 425°.

Wash the capon and pat dry. Rub with oil and sprinkle
with salt and pepper.

Separate the garlic cloves from the heads, leaving the
skins on. Blanch the garlic cloves in boiling water for
10 minutes. Plunge into cold water. When cool
enough to handle, pinch off the skins and cut off
the hard end.

Cream the butter. When it is soft, fold in the rosemary
and garlic cloves.

Stuff the capon with the mixture and truss the bird.

Place the capon on a rack in a roasting pan and
surround it with the chopped vegetables. Roast for
45 minutes.

Reduce the oven temperature to 325° and roast 2
hours more, basting every 15 minutes or until the
juices run clear after piercing the leg joint with a
sharp paring knife.

Remove the bird to a warm platter and keep warm.

Pour off most of the butter and fat in the roasting pan
and place the pan over high heat. Add the stock
and deglaze, scraping up the brown particles and
mashing the vegetables. Strain the sauce into a
heated pitcher.

Serve the capon and the garlic cloves with parsleyed
boiled potato culls.

Serves 6

POACHED PEACHES WITH
RED PEPPERCORN SAUCE

INGREDIENTS

8 unblemished ripe peaches, unpeeled
1½ to 2 cups sugar (depending on the sweetness of
the fruit)
Juice of ½ lemon
1 cinnamon stick

Syrup
2 cups sugar
3 cups dry white wine
1 tablespoon red peppercorns, deep red and flaky
(not pink)

METHOD

Place the peaches in the pot with the sugar, lemon
juice and cinnamon stick. Add cold water to cover.

Cover the peaches with a round of waxed paper cut
to fit the interior of the pot.

Set the pan over moderately high heat and bring the
liquid to a simmer. Simmer until the peaches can
be pierced easily with a sharp paring knife, about
10 to 15 minutes after the water begins to simmer.
Cool the peaches in the liquid.

Remove the skins with a paring knife. Strain the juice
and reserve 3 cups for the syrup. Pour the remaining juice over the peaches.

To prepare the syrup:

Melt the sugar over high heat just until it turns a
golden caramel color. Stir with a wooden spoon
and watch carefully. Immediately add the reserved
juice and the wine. Simmer for 10 minutes. Slightly
crush the peppercorns between your fingers and
add them to the syrup and remove from the heat.

Using a slotted spoon, transfer the peaches to a bowl
or beaker and pour the syrup over them. Allow to
sit in the syrup for 2 hours before serving at room
temperature.

Serves 8

Tiny lemon tartlets with after-dinner coffee.

BAKED CHÈVRE

INGREDIENTS

Chèvre cheese, in log form, 2 inches in diameter
    (Montrachet, without the ash, is ideal)
Virgin olive oil
1 sprig each fresh rosemary, thyme, chervil and sage
    or a combination of the herbs of your choice,
    chopped
1 cup finely diced bread crumbs
Ruby Red lettuce leaves for serving

TOOLS

Baking sheet
Long thin spatula

METHOD

Cut the chèvre into 1-inch-thick rounds.
Coat a shallow pan with oil and place the cheese
    rounds in the pan. Coat them with oil and sprinkle
    with the herbs. Cover and refrigerate for about 1
    hour.
Preheat the oven to 400°.
Remove the chèvre from the oil and herb mixture
    and dust well with the bread crumbs. Transfer to a
    baking sheet and bake for 10 minutes.
Carefully remove the rounds with a spatula and serve
    each one on a lettuce leaf.

Serves 6

LEMON TARTLETS

INGREDIENTS

Pâte brisée (see Appendix, page 248)
1 ½ teaspoons arrowroot
½ cup lemon juice
3 egg yolks
½ cup sugar

TOOLS

Double boiler

METHOD

Make 24 tartlet shells from the *pâte brisée*.
In the top of the double boiler, over simmering water,
    whisk the arrowroot into the lemon juice until thick
    and shiny. Warm the mixture over simmering water.
In a small bowl, whisk the yolks with the sugar until
    the mixture becomes smooth and lemon colored.
    Add the lemon juice mixture to the sugar and yolks
    and stir.
Return the mixture to the double boiler over simmer-
    ing water and whisk for 10 minutes or until thick.
    Set aside to cool.
Whisk again and fill each shell with 1 teaspoon of the
    mixture just before serving.

Yield: 24 tartlets

THE WHITE PLATE

Appeal to the palate through the eye. The white plate, unadorned except by the food, is the perfect palette for mixing colors and textures. The plain white plate provides the opportunity for interesting food arrangements, simplicity always being the guideline. A true cook does not "garnish" dishes with furls of parsley, coils of carrots or cherry tomatoes impaled on toothpicks. A twelve-inch plate, known as the "chop plate," is ideal, offering a pleasant background for the small portion—in this meal, the scallop course—or the larger, main course.

The scallop course can be made in a matter of minutes, leaving ample time for preparing the duck. Muscovy ducks are lean, meaty birds. Having the flavor of a gamey steak, these ducks are sparked by the tartness of the lime and the zest of the lemon.

For dessert, the poached pear satisfies the craving for a sweet without being the usual rich finale to a meal.

MENU

Sautéed Bay Scallops with Chives and Red Pepper*

Breast of Muscovy Duck with Limes*

Poached Pears with Raspberry Sauce and Pistachios*

Espresso

•

Châteauneuf-du-Pape Blanc

Serves Four

Sautéed scallops are tossed with a confetti of fresh red pepper and chives.

SAUTÉED BAY SCALLOPS WITH CHIVES AND RED PEPPERS

INGREDIENTS

½ cup clarified butter (see Appendix, page 245)
½ sweet red pepper, cut into matchstick julienne and finely diced
1 pound bay scallops (do not wash)
Pinch of ground cloves
2 tablespoons finely chopped chives

TOOLS

Large sauté pan

METHOD

Heat ¼ cup of the butter in the sauté pan. Add the pepper and sauté for 1 minute. Remove the pepper with a slotted spoon and reserve.

Add the remaining ¼ cup of butter. Add the scallops and sauté for 2 minutes, just long enough to warm them through.

Add the ground cloves. Fold in the pepper and chives. Serve on warmed plates.

Serves 4

BREAST OF MUSCOVY DUCK WITH LIMES

INGREDIENTS

2 Muscovy ducks (about 3½ pounds each)
Salt and freshly milled pepper, to taste
1 Granny Smith apple, halved
Vegetable oil
½ cup white wine
½ cup duck or chicken stock (see Appendix, pages 246–247)
½ cup sugar
Zest of 2 large lemons, cut into julienne
1 pound spinach, washed, dried and stems removed
2 limes, sectioned, membrane and pith removed

TOOLS

Roasting pan and rack
Baking sheet that will fit under the broiler

METHOD

Preheat the oven to 500°.
Wash the ducks and pat them dry. Salt and pepper the cavities. (There is no need to truss the birds.)
Stuff each duck with an apple half.
Brush the ducks with vegetable oil and place them on a rack in a roasting pan. Roast for 20 minutes; the ducks will be cooked, the breast meat rare and juicy.
Remove the ducks and drain the fat from the pan. Add the wine and stock and deglaze the pan.

Strain the liquids; set aside and keep warm.
Remove the duck breasts, with the skin, from the carcasses and set them on a lightly oiled pan that will fit under the broiler. (Use the legs and thighs in another recipe.)
In a heavy saucepan, melt the sugar in ½ cup of water. Stir with a wooden spoon until the consistency is syrupy; do not allow it to caramelize.
Add the lemon zest to the syrup and stir briefly. Remove the zest with a slotted spoon and reserve.
Arrange the spinach leaves on individual plates. Tuck the lime sections around the spinach, allowing 4 sections for each portion.
Broil the duck breasts, skin side up, until the skin is crisp.
Cut each breast on the bias into 4 or 5 slices. Arrange the slices on the spinach and sprinkle with the reserved lemon zest. Spoon some of the reserved juices over the duck and spinach.

NOTE

Muscovy ducks, lean meaty birds that are filled with flavor, are available at some poultry farms, fancy butchers and purveyors. You may substitute Long Island ducklings, but these should be trimmed of all fat after roasting or before broiling. Roast Long Island ducklings for 50 minutes.

Serves 4

The slices of duck are placed on a bed of fresh spinach. The heat and juice of the duck "wilts" the spinach.

POACHED PEARS WITH RASPBERRY SAUCE AND PISTACHIOS

INGREDIENTS

4 firm ripe pears
Juice of 1 lemon
1½ cups of sugar (more or less, depending on the sweetness of the fruit)
1 cup raspberry sauce (see Appendix, page 250)
2 tablespoons coarsely chopped pistachios

TOOLS

Stainless-steel *or* enameled pot

METHOD

Peel the pears, leaving the stems intact and immediately place them in a pot with the lemon juice and enough water to cover. Add the sugar.

Cover the pears with a round of wax paper to fit the interior of the pot.

Bring the liquid to a boil over high heat. Reduce the heat and simmer until the pears can be pierced easily with a sharp paring knife.

Cool the pears in the liquid.

To serve, cut a small slice off the bottom of each pear. Pour a little raspberry sauce in the middle of each plate and place the pears, sliced side down, in the sauce. Dribble more sauce over the top of each pear and sprinkle with the pistachios.

Serves 4

The pear dessert is chosen as much for its shape as its taste.

FOR ONE

Buying the finest fare is the initial step in this extravagant experience. Begin with lobster. Buy a live lobster and ask for the female, whose roe you will need for the coral mayonnaise. (If you must buy a cooked lobster, be sure the tail is tightly curled.) A one-pound or a one-and-one-quarter-pound lobster ought to be sufficient, but you may prefer to purchase two and steam them together in vodka. The anesthetizing effect of vodka does not discriminate between animal orders.

Preparing the scene is step two. Buy flowers if you wish. Chill the blanc de blanc champagne; set the table and light candles for the dining ceremony. You may choose music as a dinner companion, or perhaps a good book, or you may prefer to be alone with your thoughts. No matter which path you take, finish the meal with a chocolate truffle ... or two.

MENU

Lobster Steamed in Vodka with
Coral Mayonnaise*
Cucumber Vinaigrette with Dill

Chocolate Truffles*

Espresso

•

Iced Saran Blanc de Blanc
Côteaux Champenois

Serves One

LOBSTER STEAMED IN VODKA WITH CORAL MAYONNAISE

INGREDIENTS

2 cups vodka
A 1- to 1¼-pound live female lobster

Coral Mayonnaise
⅓ cup mayonnaise (see Appendix, page 245)
Lemon juice

TOOLS

Steamer with lid for the lobster *or* one fashioned from
a stockpot and a colander that will rest above the
level of the vodka

METHOD

Bring the vodka to a rolling boil in a covered steamer.
Add the lobster and cook, covered tightly, for 8
minutes. Set the lobster on its back on a carving
board. Cut it from head to tail with a large, sharp
knife; do not cut through the shell.

Cut the shell, from head to tail, with poultry shears.
Crack the claws. Remove the coral and reserve.
Remove and discard the brain sac.

To prepare the coral mayonnaise:
Mash the coral with a wooden spoon against the side
of a small bowl and blend the mayonnaise into the
coral. Add lemon juice to taste.

NOTE

When cooking 4 or more lobsters, use a fifth of vodka;
the coral mayonnaise may be made in a food processor.

Serves 1

CHOCOLATE TRUFFLES

INGREDIENTS

1 cup heavy cream
½ pound (2 sticks) unsalted butter
½ pound best-quality semisweet chocolate, chopped
4 ounces imported cocoa

TOOLS

6 x 10 x 2½" baking pan

METHOD

In a heavy saucepan, bring the heavy cream and
butter to a boil. Remove from the heat and stir in
the chopped chocolate, mixing thoroughly until all
the chocolate has melted.

Line the pan with waxed paper and pour the chocolate mixture through a strainer into the pan. Freeze
for 5 to 6 hours.

Liberally sprinkle a sheet of waxed paper with cocoa
powder and turn the truffle mixture onto it.

Remove the waxed paper from the frozen chocolate
mixture and sprinkle the top of the mixture with
cocoa powder.

Cut into 30 1½-inch square truffles.

One at a time, shake off the excess cocoa from each
truffle, making sure the sides are coated. Store in a
covered container and refrigerate until ready to
serve.

Yield: 2½ dozen truffles

Overleaf: The ultimate self-indulgence,
surrounded by inherited Depression glass.

THE PERFECT DINNER

Pages have been written about the possibilities of menus, the variations of food, the kaleidoscope of settings and table arrangements. Before all is done, and after all is done, there is finally only one essential concern in entertaining, one enduring ingredient without which there is nothing...the guests.

FAVORITE KITCHEN ACCESSORIES

Chopping (chef's) knife, stainless steel, 10 inches long

Slicing knife, stainless steel, 12 to 14 inches long

Serrated carving knife, stainless steel, 15 inches long

Boning knife, stainless steel

2 to 3 paring knives

A 10-inch-long full French whisk, tin or stainless steel

Wooden spoons and spatulas

Ladles, strainers, sieves and skimmers of various sizes and materials

Vegetable peelers

Flexible metal spatulas

Apple corer

Stainless-steel bulb baster

Electric mixer with a 5-quart stainless-steel bowl, attachments to include balloon whisk, paddle, dough hook

and meat grinder attachment

A food processor

A blender

A French rolling pin

A marble pastry slab

Pastry brushes

Pastry bags and tubes

Imported tartlet forms, 2 inches in diameter

Imported, fluted, loose-bottomed tart pans

Baking sheets

Shallow roasting pans and racks

Measuring cups with metric equivalent and measuring spoons

A kitchen scale, to measure up to 25 pounds with metric equivalents

Large and small stoneware bowls

Stainless-steel mixing bowls of various sizes

8- and 10-quart stainless-steel pots for cooking pastas and lobster

A 20-quart stainless-steel stockpot and cover

A 14-quart stainless-steel sauté pan and cover

A variety of stainless-steel pots up to 5 quarts

An 8- to 10-quart earthenware casserole with cover

A variety of glass and porcelain soufflé dishes

A 13 x 9 x 1½" tin-lined copper pan

2 oven-proof porcelain pâté molds, 2½ quarts each

2 oven-proof porcelain tureens, 3 quarts each

A tinned-steel fish poacher

A sorbet machine (the two Italian imports are best)

CONVERSION TABLE FOR FOREIGN EQUIVALENTS

Liquid Ingredients

Liquid Ounces	Milliliters	Milliliters	Liquid Ounces
1	29.573	1	0.034
2	59.15	2	0.07
3	88.72	3	0.10
4	118.30	4	0.14
5	147.87	5	0.17
6	177.44	6	0.20
7	207.02	7	0.24
8	236.59	8	0.27
9	266.16	9	0.30
10	295.73	10	0.33

Quarts	Liters	Liters	Quarts
1	0.946	1	1.057
2	1.89	2	2.11
3	2.84	3	3.17
4	3.79	4	4.23
5	4.73	5	5.28
6	5.68	6	6.34
7	6.62	7	7.40
8	7.57	8	8.45
9	8.52	9	9.51
10	9.47	10	10.57

Gallons	Liters	Liters	Gallons
1	3.785	1	0.264
2	7.57	2	0.53
3	11.36	3	0.79
4	15.14	4	1.06
5	18.93	5	1.32
6	22.71	6	1.59
7	26.50	7	1.85
8	30.28	8	2.11
9	34.07	9	2.38
10	37.86	10	2.74

Dry Ingredients

Ounces	Grams	Grams	Ounces
1	28.35	1	0.035
2	56.70	2	0.07
3	85.05	3	0.11
4	113.40	4	0.14
5	141.75	5	0.18
6	170.10	6	0.21
7	198.45	7	0.25
8	226.80	8	0.28
9	255.15	9	0.32
10	283.50	10	0.35
11	311.85	11	0.39
12	340.20	12	0.42
13	368.55	13	0.46
14	396.90	14	0.49
15	425.25	15	0.53
16	453.60	16	0.57

Pounds	Kilograms	Kilograms	Pounds
1	0.454	1	2.205
2	0.91	2	4.41
3	1.36	3	6.61
4	1.81	4	8.82
5	2.27	5	11.02
6	2.72	6	13.23
7	3.18	7	15.43
8	3.63	8	17.64
9	4.08	9	19.84
10	4.54	10	22.05
11	4.99	11	24.26
12	5.44	12	26.46
13	5.90	13	28.67
14	6.35	14	30.87
15	6.81	15	33.08

APPENDIX

MAYONNAISE

INGREDIENTS

4 egg yolks
1 teaspoon Dijon-style mustard
Salt and white pepper, to taste
Dash of cayenne
1½ cups olive oil or ¾ cup olive oil and ¾ cup
   vegetable oil
2 tablespoons lemon juice
1 tablespoon boiling water

TOOLS

Food processor or blender

METHOD

Place the egg yolks, mustard, salt, pepper and cayenne in the bowl of a food processor or blender
and process for 1 minute. In a thin stream, gradually
add the oil. Add the lemon juice and taste for
seasoning. Add the boiling water and turn the
machine on for 1 to 2 seconds. Refrigerate the
mayonnaise in a covered container.

CRÈME FRAÎCHE

Crème fraîche is available at many food stores. Many
cooks have their own substitutes, but none approach
the real thing.

An easy makeshift *crème fraîche* requires equal
amounts of sour cream and stiffly beaten whipped
heavy cream, thoroughly mixed together.

Should you want to make the "real thing" at home,
we suggest you buy commercially packaged Solait
crème fraîche starter. It is inexpensive and one pack-
age will generate many batches. An alternate method
uses 1 cup of room-temperature heavy cream combined with 2 tablespoons of buttermilk. Pour the
mixture into a clean, warm glass jar. Set the container
in a warm place (over the pilot light or in the oven of
a gas range or on the stove top, if electric), cover
securely and allow to thicken, 6 to 8 hours or more.
The mixture will gel and become firm; refrigerate and
use as required. *Crème fraîche* made from buttermilk
will keep for up to 10 days.

CLARIFIED BUTTER

METHOD

Over a medium flame, heat unsalted butter in a
heavy skillet or saucepan until completely melted.
   Set aside in a warm place for 30 minutes.
Skim off the foam.
Slowly pour the clear liquid into a clean container,
   stopping before any of the milky sediment from the
   bottom of the skillet is included.

VINAIGRETTE

Vinaigrettes vary depending on the quality and pun-
   gency of the oil and vinegars used.
Delicate greens such as Boston, Bibb, salad bowl and
   cress marry well with tarragon-flavored white wine
   vinegar and light olive oil or a combination of olive
   oil and bland vegetable oil. Chicory, romaine,
   radicchio and escarole stand up to hearty red wine
   vinegars and the more pungent Italian and French
   olive oils. Walnut oil is a pleasant complement to
   endive, especially when mixed with light red wine
   vinegar flavored with tarragon. Chicory with walnuts and Roquefort cheese is best served with a
   vinaigrette of walnut oil and red wine vinegar.
   Balsamic vinegar is the richest and most flavorful of
   all red wine vinegars. It can almost be drunk
   straight, it is so delicious. Fruit vinegars such as
   raspberry vinegar are more of a novelty; when
   mixed with twice as much light olive oil, they are a
   pleasant dressing for delicate greens.

A SIMPLE VINAIGRETTE

INGREDIENTS

¼ cup of good-quality red wine vinegar
1 teaspoon dry mustard
1½ teaspoons Dijon-style mustard
Salt and freshly milled black pepper, to taste
About ¾ cup olive oil (or more depending on the
   pungent quality of the vinegar)

METHOD

Combine the vinegar and the seasonings and mix
   thoroughly. Gradually add the olive oil.

NOTE

To make a creamy vinaigrette: Combine the vinegar
and seasonings in a food processor. Gradually pour in
the oil as you would when making mayonnaise.

Yield: 1 cup

COURT BOUILLON

INGREDIENTS

1 large carrot
3 shallots
1 leek, green part only
½ cup celery leaves
1 quart dry white wine
½ teaspoon crushed peppercorns
¼ teaspoon dried thyme
1 bay leaf
1 teaspoon salt
3 cloves garlic, crushed

TOOLS

Large stockpot
Strainer

METHOD

Chop the vegetables coarsely. Combine all the ingredients in a large stockpot or kettle and add 2 quarts of cold water. Bring the bouillon to a boil, skim and simmer for 30 minutes.
Strain the bouillon into a pot.
Refrigerate until ready to use or freeze in 1-quart containers.

Yield: Approximately 2½ quarts

FISH STOCK

INGREDIENTS

5 pounds assorted fish bones, including heads, tails and spines (use the bones of any white fish; avoid oily fish such as bluefish, salmon, etc.)
2 medium onions, peeled and roughly chopped
3 celery ribs with leaves, roughly chopped
3 carrots with their tops, roughly chopped
2 teaspoons dried thyme
2 bay leaves
20 black peppercorns
6 sprigs parsley
2 cups dry white wine

TOOLS

Large stockpot
Strainer
Cotton cheesecloth or cotton towel

METHOD

Rinse the fish bones under cold running water, checking to be sure that the gills have been removed; reserve.

Place the vegetables and the remaining ingredients in a stockpot, add the fish bones and enough cold water to cover.
Bring the stock to a boil and immediately reduce to a simmer; skim the stock. Simmer for 20 to 30 minutes, skimming once or twice.
Line a strainer with a double thickness of damp cheesecloth and place it over a clean pot. Ladle the stock into the strainer. Allow the bones and vegetables to sit in the strainer for 10 minutes; do not press the juices out of the mixture. Cool the stock.
Refrigerate or freeze in 1-quart containers.

Yield: 3 quarts

CHICKEN STOCK

INGREDIENTS

5 pounds assorted chicken bones—a combination of bones, necks and wings
2 medium onions, peeled and roughly chopped
3 celery ribs with leaves, roughly chopped
3 carrots with their tops, roughly chopped
2 leeks, green parts only
2 teaspoons dried thyme
1 teaspoon dried rosemary
2 bay leaves
15 peppercorns
6 sprigs parsley
1 large clove garlic, unpeeled
1 cup tomato skins (if you are preparing a dish that requires peeled tomatoes)

TOOLS

Large stockpot
Strainer
Cotton cheesecloth or cotton towel

METHOD

Rinse the bones and chicken parts under cold running water.
Place the vegetables and remaining ingredients in the stockpot, add the bones and chicken parts. Pour in enough cold water to cover.
Bring the stock to a boil and immediately reduce to a simmer; skim the surface. Simmer for 2½ hours, skimming from time to time.
Line a strainer with a double thickness of damp cheesecloth and place it over a clean pot. Ladle the stock into the strainer and strain the stock, pressing down on the bones and vegetables to release all their liquid.
Cover the strained stock and refrigerate.
When chilled, skim off the fat that has risen to the

surface and store in 1-quart containers or freeze.

NOTE

If you keep the chicken stock in the refrigerator for more than one day, bring it to a boil daily to prevent it from spoiling.

Yield: About 4 quarts

DUCK STOCK

INGREDIENTS

1 whole duck carcass (any half-cooked or partially cooked carcass from one of the duck recipes)
1 medium onion, peeled and roughly chopped
2 carrots, roughly chopped
1 large celery rib with leaves, roughly chopped
3 sprigs parsley
1 clove garlic, unpeeled
8 peppercorns, crushed
½ teaspoon dried rosemary
Pinch dried thyme
1 bay leaf

TOOLS

Large stockpot
Strainer
Cotton cheesecloth *or* cotton towel

METHOD

Place all the ingredients in a stockpot and add enough cold water to cover.
Bring the stock to a boil and immediately reduce to a simmer; skim the surface. Simmer for 2½ hours, skimming from time to time.
Line a strainer with a double thickness of damp cheesecloth and place it over a clean pot. Ladle the stock into the strainer and strain the stock, pressing down on the bones and vegetables to release all their liquid.
Cover the strained stock and refrigerate.
When chilled, skim off the fat that has risen to the surface and store in containers or freeze.

Yield: About 4 cups

BROWN SAUCE

INGREDIENTS

5 pounds veal bones, preferably from the loin, or 4 pounds veal bones plus 1 pound chicken bones
2 cups roughly chopped onion
2 cups roughly chopped carrot
2 cups roughly chopped celery
1 tablespoon peppercorns, crushed
2 bay leaves
2 cloves garlic, crushed
1 teaspoon dried thyme
2 teaspoons dried rosemary
1 cup parsley leaves and stems
2 very ripe tomatoes, cubed, or 3 cups tomato skins (if you have them fresh and available)
2 cups dry red wine

TOOLS

Roasting pan
Large stockpot
Strainer
Cotton cheesecloth *or* cotton towel

METHOD

Preheat the oven to 400°.
Wash the bones thoroughly under cold running water; drain.
In a roasting pan large enough to comfortably hold the bones, brown them in the oven, turning every 30 minutes for about 2½ hours. Scatter the vegetables over the bones for the last 10 minutes.
Transfer the contents of the roasting pan to a stockpot.
Pour 1 quart of water into the roasting pan and deglaze, scraping up all browned particles that have stuck to the pan. Pour the liquid into the stockpot and add the remaining ingredients. Add enough water to cover all the ingredients.
Place the pot over high heat and bring the liquid to a boil; skim and reduce to a simmer. Simmer for 12 hours.
Line a strainer with a double thickness of cheesecloth and strain the liquid. Refrigerate.
When chilled, remove any surface fat and store in covered containers; refrigerate or freeze.

Yield: 2 quarts

SAVORY PASTRY

INGREDIENTS

4 cups sifted all-purpose flour
½ pound (2 sticks) unsalted butter, very cold and cut into small bits
1 teaspoon salt
1 egg
About ½ cup ice water

TOOLS

Electric mixer with paddle attachment

METHOD

Place the flour, butter and salt in a medium-size bowl.

Mix with an electric mixer at the lowest speed for 8 minutes, until the mixture is the consistency of fine cornmeal. Add the egg and combine. Increase the speed and gradually add the ice water, 1 table-spoon at a time.

The pastry will pull away from the sides of the bowl and adhere to the paddle; it will be very elastic.

Remove the pastry to a lightly floured surface and shape it into a ball.

Cover with waxed paper and refrigerate for 45 minutes before rolling it out.

NOTE

The savory pastry dough may be frozen.

Yield: Enough pastry for a 15- to 16-pound ham (see page 106), with decoration, or enough for about 144 2-inch tartlets (see page 177). The recipe may be halved.

PÂTE BRISÉE

INGREDIENTS

2 cups flour
1/8 teaspoon salt
1/2 teaspoon sugar
12 tablespoons (1 1/2 sticks) unsalted butter, chilled and cut into bits
About 2 to 3 tablespoons ice water

TOOLS

Electric mixer with paddle attachment

METHOD

Place the flour, salt, sugar and butter in a medium bowl. Using an electric mixer on low speed, mix for about 8 minutes or until the mixture is the consis-tency of fine cornmeal.

Add up to 3 tablespoons of the water; the pastry will pull away from the sides of the bowl and adhere to the paddle. It will be very elastic.

Remove the pastry to a lightly floured surface and shape into a ball.

Cover with waxed paper and refrigerate for 30 to 45 minutes before rolling out.

Pâte brisée is a delicate, but quite manageable, pastry. This recipe makes enough for 2 Tartes Tatin (page 125) or 2 Raspberry Tarts (page 224) or 72 2-inch tartlet shells (see pages 48 and 235). Roll the pastry 1/8-inch thick for all recipes.

When making tartlet shells, place the tartlet forms upside down on the pastry close to one another. Gently roll over the forms with a rolling pin.

Lift the forms, line them with the pastry and prick the dough lightly with a fork. Place the forms on a baking sheet and bake in a preheated 425° oven for 8 to 10 minutes or until the edges are golden brown.

Cool the tartlets on a wire rack and continue the process until all the pastry is used.

NOTE

The cooked tartlets may be stored in an airtight container for a few days before using. The dough may also be frozen.

BRIOCHE

INGREDIENTS

Sponge
1 ounce cake yeast
5 1/2 ounces milk
5 1/4 ounces sifted all-purpose flour

Dough
5 1/4 ounces butter
2 ounces sugar
Grated zest of 1 lemon
5 egg yolks
9 ounces all-purpose flour
1/2 teaspoon salt
Vegetable oil
1 egg

TOOLS

Electric mixer with dough hook attachment
One 2-quart bread pan *or* two 1-quart bread pans

METHOD

To make the "sponge":
In a small bowl, dissolve the yeast in the milk. Add the flour and set aside for 30 minutes.

To make the dough:
Using an electric mixer, cream the butter. Fold in the sugar and zest and blend. Add the yolks, 1 at a time, blending thoroughly. Add the flour and salt and continue to mix. Add the "sponge" and incor-porate thoroughly until the dough pulls away from the sides of the bowl (dust the dough with additional flour if necessary). Transfer the dough to a large mixing bowl and brush the top lightly with oil. Cover with a dampened kitchen towel and set aside in a warm place until it doubles in bulk, 2 to 3 hours.

Butter the bread pan(s) and dust with flour.

Place the dough in the pan(s).

Punch the dough down and shape it to the pan(s).

Brush the top of the dough with oil and cover with a damp kitchen towel. Set aside in a warm place to rise again until doubled, about 2 hours.

Preheat the oven to 350°.

Score the dough with scissors.

Beat the egg with 1 tablespoon of cold water and brush the top of the loaf with the egg wash.

Bake for 30 to 35 minutes or until golden brown. Cool on a rack and remove from the pan(s).

NOTE

You may use this recipe for individual brioche molds; it yields about 1 dozen.

PUFF PASTRY

INGREDIENTS

2 cups flour
2 teaspoons salt
½ cup ice water
4 tablespoons (½ stick) unsalted butter, melted
½ pound (2 sticks) unsalted butter, chilled

TOOLS

Electric mixer with paddle attachment
A cool marble surface to roll out the dough, optional

METHOD

Place the flour, salt, ice water and melted butter in a medium-size bowl. Using an electric mixer, beat the mixture at low speed until it becomes very firm.

On a cool surface, knead the dough until it becomes elastic. Wrap in waxed paper and refrigerate for 15 minutes.

Meanwhile, form the chilled butter into a ¼-inch-thick rectangle (beat with a rolling pin if too cold). Wrap in waxed paper and refrigerate for 15 minutes.

Place the dough on a lightly floured surface and roll it out into a ¼-inch-thick rectangle. Place the butter in the center of the dough and overlap the dough so that the butter is totally enclosed. Dust with flour, wrap in waxed paper and refrigerate for 30 minutes.

On a lightly floured surface, roll out the dough into a rectangle, ¼ inch thick. Fold in the sides to meet in the center; fold in half as though closing a book—there will be four layers, or "turns," of dough. Wrap in waxed paper and refrigerate for 30 minutes.

Roll out and fold the dough in the same manner 5 more times, refrigerating for 20 minutes between each folding.

You may freeze the prepared pastry at this point or refrigerate the dough until you are ready to roll it out for the recipe.

Yield: 1 pound of puff pastry, enough for 2 Tartes Tatin (page 125) or 1 Chicken Pot Pie (page 166).

PÂTE À CHOUX

INGREDIENTS

1 pint (2 cups) milk
½ pound (2 sticks) unsalted butter
9 ounces flour, preferably bread flour
8 large eggs
Pinch salt

TOOLS

Electric mixer with paddle attachment
Pastry bag and metal tips

METHOD

In a saucepan, bring the milk and butter to a rolling boil over high heat. Add the flour, mix thoroughly and cook for 4 minutes, stirring continuously. Remove the mixture to the bowl of an electric mixer.

Mix until most of the steam has subsided. Begin adding the eggs, 2 at a time, making sure they are thoroughly incorporated before adding more. After all the eggs have been incorporated, place the mixture in the pastry bag and pipe onto baking sheets as instructed in the recipe.

Work with the dough while it is still warm.

APRICOT GLAZE

INGREDIENT

1 cup apricot jam

METHOD

Heat the jam with 2 tablespoons of water, stirring until it melts and is just warmed through.

Remove from the heat when melted.

NOTE

If using pulpy jams or preserves, strain after heating.

A cup of currant jam, dissolved until liquid, can be used for red berry fruits.

Brush or spoon the glaze over the Fruit Tartlets (page 48), Raspberry Tart (page 224) and Poached Peaches with Zabaglione Cream (page 143).

APRICOT SAUCE

INGREDIENTS

1 cup apricot jam
2 ounces bourbon

METHOD

In a heavy saucepan, bring the jam, bourbon and ¼ cup of water to a boil over medium heat. When the sauce begins to boil, remove from the heat and strain.

NOTES

If using pulpy jams or preserves, strain after heating.

Serve the sauce at room temperature when accompanying fruit or sorbets; when using it as a glaze for the fruitcakes, omit the water and brush the sauce directly on the cakes while they are still hot. If the sauce becomes too thick, add more water or bourbon.

RASPBERRY SAUCE

INGREDIENTS

1 pint fresh raspberries
Juice of ½ lemon
½ cup sugar
½ teaspoon arrowroot
1 ounce *framboise* or *kirsch*

TOOLS

Food processor or blender

METHOD

Combine the raspberries and lemon juice and ¼ cup water in a food processor or blender. Purée until smooth and strain through a fine sieve to remove all seeds.

Pour the raspberry mixture into a saucepan and add the sugar. Bring to a boil over a moderately high heat; simmer for 15 minutes.

Dissolve the arrowroot in the *framboise* and stir into the raspberry mixture. Remove from the heat and cool. Cover and refrigerate.

CARAMEL SAUCE

INGREDIENTS

1½ cups sugar
About 1⅓ cups water

TOOLS

Heavy enamel saucepan *or* solid copper saucepan

METHOD

Heat the sugar and ½ cup of water in a heavy saucepan over medium heat. Stir with a wooden spoon only until the sugar has dissolved. When the sugar begins to turn golden, rotate the pan to even the color. Caramel burns quickly, so watch it carefully. When the caramel turns amber, place the pan in a sink of cold water to cool. The caramel will become rock hard.

When the caramel is cool, return the saucepan to the heat and add the remaining water, ⅓ cup at a time. The caramel sauce will liquify and become a little darker. The sauce should flow in ribbons from a spoon; if it is too thick, add a little more water.

Cool and serve at room temperature.

NOTE

Caramel sauce will keep for weeks under refrigeration.

ORANGE ZEST GRENADINE

INGREDIENTS

18 navel oranges
1½ cups granulated sugar
1½ cups grenadine syrup

METHOD

Using a vegetable peeler, peel the zest from the oranges in long, wide strips.

Cut the zest into fine, needle-thin julienne. Refrigerate the oranges for a dessert.

Combine the sugar, grenadine and 1½ cups cold water in a heavy saucepan and bring to a boil over high heat. Boil for 5 minutes; fold in the orange julienne and cook for 5 minutes more, stirring with a wooden spoon.

Cool, cover and refrigerate until ready to serve.

NOTE

In all recipes requiring the Orange Zest Grenadine, use only the julienne; do not use the syrup.

Yield: 3 to 4 cups

LIGHT SUGAR SYRUP

INGREDIENTS

2 cups sugar

METHOD

Place the sugar and 4 cups of cold water in a saucepan and cook over a high heat, stirring with a wooden spoon until the sugar has dissolved. Bring the mixture to a boil and boil for 5 minutes.

Cool and refrigerate in a covered container. The syrup keeps for weeks under refrigeration and can be frozen indefinitely.

Yield: 1 quart

PASTRY CREAM

INGREDIENTS

3 egg yolks
¼ cup sugar
1 tablespoon arrowroot
1 cup cold milk
¼ teaspoon vanilla
1 tablespoon heavy cream (optional)

TOOLS

Double boiler

METHOD

In the top of a double boiler over simmering water, whisk the egg yolks and sugar until the mixture becomes lemon colored and falls like a ribbon from the whisk.

In a small bowl, whisk the arrowroot with the milk and fold it into the egg mixture. Whisk 5 to 10 minutes, until thick. Add the vanilla and remove from the heat.

Whisk over a bowl of ice to cool; cover and refrigerate.

If the mixture is too thick, add the heavy cream and whisk vigorously.

NOTE

When making Fruit Tartlets (see page 48) replace the vanilla with *eau de vie* (unsweetened fruit alcohol), such as *framboise*, *poire* or *kirsch*.

Yield: 1½ cups

CRÈME ANGLAISE

INGREDIENTS

1 quart milk
2 vanilla beans, split lengthwise
12 very fresh egg yolks
1 cup sugar

TOOLS

Double boiler or a makeshift double boiler consisting of a stainless-steel bowl fit over a pot of simmering water

METHOD

Scald the milk with the vanilla beans and set aside.

In the top of the double boiler, off the heat, whisk the yolks and sugar until lemon colored.

Warm the yolk mixture over simmering water, stirring the yolk mixture continuously with a wooden spoon. Slowly pour in the scalded milk and vanilla beans and continue to stir until the mixture coats a *metal* spoon, about 20 minutes. Strain.

Cool the *crème anglaise* over a bowl of ice, stirring from time to time.

Cover and refrigerate.

NOTES

When serving the *crème anglaise* with the Chartreuse Soufflé (page 61), do not cool it. Place it on the warm side of the stove and stir occasionally until ready to serve.

If the *crème* curdles, immediately remove the bowl from the heat and whisk in a little cold heavy cream. If you think it is unsalvageable, place two cups at a time in a food processor for a couple of seconds to return it to the smooth texture.

Yield: Approximately 1 quart

ACKNOWLEDGMENTS

Though Glorious Food was the brainchild of but two people, its success was brought about by a collaboration of very devoted friends, clients and hard workers. They have offered help and love in many ways, both to the company and to us as individuals. This book, too, has come about through their kind efforts, and though I cannot mention every one of them, I wish to propose a toast to those who have made it possible.

To Sean Driscoll for his friendship and his dream. To Jean-Claude Nedelec for his attention and devotion to detail and his enthusiasm and love for the big event. To the Glorious Food kitchen crew. And to the waiters—those incredible young men who thrive on pleasing the guests—especially four of them, who from the beginning taught the others well: Patrick Riordan, Vitor Faria, Gerassimos Nicoloutsos and Serge Cluny. To Bridie McSherry and my brother Peter, whose hard work and humor during those formative years are cherished by many of us. And for the "upstairs," my special thanks to Philippe Maleval, Ruth Newman and Lon Sulkowski.

There are not enough grapes in the world to toast Joan Gates, who devoted a year and more to this project and made it hers. And to Monie Begley, dear friend and savior, who worked so hard to help write this book.

To Marya Dalrymple and Susan Meyer—patient editors—who guided me through this endeavor, and to Nai Chang and Jim Wageman—art directors—whose suggestions and sensitivity have made this a beautiful book. To *House & Garden*, who so generously permitted us to draw on photographs of our work. To those photographers who gave their permission and their wonderful eyes—Horst and John Marmaras.

And especially to Karen Radkai and Rico Puhlmann, who taught me how food could come alive in pictures and so generously helped with this book.

But most of all to Richard Jeffery—the principal photographer of this book—who made every photo session a joy.

To Mary Allen, my Roxbury "staff." And to Rena Coyle, who tested and retested so many of these recipes. For Claudia Schwide, whose talents have thrown the ancient art of pottery into the modern idiom with intelligence and style. To Dan Danoff at Bob Pryor Antiques, for being so generous when enough was not enough.

For Enid Futterman, who named the company—we all thank her—and dear Allen Kupchick, who did more than store radishes in his refrigerator. For Miki

252

Denhof, whose subtle voice encouraged this book and whose vision made it possible. For Catherine Campaigne Vaisse, who gave me a field of rosemary and a tray of tea each morning when I first started writing the book. And to Bob Reynolds—best friend—whose quiet encouragement helped me finish it.

To David Easton, whose genius and "eye" has been a guide throughout my life. For James Steinmeyer, who so often jumped in to help and unruffle the edges. To Felicite Love Morgan, who gave me syllabub and makes every dinner she cooks a pleasure and an event. To Lee Bailey, who has reduced the trappings of life to the simplest and is my favorite home cook.

To my parents, who taught me the goodness and value of food.

For Lorna de Wangen—my *bec fin*—and favorite trumpet. To Nanette Kreizel, one of my favorite charity organizers, who thought she was coming to dinner but peeled a hundred peaches instead. For Geraldine Stutz for being a loving critic. And to Jean-Pierre Denet—best French import.

To Helen O'Hagan at Saks Fifth Avenue, and to all her "troops," for giving us the smallest "kitchen" in the world and making it home. For the Metropolitan Museum of Art—but most especially for Richard Morsches and his wonderful staff, who have taught and supported us and given so much. And to Chris Giftos and John Funt, whose talent and designs make every museum party a success. And to Sisi Cahan, arch organizer of "The Party of the Year." To Renny, for his collaboration on the Tea Party.

For John Williamson, brilliant gardener and supplier of herbs, folklore and myth. For the wonderful purveyors, producers and farmers, who have been a constant source of quality. I particularly single out those who helped when we were small and continue to help now that we are big: Ceil and Stanley Knight at Knight's Farm and all the Halseys at the Green Thumb; Catinas and Pisacane fish markets, and Tony at the A & L Meat and Poultry Market.

And to the following friends and clients, who gave their homes, apartments, offices, lakes, boats, woods and lawns to make this happen: I thank Eileen Barrett at the New York Botanical Garden, Carol Anthony, Libba and Kim Esteve, Jimmy Goslee, Barbara and Philip Isles, Bob Dash, Halston, Knoll International, Annette and Sam Reed, Mark Hulla, Susan and Peter Nitze, Rosemary and Bill Weaver, Bill Blass, Paul Jenkins, Melissa and Christopher Brumder, Peter Gates and his entire family, Jersey Party for dazzle, Brian Leahy at Frost Lighting for tents and magic, and Tom Dillow for music and laughter.

INDEX

255

Composition
by U.S. Lithograph Inc., New York, New York

Printing in four-color offset on 150 gsm gloss-coated paper
by Amilcare Pizzi s.p.a., Arti Grafiche, Milan, Italy.
Bound in Italy by Amilcare Pizzi.